The Tessels

THIS IS TODAY

A WINDOW ON OUR TIMES

THIS IS TODAY

A WINDOW ON OUR TIMES

INTRODUCTION BY KATIE COURIC AND MATT LAUER

WRITTEN BY ERIC MINK • EDITED BY LAURIE DOLPHIN AND CHRISTIAN BROWN

Andrews McMeel
Publishing

Kansas City

03 04 05 06 07 QGR 10 9 8 7 6 5 4 3 2 1

Library of Congress Cataloging-in-Publication Data

Mink, Eric.
This is today : a window on our times / Eric Mink ; edited by Laurie Dolphin and Christian Brown ; introduction by Katie Couric and Matt Lauer.
    p. cm.
ISBN 0-7407-3853-4
    1. Today show (Television program) I. Dolphin, Laurie. II. Couric, Katie, 1957 - III. Lauer, Matt, 1957 - IV. Title.

PN1992.77.T6M56 2003
791.45'72—dc21

2003052151

Book Design by Laurie Dolphin Design
DVD Menus by Laurie Dolphin Design
This Is Today is an Authorscape book/DVD production

ATTENTION: SCHOOLS AND BUSINESSES

ACKNOWLEDGMENTS

Author Thanks:

Writing may be a solitary endeavor, but publishing—like television—is inevitably collaborative. It has been my good fortune to have had collaborators, official and unofficial, who made my work far easier and better than it ever could have been without them. At NBC Enterprises, April Brock brought efficiency and remarkable diplomacy to the management of this project's disparate elements. Allison Gollust and Lauren Kapp of NBC News always found time to help solve logistical problems for me, despite the pressing demands of their full-time duties. Former *Today* producer Chris Brown was, simply, the perfect editor. Bill Carter of the *New York Times*, a close friend for more than two decades, provided critical advice and perspective during the research and writing process. And Claudia Mink gave me, as always, unwavering support and honest, crucially important assessments through exceptionally difficult times.

Eric Mink
St. Louis, 2003

NBC Acknowledgments:

Very special thanks to: Katie Couric, Matt Lauer, Al Roker, Ann Curry, Bob Wright, Neal Shapiro, Frank Radice

The day-to-day team who worked diligently together to bring this project to fruition: Meredith Ahr, April Brock, Chris Brown, Nancy Cole, Laurie Dolphin, Allison Gollust, Lauren Kapp, Eric Mink, Kim Niemi, Mary-Alice O'Rourke, Chris Schillig, Stuart Shapiro, Deborah Warren

Any project of this magnitude is a truly collaborative effort. NBC would like to thank the many people who gave their time and energies so generously including:

Jackie Agnolet, Pat Ambrose, Jim Andrews, Ernie Angstadt, David Atlas, William Bartlett, Jenness Brewer, B. J. Carretta, Courtney Chapman, Yuien Chin, Bari Cohen, Loretta Desmond, Maryanne Dicandia, Leslie Duong, Frank Fernandez, Globe Photos, Lawnie Grant, Martha Hanrahan, Arthur Hogan, Jon Hookstratten, Stacey Irvin, Loretta Kraft, Debra Levinson, David Lipsius, Gillian Lusins, Peter Mahler, Lauren McCollester, David McCormick, Allison Meierding, Lauren Mitchell, Jim Nichols, George Nunes, Miranda Patterson, Jerry Petry, Zinta Poilovs, Kerry Prendergast, Willard Scott, Alan Seiffert, Judy Simanello, Traecy Smith, Patricia Steele, Lori Stethers, Cressida Suttles, Steve Tom, Tom Touchet, Justin Weinstein, Bill Wheatley, Ed Wilson, Sharon Zink, Jeff Zucker.

Authorscape Acknowledgments:

Thanks to NBC and Kim Niemi for giving us the opportunity to be a part of one of the most exceptional families in entertainment. We want to especially thank and applaud our team: April Brock, Christian Brown, Craig Cefola, Dayna Elefant, Alex Halpern, Christi Hoffman, Robert Krulwich, Allison Meierding, Eric Mink, Nick Mougis, Yusuf Sayman, Chris Schillig, Deborah Warren, and Justin Weinstein for their hard work, diligence, and attention to details. We are equally thankful to Paul Bacon, Selma Shapiro, Jim Silberman, Murray and Rita Stichman for their inspiration and insight.

DVD CONTENT

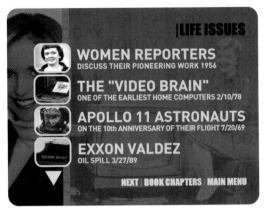

As a '48 baby, I grew up with *Today*, just old enough to watch it with my parents from the beginning. Big round knobs and a chimp loom large in my early memories. But half a century later, as I screened NBC's *Today* archives for the DVD, I felt I was going back to school for a crash course in twentieth century history and popular culture. These archives reflect moments in time that have been frozen for us to enjoy forever—the interactions between the cast, their guests, and the events of the day, all as if still live and in real time.

The sum total of this companion DVD is a testament to the magic of the times in which I have been so lucky to live, and now to revisit with digital random access.

Hard as it was to select from fifty years of *Today* for a single DVD with only seventy segments and 210 minutes, I hope this sampling is still a testament to a legacy unique in our culture.

And I hope you enjoy watching it as much as I have enjoyed assembling it.

Stuart S. Shapiro

DVD MAIN MENU

BOOK CONTENTS

WE'LL PUT YOU IN TOUCH WITH THE WORLD, AND NOT GET STUFFY ABOUT IT

DAVE GARROWAY

By Katie Couric and Matt Lauer

On a chilly New York morning in the winter of 1952, a transplanted Chicagoan with big glasses and a genial manner looked into the lens of a massive television camera and made viewers a simple, straightforward promise:

"We'll put you in touch with the world," Dave Garroway vowed. "And," he added minutes later, "not get stuffy about it."

That doesn't sound like much today, when we take for granted that our TV sets will show us anything that happens at any time anywhere on this earth or beyond—and show it to us live. But more than half a century ago, when television was just beginning to find its way in a media world defined, at that point, by newspapers and radio, Garroway's pledge sounded bold, even audacious. Ever since that January 14, fulfilling Garroway's commitment has been the goal of *Today* men and women. You may recognize those who have appeared on your TV screen, but hundreds more have worked unseen in NBC News offices, bureaus, studios, and control rooms around the world gathering, organizing, and transmitting the words, sounds, and images you see and hear.

That *Today* is still alive and well more than fifty years later—despite dizzying and sometimes wrenching technological, social, and political changes—is a testament to the genius of the late Sylvester "Pat" Weaver. As NBC's chief programmer in the early 1950s—he later served as president and chairman—Weaver created *Today* and the *Tonight* show and had a hand in countless other innovations. And by figuring out how to shift control of programs from advertisers to networks, the visionary ad executive–turned-broadcaster laid the foundation for commercial television as it exists today.

In developing *Today*, Weaver realized that his pioneering morning show would have to accommodate the real-life rhythms of its awakening audience: people gearing up for work, parents getting children off to school, and homemakers catching their breath after the breadwinners and kids cleared out. Like radio, it would have to deliver information people needed first thing in the morning: dependably scheduled, up-to-date news stories, weather reports, and a preview of the day to come. It would also have to communicate with people who were busy dressing, talking, and eating—people, in other words, who had no more than a few minutes at a time to actually focus on their TV screens.

They were radio listeners, really, but Weaver figured *Today* could convert them into television viewers if it gave them everything radio did—and then something more: moving pictures of news events from around the world, a peek at the workings of a real newsroom and face-to-face contact with a company of engaged and engaging on-camera personalities.

Weaver's concept remains the essence of *Today*. And, truth be told, it has proved to be the model for all the other successful morning TV programs that have followed on networks, local stations, and cable channels.

Think of this book, then, not as a history of *Today* but as a kind of thumbnail sketch of fifty-plus years of history illustrated and illuminated

Dave Garroway on the left, Sylvester "Pat" Weaver on the right.

with highlights culled from the *Today* archives. There are moments of tragedy and crisis; there are moments of triumph and hope. It traces the forces and issues that have shaped our world and looks at some of the performers and artists who have crafted our popular culture. You'll also hear the reflections and recollections of some of *Today*'s cast and contributors, past and present.

The documentary record, we should mention, is incomplete. In the rush toward the next day's program, much of the early material was neglected and lost. Fortunately NBC changed its preservation practices in the 1970s, so the record is more comprehensive after that. Still, readers will surely notice that this book and its companion DVD can't help but reflect the gaps in the record.

In the end, though, the mission of *Today* has never been to make history; our job has always been to bear witness to each present day, to offer it to you and to try to make some sense of it on your behalf. On January 14, 1952, Dave Garroway articulated the show's broader aspirations: "We hope," he said, "to keep you more free, more informed. Because I believe, as I hope you do, that an informed people tends to be a free people."

That is every bit as true today as it was then, and all who have followed in Garroway's footsteps, both in front of and behind the cameras, have tried to live up to that responsibility—without getting stuffy about it.

Frank Blair, Dave Garroway, Florence Henderson, and Jack Lescoulie having a good time.

TIMELINE

1952 1953 1954 1955 1956 1957 1958

JANUARY 14, 1952
Dave Garroway becomes first host of *Today*.
1/14/52–6/16/61

Jack Lescoulie becomes first *Today* "panelist."
1/14/52–1/18/57

Jim Fleming becomes *Today* news anchor.
1/14/52–8/53

NOVEMBER 1, 1952
World's first hydrogen bomb exploded in test by U.S. on Eniwetok, an island in the Pacific Ocean.

NOVEMBER 4, 1952
Dwight D. Eisenhower defeats Adlai Stevenson in U.S. presidential election.

1952
Mr. Potato Head is patented.

FEBRUARY 3, 1953
Ratings climb after chimpanzee J. Fred Muggs becomes *Today* regular.
2/3/53–12/3/54, occasional appearances through 3/1/57

MAY 29, 1953
Sir Edmund Hillary and Tenzing Norgay become first to reach summit of Mt. Everest.

JULY 27, 1953
Armistice ends the Korean War.

AUGUST 3, 1953
Frank Blair becomes *Today* news anchor.
8/3/53–3/14/75

1953
Francis Crick and James Watson become first to describe the structure of DNA.

Arthur Miller's *The Crucible* wins Tony award for best play.

I Love Lucy is the most popular show of '52–'53 TV season.

MARCH 1, 1954
Five U.S. congressmen are wounded on the floor of the House by shots fired from the visitors' gallery by members of an extremist group advocating Puerto Rican independence.

APRIL–JUNE 1954
Wisconsin Senator Joseph McCarthy conducts hearings into alleged Communist influences in the U.S. Army.

MAY 17, 1954
In *Brown v. Board of Education* of Topeka, Kansas, U.S. Supreme Court rules that separate public schools for whites and blacks are unconstitutional.

SEPTEMBER 27, 1954
The Tonight Show with Steve Allen premieres on NBC.

1954
Dr. Jonas Salk's polio vaccine becomes available.

Movie *On the Waterfront* is released. Wins Oscar for best picture.

Elvis Presley records "That's All Right."

OCTOBER 1, 1955
The Honeymooners premieres on CBS.

OCTOBER 17, 1955
Lee Ann Meriwether becomes first *Today* Girl.
10/17/55–11/30/56

DECEMBER 1, 1955
Rosa Parks, a 42-year-old black seamstress, is arrested in Montgomery, Alabama, for refusing to give up her seat on the public bus to a white man. Bus boycott follows.

1955
Fiber optics are invented.

DECEMBER 7, 1956
Helen O'Connell becomes *Today* Girl.
12/7/56–8/15/58

SEPTEMBER 4, 1957
National Guard troops are called in by Arkansas Governor Orval Faubus to turn back the first black students trying to attend Little Rock's Central High School.

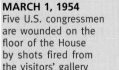

OCTOBER 4, 1957
Soviet Union launches Sputnik, the world's first space satellite.

1957
My Fair Lady wins Tony for best musical play.

Nevil Shute's novel *On the Beach*, about a nuclear war, becomes a best-seller.

AUGUST 18, 1958
Betsy Palmer becomes *Today* Girl.
8/31/58–10/31/58

1959 1960 1961 1962 1963 1964

JANUARY 1, 1959
Cuban dictator Fulgencio Batista flees country; Fidel Castro assumes power.

SEPTEMBER 12, 1959
Bonanza premieres on NBC.

OCTOBER 19, 1959
Florence Henderson becomes *Today* Girl. 10/19/59–5/20/60

MAY 1, 1960
U.S. spy plane piloted by Francis Gary Powers shot down over Soviet Union. Powers taken prisoner.

SEPTEMBER 12, 1960
Beryl Pfizer becomes *Today* Girl. 9/12/60–4/28/61

SEPTEMBER 26, 1960
The first of four nationally televised debates between presidential candidates John F. Kennedy and Richard M. Nixon airs.

NOVEMBER 8, 1960
Democrat Kennedy defeats Republican Nixon in U.S. presidential election.

APRIL 12, 1961
Soviet Cosmonaut Yuri Gagarin becomes first human in space.

APRIL 17, 1961
Ill-fated Bay of Pigs invasion of Cuba by anti-Castro Cuban exiles begins.

MAY 4, 1961
A multiracial group of civil rights activists organized by the Congress for Racial Equality leaves Washington, D.C., on a bus for the first Freedom Ride to integrate public accommodations in the South.

MAY 5, 1961
Astronaut Alan Shepard becomes first American in space.

JULY 17, 1961
John Chancellor becomes *Today* host. 7/17/61–9/7/62

JULY 24, 1961
Edwin Newman becomes *Today* co-host. 7/24/61–12/22/61

SEPTEMBER 18, 1961
Robbin Bain becomes *Today* Girl. 9/18/61–12/29/61

1961
Barbara Walters is hired as freelance *Today* writer.

Jackie Gleason and Paul Newman star in *The Hustler.*

Motown Records releases "Shop Around," by the Miracles.

JANUARY 1, 1962
Louise King becomes *Today* Girl. 1/1/62–6/29/62

FEBRUARY 20, 1962
Astronaut John Glenn becomes first American to orbit earth.

SPRING 1962
Silent Spring, written by Rachel Carson about the dangers of pesticides, is published. It is generally regarded as beginning of modern environmental movement.

AUGUST 14, 1962
Pat Fontaine becomes *Today* Girl. 8/14/62–2/6/64

SEPTEMBER 10, 1962
Hugh Downs becomes *Today* anchor. 9/10/62–10/8/71

OCTOBER 1, 1962
Johnny Carson takes over as host of *The Tonight Show* on NBC.

OCTOBER 11, 1962
Pope John XXIII opens Second Vatican Council in Rome.

OCTOBER 22, 1962
U.S. discovery of Soviet missiles in Cuba triggers Cuban Missile Crisis.

1962
Chubby Checker releases "The Twist."

AUGUST 28, 1963
Rev. Dr. Martin Luther King Jr.'s "I Have a Dream" speech marks climax of March on Washington for civil rights.

NOVEMBER 22, 1963
President Kennedy is assassinated in Dallas by Lee Harvey Oswald.

NOVEMBER 24, 1963
Oswald is murdered on live TV by Dallas strip-club owner Jack Ruby.

1963
Cleopatra, starring Elizabeth Taylor and Richard Burton, becomes most expensive movie ever made.

Who's Afraid of Virginia Woolf? wins Tony for best play.

FEBRUARY 9, 1964
Beatles make first appearance on CBS's *Ed Sullivan Show.*

MAY 4, 1964
Maureen O'Sullivan becomes *Today* Girl. 5/4/64–9/18/64

JULY 30, 1964
Legislation creating Medicare becomes law.

AUGUST 4, 1964
Bodies of three civil rights workers are found buried in earthen dam in Mississippi.

AUGUST 7, 1964
Congress passes Gulf of Tonkin Resolution, used as legal basis for U.S. war in Vietnam.

1964
Barbara Walters becomes *Today* Girl/reporter. 1964–1966

1965

FEBRUARY 21, 1965
Malcolm X is murdered in New York City.

MARCH 7, 1965
Civil rights marchers are beaten as they leave Selma for Montgomery, Alabama.

AUGUST 11, 1965
Riots begin in Watts area of Los Angeles.

SEPTEMBER 15, 1965
I Spy premieres on NBC.

NOVEMBER 9, 1965
Electric power grid failures plunge northeastern U.S. into darkness. New York City residents display spirit of cooperation deemed unusual by outsiders.

1966

JUNE 29, 1966
U.S. begins bombing Hanoi, capital of North Vietnam.

SEPTEMBER 19, 1966
Barbara Walters becomes *Today* panelist.
9/19/66–4/22/1974

OCTOBER 1966
Black Panther Party is founded in Oakland by Bobby Seale and Huey P. Newton.

1966
The Beach Boys release "Good Vibrations."

1967

FEBRUARY 5, 1967
The Smothers Brothers Comedy Hour premieres on CBS. Cancelled in 1969 for being too controversial.

JUNE 5, 1967
Start of Six-Day War; Israel defeats allied Arab armies.

JULY 1967
Racial rioting erupts in Newark and Detroit.

OCTOBER 2, 1967
Thurgood Marshall is sworn in as first African-American Supreme Court justice.

OCTOBER 21–22, 1967
Antiwar demonstrators stage massive March on Pentagon in Washington.

DECEMBER 3, 1967
In South Africa, Dr. Christiaan Barnard performs the first human heart transplant.

DECEMBER 5, 1967
Joe Garagiola becomes *Today* co-host.
12/5/67–1/12/73

1967
Sgt. Pepper's Lonely Hearts Club Band wins Grammy for best album.

Cabaret wins Tony for best musical.

1968

JANUARY 22, 1968
Freewheeling comedy-variety show *Rowan and Martin's Laugh-In* premieres on NBC.

MARCH 12, 1968
Antiwar Sen. Eugene McCarthy runs close second to President Lyndon Johnson in New Hampshire Democratic primary.

MARCH 31, 1968
President Johnson announces he will not run for re-election.

APRIL 4, 1968
Rev. Dr. Martin Luther King Jr. is assassinated by James Earl Ray in Memphis. His death sparks rioting in dozens of U.S. cities.

JUNE 5, 1968
Following California primary victory, Sen. Robert F. Kennedy shot and mortally wounded by Sirhan Sirhan in Los Angeles.

AUGUST 20, 1968
Communist armies invade Czechoslovakia to squelch liberalization known as Czech Spring.

AUGUST 26–29, 1968
Antiwar demonstrations turn violent at Democratic National Convention in Chicago; later judged a "police riot."

SEPTEMBER 17, 1968
Julia premieres on NBC.

SEPTEMBER 24, 1968
60 Minutes premieres on CBS.

NOVEMBER 5, 1968
Republican Richard Nixon defeats Democrat Hubert H. Humphrey for the presidency.

1969

APRIL 1969
U.S. troop strength in Vietnam peaks at 543,400.

JULY 8, 1969
U.S. begins gradual withdrawal from Vietnam.

JULY 20, 1969
Neil Armstrong becomes first man to walk on moon.

AUGUST 15–18, 1969
Woodstock music festival draws hundreds of thousands of young people to upstate New York farm pasture.

SEPTEMBER 23, 1969
Marcus Welby, M.D. premieres on ABC.

1969
Norman Mailer's *Armies of the Night* becomes best-seller, wins Pulitzer Prize.

Great White Hope wins Tony for best play.

Sam Peckinpah directs the movie *The Wild Bunch*.

Midnight Cowboy wins Oscar for best picture.

1970

APRIL 22, 1970
Environmentalists stage first Earth Day celebrations.

MAY 4, 1970
Four students are killed by National Guard troops at Kent State University in Ohio.

SEPTEMBER 19, 1970
The Mary Tyler Moore Show premieres on CBS.

1970
The Sensuous Woman by "J" becomes best-seller.

1971 1972 1973 1974 1975 1976 1977

JANUARY 12, 1971
All in the Family premieres on CBS.

JUNE 13, 1971
Publication of Pentagon Papers begins, further damaging credibility of U.S. Vietnam War policies.

JUNE 30, 1971
Ratification of the 26th Amendment to the U.S. Constitution lowers voting age to 18.

OCTOBER 11, 1971
Frank McGee becomes *Today* host.
10/11/71–4/10/74

1971
Godfrey Hounsfield creates first CT scan medical diagnostic system.

Team at Intel develops microprocessor chip.

FEBRUARY 21, 1972
President Richard Nixon challenges conservative orthodoxy by traveling to People's Republic of China.

MARCH 15, 1972
While campaigning for president, Alabama Gov. George Wallace is shot by Arthur Bremer and permanently disabled.

MAY 22, 1972
Nixon becomes the first U.S. president to visit Moscow and forges strategic arms limitation agreement.

JUNE 17, 1972
Five Republican-paid operatives are arrested during espionage caper at Democratic National Committee offices in Washington's Watergate complex.

1972
Nolan Bushnell develops first video game: Pong.

The Godfather, directed by Francis Ford Coppola, wins Oscar for best picture; Marlon Brando wins best actor. Brando declines.

JANUARY 15, 1973
Gene Shalit becomes *Today* panelist and arts editor.
1/15/73–present

JANUARY 22, 1973
In *Roe v. Wade* decision, U.S. Supreme Court rules abortion legal in limited circumstances.

JANUARY 27, 1973
Vietnam peace agreement is signed in Paris; military draft ends in U.S.

MARCH 29, 1973
Last U.S. troops leave Vietnam.

OCTOBER 10, 1973
Vice President Spiro Agnew resigns, pleads "no contest" to tax evasion.

OCTOBER 19, 1973
Arab oil-producing nations declare embargo on exports to U.S. because of support for Israel in Yom Kippur War.

APRIL 17, 1974
Today anchor Frank McGee dies.

APRIL 22, 1974
Barbara Walters becomes *Today* co-anchor.
4/22/74–6/4/76

MAY 9, 1974
House Judiciary Committee begins impeachment hearings against President Nixon.

JULY 1974
Betty Furness becomes *Today* weekly consumer-news contributor.
7/74–3/92

JULY 29, 1974
Jim Hartz becomes *Today* co-anchor.
7/29/74–8/20/76

AUGUST 8, 1974
Nixon announces resignation, effective August 9. Vice President Gerald Ford becomes president.

MARCH 1975
Lew Wood becomes *Today* news anchor.
3/75–10/76

APRIL 30, 1975
South Vietnamese government officially surrenders power to North Vietnam.

OCTOBER 11, 1975
Saturday Night Live premieres on NBC.

1975
Jaws, directed by Steven Spielberg, becomes first summer blockbuster.

Michael Shaara writes *The Killer Angels* about Civil War's Battle of Gettysburg; wins Pulitzer Prize.

1975–1976
Today lauches year-long, state-by-state series of reports, airing each Friday, leading up to the nation's bicentennial.

JANUARY 1976
Mary Hartman, Mary Hartman premieres in first-run TV syndication.

JULY 4, 1976
Ceremonies nationwide mark 200th anniversary of U.S. Declaration of Independence.

JULY 20, 1976
Viking I probe lands on surface of Mars.

AUGUST 23, 1976
Jim Hartz becomes *Today* traveling co-anchor.
8/23/76–4/25/77

AUGUST 30, 1976
Tom Brokaw becomes *Today* anchor.
8/30/76–12/18/81

SEPTEMBER 9, 1976
China's Mao Zedong dies after ruling People's Republic for 27 years.

OCTOBER 1976
Floyd Kalber becomes *Today* news anchor.
10/76–Summer '79

OCTOBER 11, 1976
Jane Pauley becomes *Today* panelist.
10/11/76–1/1/82

NOVEMBER 9, 1976
Georgia Gov. Jimmy Carter defeats President Ford to win presidency.

1976
First Apple computer created by Steve Jobs and Steve Wozniak.

All the President's Men, directed by Alan Pakula, dramatizes events of Watergate.

A Chorus Line wins Tony for best musical.

JANUARY 21, 1977
On first full day in office, President Carter pardons most Vietnam-era draft evaders.

1977
Bill Gates and Paul Allen incorporate Microsoft.

JULY 13, 1977
Electrical blackout plunges New York City into darkness.

AUGUST 10, 1977
David Berkowitz, "Son of Sam" serial killer, is arrested in New York.

1977
Annie Hall, directed by Woody Allen, wins Oscar for best picture.

Hotel California, by the Eagles, wins Grammy for record of the year.

1978 1979 1980 1981 1982 1983 1984

APRIL 2, 1978
Dallas premieres on CBS.

NOVEMBER 18, 1978
More than 900 members of the so-called People's Temple follow leader Jim Jones to mass suicide/murder at Jonestown, Guyana. Also murdered are visiting U.S. Congressman Leo Ryan, NBC News correspondent Don Harris, and NBC photographer Bob Brown.

MARCH 26, 1979
Egypt and Israel sign peace treaty.

MARCH 28, 1979
Accident creates emergency at Three Mile Island nuclear power plant in Middletown, Pennsylvania.

NOVEMBER 4, 1979
Radical Islamist students seize U.S. embassy in Tehran, taking some ninety hostages.

1979
Sony develops compact disc player.

Stephen King writes novel *The Dead Zone*.

JANUARY 4, 1980
President Carter announces sanctions against the Soviet Union after it invades Afghanistan.

MARCH 10, 1980
Willard Scott becomes *Today* weathercaster. 3/10/80–present

APRIL 12, 1980
U.S. Olympic Committee announces boycott of summer games in Moscow.

MAY 18, 1980
First of a series of spectacular eruptions by Mount St. Helens volcano in Washington state.

NOVEMBER 4, 1980
California Gov. Ronald Reagan defeats Jimmy Carter for U.S. presidency.

DECEMBER 8, 1980
Former Beatle John Lennon is shot and killed by Mark David Chapman outside New York's Dakota apartment building.

1980
World Health Organization declares smallpox eradicated from the Earth.

3M Company develops Post-it notes.

Bruce Springsteen and E Street Band release "Hungry Heart."

JANUARY 12, 1981
Dynasty premieres on ABC.

JANUARY 20, 1981
Ronald Reagan is inaugurated as president; hostages in Iran are released.

OCTOBER 6, 1981
Egyptian President Anwar Sadat is assassinated by Islamist extremists during military parade.

Sadat

MARCH 30, 1981
President Reagan is shot and seriously wounded by John Hinckley Jr. outside Washington, D.C., hotel.

AUGUST 1, 1981
MTV is launched on cable-TV systems.

SEPTEMBER 21, 1981
Sandra Day O'Connor is confirmed as first female Supreme Court justice.

DECEMBER 13, 1981
Communist government of Poland declares martial law, arrests leaders of Solidarity labor union.

JANUARY 4, 1982
Bryant Gumbel becomes *Today* anchor. 1/4/82–1/3/97

JANUARY 4, 1982
Jane Pauley becomes *Today* co-anchor. 1/4/82–12/29/89

JANUARY 4, 1982
Chris Wallace becomes *Today* co-anchor. 1/4/82–9/24/82

FEBRUARY 2, 1982
Late Night with David Letterman premieres on NBC.

SEPTEMBER 27, 1982
John Palmer becomes *Today* news anchor. 9/27/82–9/1/89

SEPTEMBER 30, 1982
Cheers premieres on NBC.

OCTOBER 26, 1982
St. Elsewhere premieres on NBC.

1982
A Few Minutes with Andy Rooney by Andy Rooney of *60 Minutes* becomes a best-seller.

OCTOBER 23, 1983
In Beirut, terrorist truck bomb kills 241 U.S. Marines.

1983
Researchers in the United States and France isolate AIDS-causing virus, later dubbed HIV.

Alice Walker wins Pulitzer Prize for her novel *The Color Purple*.

JANUARY 1984
Apple launches Macintosh computer.

JUNE 6, 1984
Democratic presidential candidate Walter Mondale names Geraldine Ferraro as running mate, the first female nominee on a national party ticket.

NOVEMBER 6, 1984
President Reagan defeats Mondale in landslide vote.

1984
The Real Thing wins Tony for best play.

1985 1986 1987 1988 1989 1990

SUMMER 1985
World shocked by news of widespread famine in sub-Saharan Africa.

JUNE 14, 1985
Islamist terrorists hijack TWA jet in Athens.

OCTOBER 7, 1985
Palestinian terrorists seize *Achille Lauro* cruise ship, kill American Leon Klinghofer.

JULY 13, 1985
Rock stars present "Live Aid" performance telethon to benefit famine relief efforts in Africa.

JANUARY 28, 1986
Challenger space shuttle explodes shortly after launch, killing all six crew members and teacher Christa McAuliffe.

NOVEMBER 1986
Stories detailing Iran-contra affair are first published.

1986
Oliver Stone directs *Platoon*, which wins Oscars for best film, best director.

Paul Simon's *Graceland* wins Grammy for album of year.

MAY–AUGUST 1987
Congress holds hearings into Iran-contra abuses of power.

OCTOBER 19, 1987
Stock market crashes; Dow Jones industrial average plummets 508 points.

DECEMBER 8, 1987
President Reagan and reformer Mikhail Gorbachev, Communist leader of Soviet Union, sign agreement to dismantle all medium-range ballistic missiles.

DECEMBER 1987
First *intifada* by Palestinians against Israeli occupation begins in Gaza strip.

1987
Steven Spielberg directs *E.T. the Extra Terrestrial*.

OCTOBER 18, 1988
Roseanne premieres on ABC.

NOVEMBER 8, 1988
Republican Vice President George H. W. Bush easily defeats Democrat Michael Dukakis for presidency.

DECEMBER 21, 1988
Terrorist bomb destroys Pam Am Flight 103 over Lockerbie, Scotland.

1988
Tom Hanks stars in the movie *Big*.

FEBRUARY 1989
Soviet troops complete withdrawal from Afghanistan.

MARCH 24, 1989
Oil tanker *Exxon Valdez* runs aground in Prince William Sound, Alaska, creating environmental disaster.

MAY 4, 1989
Students and workers stage massive demonstrations in Tiananmen Square in Beijing, China; troops crush movement June 3.

SUMMER–FALL 1989
Communist governments collapse throughout Eastern Europe.

AUGUST 9, 1989
President Bush signs law bailing out savings-and-loan industry.

AUGUST 10, 1989
Gen. Colin Powell is nominated as the first African-American chairman of the Joint Chiefs of Staff.

SEPTEMBER 4, 1989
Deborah Norville becomes *Today* news anchor. 9/4/89–1/8/90

OCTOBER 17, 1989
Earthquake strikes San Francisco as World Series game about to start.

NOVEMBER 1989
Berlin Wall dividing East and West Germany is dismantled.

DECEMBER 17, 1989
The Simpsons premieres on Fox.

DECEMBER 20, 1989
U.S. invades Panama, seizes Gen. Mañuel Noriega.

1989
Movie director Spike Lee releases *Do the Right Thing*.

JANUARY 8, 1990
Deborah Norville becomes *Today* co-anchor. 1/8/90–2/22/91

FEBRUARY 11, 1990
Nelson Mandela released after 27 years in South African prison.

MAY 31, 1990
Seinfeld premieres on NBC.

JUNE 1990
Katie Couric becomes *Today* national correspondent. 6/90–4/91

JUNE 1990
Joe Garagiola becomes *Today* correspondent-at-large.

JUNE 11, 1990
Faith Daniels becomes *Today* news anchor. 6/11/90–5/92

AUGUST 2, 1990
Iraq invades Kuwait.

OCTOBER 3, 1990
East and West Germany are officially reunified.

1991　1992　1993　1994　1995　1996

1991

JANUARY 17, 1991
U.S.-led coalition begins Desert Storm air war against Iraq.

FEBRUARY 24, 1991
Ground war against Iraq begins.

FEBRUARY 27, 1991
Iraq is defeated; cease-fire declared.

FEBRUARY 1991
South African President F. W. de Klerk announces plan to repeal apartheid laws.

APRIL 4, 1991
Katie Couric becomes *Today* co-anchor. 4/4/91–present

AUGUST 19, 1991
Futile coup attempt begins against Soviet leader Mikhail Gorbachev.

SEPTEMBER 17, 1991
Home Improvement premieres on ABC.

OCTOBER 15, 1991
Senate confirms Clarence Thomas as associate justice of U.S. Supreme Court.

DECEMBER 1991
Former Solidarity leader Lech Walesa is elected president of Poland.

DECEMBER 26, 1991
Soviet Union is officially dissolved.

1991
The Silence of the Lambs wins Oscars for best picture, best director (Jonathan Demme), best actor (Anthony Hopkins), and best actress (Jodie Foster).

R.E.M. records "Losing My Religion."

1992

APRIL 29, 1992
LAPD officers are found not guilty of criminal charges in beating of motorist Rodney King. Days of rioting begin.

MAY 1992
Margaret Larson becomes *Today* news anchor. 5/92–1/94

1992
The Way Things Ought to Be, by Rush Limbaugh, becomes a best-seller.

1993

FEBRUARY 26, 1993
Terrorist bomb explodes in underground parking area of World Trade Center.

FEBRUARY 28, 1993
Federal agents and civilians are killed in raid on Branch Davidian cult compound outside Waco, Texas. Compound is placed under siege.

APRIL 19, 1993
Siege at Waco ends. Seventy people die.

SUMMER 1993
So-called 100-year floods ravage U.S. Midwest.

SEPTEMBER 13, 1993
Israel reaches agreement with Palestine Liberation Organization.

OCTOBER 3–4, 1993
Eighteen U.S. Army Rangers are killed on mission in Somalia.

NOVEMBER 30, 1993
President Clinton signs Brady Bill requiring waiting period before gun purchases.

DECEMBER 1993
Repairs are completed on orbiting Hubble telescope; begins transmitting spectacular interstellar images back to Earth.

1993
Angels in America wins Tony for best play.

1994

JANUARY 1994
Matt Lauer becomes *Today* news anchor. 1/94–1/97

JANUARY 20, 1994
U.S. Attorney General Janet Reno appoints special prosecutor to investigate Whitewater land deal involving past actions by President and Mrs. Clinton.

FEBRUARY 5, 1994
Byron de La Beckwith is convicted of 1963 murder of civil rights activist Medgar Evers.

APRIL 6, 1994
Rwandan genocide begins; Hutu rebels slaughter 800,000 Tutsis and others in 100 days.

APRIL 26–29, 1994
Nelson Mandela is elected president of South Africa.

JUNE 12, 1994
Nicole Brown Simpson and Ronald Goldman are murdered in Los Angeles. Her ex-husband, former football great O. J. Simpson, is arrested and charged days later.

JUNE 20, 1994
Today begins broadcasting from new glass-windowed Studio 1A on 49th Street in Rockefeller Center.

OCTOBER 26, 1994
Israel and Jordan sign peace treaty.

NOVEMBER 8, 1994
Republicans sweep to victory in midterm congressional elections.

1994
New computer program developed by Netscape Communications, a browser, fuels rapid growth of Internet.

Men Are from Mars, Women Are from Venus by John Gray becomes best-seller.

1995

APRIL 19, 1995
Truck bomb explodes outside Murrah Federal Building in Oklahoma City, killing 168.

OCTOBER 3, 1995
O. J. Simpson is found not guilty of murders of ex-wife and her friend.

NOVEMBER 14, 1995
Budget impasse leads to shutdown of federal government.

NOVEMBER 21, 1995
Ethnic/political factions fighting in Bosnia agree to peace terms of Dayton Accords.

1995
Babe, a film about a pig that herds sheep, triumphs at the box office.

1996

JANUARY 2, 1996
Al Roker becomes *Today* weathercaster and feature reporter. 1/2/96–present

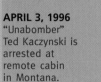

APRIL 3, 1996
"Unabomber" Ted Kaczynski is arrested at remote cabin in Montana.

JULY 27, 1996
Bomb explodes in midst of Summer Olympics activities in Atlanta.

SEPTEMBER 1996
The Taliban, an ultraconservative Islamic faction, takes control of Afghanistan.

SEPTEMBER 8, 1996
Ally McBeal premieres on Fox.

JANUARY 6, 1997
Matt Lauer becomes *Today* co-anchor.
1/6/97–present

JANUARY 1997
Bombs explode at abortion clinics in Atlanta and Tulsa.

JANUARY 23, 1997
Madeline Albright is sworn in as first female Secretary of State.

FEBRUARY 1997
Researchers in England announce they have produced a cloned mammal, a sheep named Dolly.

MARCH 1997
Ann Curry becomes *Today* news anchor.
3/97–present

MARCH 26, 1997
Members of Heaven's Gate cult commit mass suicide in Rancho Santa Fe, California. Thirty-nine die.

JUNE 2, 1997
Timothy McVeigh is convicted in 1995 bombing of Oklahoma City federal building.

1997
Titanic sets box-office records, wins Oscar for best picture.

Into Thin Air by Jon Krakauer becomes best-seller.

JANUARY 21, 1998
The Washington Post reports that Independent Counsel Kenneth Starr is investigating President Clinton for possible crimes in connection with alleged affair with White House intern Monica Lewinsky.

APRIL 10, 1998
Historic peace agreement is reached in Northern Ireland, approved by voters May 22.

AUGUST 7, 1998
Islamist terrorists explode truck bombs at U.S. embassies in Kenya and Tanzania, killing hundreds

FALL 1997– SPRING 1998
Flurry of shootings occur at public schools, including Pearl, Mississippi; Paducah, Kentucky; Jonesboro, Arkansas; and Springfield, Oregon.

NOVEMBER 23, 1998
Major tobacco companies are ordered to pay $260 billion over 25 years to settle lawsuits filed by states.

DECEMBER 19, 1998
Clinton becomes first elected U.S. president to be impeached.

JANUARY 7– FEBRUARY 12, 1999
Clinton impeachment trial in Senate ends with acquittal.

APRIL 20, 1999
Two students kill 14 students, including themselves, and a teacher at Columbine High School in Littleton, Colorado.

JULY 16, 1999
John F. Kennedy Jr., his wife, and his sister-in-law die in small plane crash off the coast of Martha's Vineyard.

DECEMBER 31, 1999
Control of Panama Canal reverts to Panama.

Worldwide celebrations and observances mark turn of millennium.

JUNE 26, 2000
Competing groups of scientists jointly announce successful decoding of human genome.

JULY 2000
South Africa hosts international AIDS conference; 20% of its population is infected with HIV.

OCTOBER 2, 2000
Today goes to three-hour format.

OCTOBER 12, 2000
Islamist terrorists bomb U.S.S. *Cole* in harbor at Aden, Yemen; seventeen killed.

NOVEMBER 7, 2000
Close presidential election produces no clear victor; candidates' organizations and media focus on voting irregularities in Florida; recounts and legal actions go on for weeks.

DECEMBER 12, 2000
U.S. Supreme Court orders end to Florida recounts. Democratic Vice President Albert Gore concedes to Republican Texas Governor George W. Bush the next day.

2000
Steeley Dan's *Two Against Nature* wins Grammy for album of year.

JUNE 11, 2001
Timothy McVeigh is executed for Oklahoma City bombing murders.

SEPTEMBER 11, 2001
Islamist terrorists hijack four planes on East Coast; crash two into World Trade Center towers in New York, one into Pentagon in Washington. Fourth plane crashes into field in Pennsylvania. Both towers collapse. Close to 3,000 die.

OCTOBER 5– NOVEMBER 21, 2001
Envelopes containing anthrax, origin unknown, are discovered at U.S. Senate and media organizations, including the office of NBC's Tom Brokaw. Five die. Postal workers are most affected.

OCTOBER 7, 2001
U.S. begins military actions in Afghanistan after Taliban government fails to turn over terrorist leader Osama bin Laden.

DECEMBER 2, 2001
Energy-trading giant Enron declares bankruptcy.

2001
The Producers wins Tony for best musical play.

JANUARY 1, 2002
Twelve countries in Europe begin phase-in of common currency, the euro.

JANUARY 23, 2002
Daniel Pearl, *Wall Street Journal* reporter, is kidnapped in Pakistan; confirmed dead February 20.

FEBRUARY 12, 2002
Former Yugoslav President Slobodan Milosevic is put on trial at The Hague for war crimes.

MARCH 27, 2002
President Bush signs McCain-Feingold campaign finance–reform act.

MAY 30, 2002
Solemn ceremonies mark completion of clean-up of World Trade Center site in New York.

JUNE 6, 2002
FBI agent Coleen Rowley testifies to Senate Intelligence Committee about problems and mistakes in agency's terrorism investigation.

OCTOBER 2002
Snipers kill ten, wound three, in spree near Washington. Two men are arrested October 24 and charged with multiple murders.

OCTOBER 10, 2002
Former President Jimmy Carter receives Nobel Peace Prize for lifetime of work for peace and human rights.

OCTOBER 12, 2002
Islamist terrorists explode bomb in Bali resort, killing 180.

NOVEMBER 5, 2002
Republicans dominate midterm elections. Now control both houses of Congress.

MARCH 19, 2003
Air attacks mark beginning of U.S. campaign to oust regime of Iraqi dictator Saddam Hussein. Like much of the war, the fall of Baghdad on April 9 is covered live.

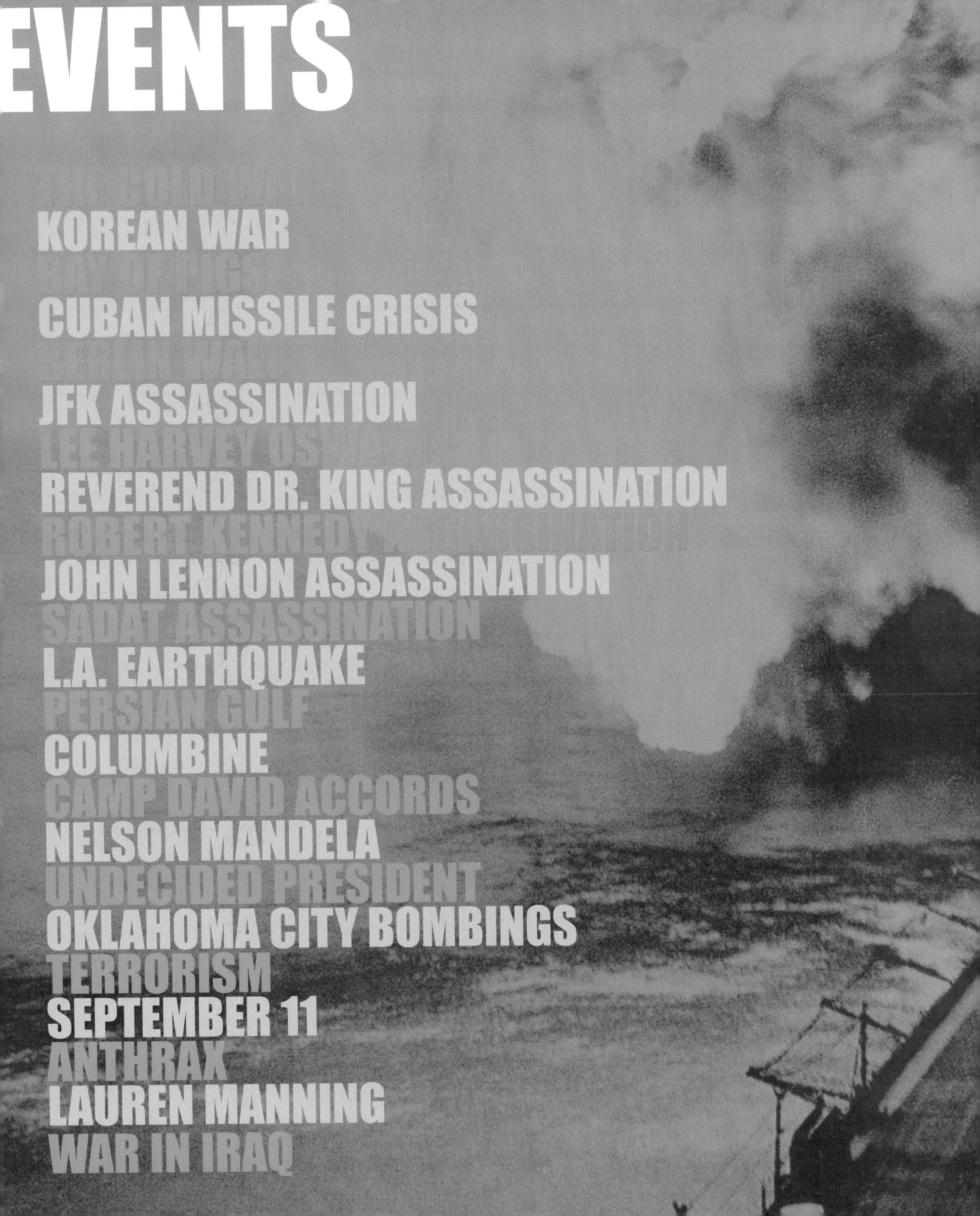
EVENTS
THE COLD WAR
KOREAN WAR
BAY OF PIGS
CUBAN MISSILE CRISIS
BERLIN WALL
JFK ASSASSINATION
LEE HARVEY OSWALD
REVEREND DR. KING ASSASSINATION
ROBERT KENNEDY ASSASSINATION
JOHN LENNON ASSASSINATION
SADAT ASSASSINATION
L.A. EARTHQUAKE
PERSIAN GULF
COLUMBINE
CAMP DAVID ACCORDS
NELSON MANDELA
UNDECIDED PRESIDENT
OKLAHOMA CITY BOMBINGS
TERRORISM
SEPTEMBER 11
ANTHRAX
LAUREN MANNING
WAR IN IRAQ

Today was born January 14, 1952, in the radiant afterglow of America's victory over fascism in World War II. The nation's military might tested and proved, the potency of its democratic ideals reaffirmed, it was now leading the world into the second half of the twentieth century.

Since the end of the war, millions of former soldiers had been going to college—subsidized by the G.I. Bill—getting married, starting families, creating communities, and fueling a vibrant new consumer-oriented economy. The postwar boom, the population shift to cities, and the release of technologies bottled up during the war created perfect conditions for the rapid development of television.

By the time *Today* premiered in 1952, the number of U.S. homes with TVs had rocketed to fifteen million from just over three million two years earlier. Prime-time entertainment shows like Milton Berle's *Texaco Star Theater*—and, even before that, coverage of the Yankees–Dodgers World Series in 1947—had stoked sales of sets, but it wasn't until September of 1951 that full-time coast-to-coast network connections became a reality, making an information-driven show like *Today* at least theoretically viable.

As the first of its kind, *Today*'s debut was an event in and of itself; half a century later, it looks quaint, sweet, even naive. But except for host Dave Garroway's declarations of principles and intentions, the premiere was feather-light on content and heavy on technical glitches.

There was within it, however, one example of television's extraordinary ability to meld news and information with universal emotions. In the ongoing Korean War, American troops were part of a United Nations action to prevent the forces of Communist North Korea from seizing the South. *Today* wanted to link a couple of U.S. soldiers fighting in Korea with their families back home, but a live hookup, a routine matter today, would not be possible for years.

Instead, days before the show's premiere, the *Today* staff brought members of the Sinnot and Cassidy families to NBC studios in Manhattan from Brooklyn. Waiting by a telephone in Seoul, South Korea, were Sergeant Daniel "Mickey" Sinnot and Sergeant Bill Cassidy, both having been pulled off the front lines for the occasion. As the young men talked on the phone with their parents, a *Today* camera crew in Seoul recorded the soldiers' half of the conversation, then rushed the film back to New York for processing.

On the morning of the first *Today* show, the Sinnots and Cassidys were brought back to the New York studio to watch the film that had been made of their sons during the phone call. A TV camera showed the parents' reactions—live. The moment was real, raw, and poignant in 1952, and, seen today, it remains so—a testament to the young medium's affective power.

The Korean conflict was an early and not very cool episode in the Cold War pitting the tyranny of the authoritarian Soviet state against the freedom of the United States' representative democracy. The Cold War, made all the more ominous by the ever-present threat of nuclear war, cast a dark shadow on the otherwise bright promise of postwar America.

Today
January 14, 1952
Televised phone conversation between U.S. soldier in Korea and family back home.

SGT. MICKEY SINNOT: Hello, Mom.

SINNOT'S MOTHER: How are you?

SGT. SINNOT: I'm fine. How are you?

SINNOT'S MOTHER: When are you coming home?

SGT. SINNOT: I'll be home soon, Mom. Don't worry about it.

SINNOT'S MOTHER: Are you all right?

SGT. SINNOT: Yeah, I'm fine, Mom.

May 23, 1952: The eight-inch main battery guns of the heavy cruiser USS *St. Paul*, operating off Korea's east coast, throw out a ball of flame and smoke as the ship blasts Communist targets in North Korea.

Many more incidents—all arising from the superpowers' clash of political ideologies and economic systems—would unfold as *Today* came of age. The anti-Communist witch hunts of Wisconsin Senator Joseph McCarthy blew through America on the icy winds of the Cold War, of course, and even after McCarthy's censure by his Senate colleagues at the end of 1954, the inquisitions continued.

"The House Un-American Activities Committee," *Today* newsman Frank Blair reported in 1957, "has summoned leading publishers, editors, and distributors of left-wing publications to testify up here in New York today."

The battle against Communism obviously drove the ill-fated 1961 Bay of Pigs invasion of Cuba by anti-Communist, anti-Castro Cuban exiles. Later that year, along the dividing line between East Berlin and West Berlin, the Communists erected a massive wall that was both physically intimidating and grimly symbolic.

No Cold War incident proved more frightening, however, than the Cuban missile crisis. In October 1962, just months after Lieutenant Colonel John Glenn had boosted national confidence and spirit when he became the first American to orbit the earth (in a Mercury capsule dubbed *Friendship 7*), the world stood teetering on the knife's edge of nuclear extinction.

In a nationally televised address on October 22, President John F. Kennedy presented aerial photographs revealing the presence of offensive Soviet missiles in Cuba, ninety miles off the coast of Florida. If allowed to remain, the missiles would radically upset the balance of power that acted as a

December 7, 1952: U.S. President-elect Dwight D. Eisenhower is flanked by General Mark W. Clark, left, commanding general, U.S. Armed Forces Far East; and by General James Van Fleet, U.S. 8th Army commander, in South Korea during the Korean War.

deterrent to war. Kennedy demanded that the Cubans and Soviets dismantle the installations and ship the missiles back to Russia. He also ordered the U.S. Navy to set up a blockade to stop any more military equipment from reaching Cuba; Soviet ships were already en route.

It wasn't until November 2 that Kennedy announced the crisis had ended with a Soviet promise to remove the missiles, but tensions had eased several days earlier when the Soviet vessels veered away from the U.S. blockade and avoided a confrontation at sea. "The reported diversion of some Russian supply ships en route to Cuba," Blair reported on October 25, "appears to have stalled off an immediate showdown on the high seas between the Soviet Union and the United States. This would allow time for diplomats to try to find a peaceful way out of the potentially explosive crisis. President Kennedy reportedly has left the door open for a possible summit conference with Premier Khrushchev. But Mr. Kennedy is sticking firmly to his immediate objective: to put an end to Soviet nuclear missile bases in Cuba."

Seven years later, in 1969, Hugh Downs and *Today* regular Barbara Walters took the program to Berlin itself, showing America what life was like at the edge.

"Good morning," Downs began. "This is *Today* in West Berlin, an island of freedom ten miles inside Soviet-controlled East Germany . . . the grotesque scar of the wall a constant reminder of political division."

In one memorable exchange during *Today*'s visit, Downs asked German publishing magnate Axel Springer how long he thought it would take for East and West Germany to reunite. Springer guessed five years or so.

In May of 1971, *Today* took an even bolder step, sending Downs, Walters, and co-host Joe Garagiola to Romania for a week of shows from behind the Iron Curtain. Walters took every opportunity to question guests about freedom of expression and censorship in the Communist country.

The next year, *Today* accompanied President Richard Nixon to the very center of Communist power, Moscow, with anchor Frank McGee broadcasting live daily. The show returned with Nixon in 1974, this time with Garrick Utley reporting.

In September of 1984, anchor Bryant Gumbel and a small *Today* production staff traveled to Moscow to broadcast a wide range of reports. These included interviews with Sergei Akhromeyev, the Soviets' newly appointed military chief of staff, which may well have had an impact on then-stalled arms talks between the U.S. and the Russians. Within days of the broadcasts, President Ronald Reagan, in a speech at the United Nations, offered a new proposal, and discussions resumed several months later.

Publisher Springer's 1969 prediction of German reunification in five years was a tad optimistic; it took until 1990. But the despised Berlin Wall came down a year sooner, and former *Today* anchor Tom Brokaw, who had since taken over *NBC Nightly News*, was there.

"Mark the date on your calendar, Deborah," Brokaw said to *Today* co-anchor Deborah Norville. "This is the tenth of November, 1989. It is the beginning, it appears, of a new age not only in Europe, but throughout the world. This is the day that the Cold War ended not with a bang, but with a street party

October 25, 1962: Frank Blair reports on Kennedy's objective regarding the Cuban Missile Crisis.

West Berlin, 1969: Hugh Downs and Barbara Walters in the Springer House, which Downs called "a skyscraper that stands symbolically and boldly right up against the wall that separates East and West Berlin."

November 23, 1961: West Berlin police stand guard behind barbed wire along the new 250-yard massive concrete wall at Berlin's Brandenburg Gate.

throughout East and West Berlin. A remarkable development here. Not so long ago, I was atop the wall with all those young people. Just as I got up there, a group of them dropped off onto the other side, and this is what happened: They began to approach the East German guards who were aligned in front of the Brandenburg Gate. They offered them roses, a gesture of peace, as their colleagues and their comrades cheered them on. The East German police made no threatening moves, highly unusual. On another day not so long ago, these young people would have been shot or certainly imprisoned. Today, they are escorted gently back toward the wall. And later, one of the young men who went down to greet the guards said to me, 'They had tears in their eyes.'"

The final curtain fell on the Cold War two years later, after a last-gasp abortive attempt by Soviet hard-liners to oust the reform-minded Mikhail Gorbachev. On December 26, 1991, the Soviet Union was officially dissolved.

While the strategic and ideological battles with Russia dwarfed all other international concerns from 1952 on, events in the United States were prodding *Today*—and television news in general—to discover its unique place in society.

After a decade on the air, *Today* had evolved. It was hardly stuffy, but covering tough stories—the missile crisis and the civil rights movement among them—had given the show a certain maturity. J. Fred Muggs and his successor chimpanzees, having done exactly what they were supposed to do in the mid-fifties—boost ratings—were gone. On a day-to-day basis, *Today* focused on its basic mission of satisfying the information needs of viewers at the start of each ordinary day.

Nothing, however, was ordinary about November 22, 1963, or the days that followed. At 12:30 P.M. Central time, President John F. Kennedy was shot while riding in an open limousine through downtown Dallas with his wife,

THIS IS THE DAY THAT THE COLD WAR ENDED NOT WITH A BANG, BUT WITH A STREET PARTY THROUGHOUT EAST AND WEST BERLIN.

TOM BROKAW

November 10, 1989: Berliners sing and dance on top of the Berlin Wall to celebrate the opening of East–West border.

7

November 10, 1989: Deborah Norville reporting from the NBC building, and Tom Brokaw at the Brandenburg Gate in West Berlin.

DEBORAH NORVILLE: I don't think any of us have reported a story like this before. The wall in Berlin physically does still stand, but it no longer is a barrier. The party that began with Thursday's ending of travel restrictions by the East German government shows no signs of ending. East Germany had planned to implement visa requirements today, but given the crush of people, it has decided to wait until next week. At least eighty people have died trying to scale the wall to freedom, but today thousands of Berliners stand atop the wall in full view of East German police.

The question "What next?" is prominent this morning, given the rapid turn of events, but it is probably unanswerable. NBC's Tom Brokaw is at the Brandenburg Gate in West Berlin this morning, I guess sort of watching history unfold, Tom.

TOM BROKAW: Mark the date on your calendar, Deborah. This is the tenth of November, 1989. It is the beginning, it appears, of a new age not only in Europe, but throughout the world. This is the day that the Cold War ended not with a bang, but with a street party throughout East and West Berlin.

A remarkable development here. Not so long ago, I was atop the wall with all those young people. Just as I got up there, a group of them dropped off onto the other side and this is what happened. They began to approach the East German guards who were aligned in front of the Brandenburg Gate. They offered them roses, a gesture of peace, as their colleagues and their comrades cheered them on.

The East German police made no threatening moves, highly unusual. On another day not so long ago, these young people would have been shot or certainly imprisoned. Today, they are escorted gently back toward the wall. And later, one of the young men who went down to greet the guards said to me, "They had tears in their eyes. I told them I simply wanted to go to East Berlin." But today at least he was not able to, through this way at least.

Deborah, I don't know what's going to happen here politically. Chancellor Kohl of West Germany, as you know, is en route back now from Poland to Bonn for emergency meetings with his government. We have not yet heard from the East German party chief about what his plans are. I have the very strong impression that they are making a policy hour by hour. When they announced this yesterday, I cannot imagine they expected this to happen.

DEBORAH NORVILLE: Tom, all along, the East German government has said once the restrictions were lifted that we want to be able to show our people that they can go across. They can travel freely and then they can return. Do you have the sense that those East Berliners who crossed over, in fact, will be doing that?

TOM BROKAW: Yes. Most of them that I talked to today, in fact, Deborah, were saying to me, "We're coming for a visit." One man in a car full of friends, I said to him, "How long has it been since you've seen West Berlin?" He thought for a moment and said, "Thirty years. I just want to spend an hour driving around the streets, taking a look."

Another young woman with her baby in a baby carriage who has never been here for a long, long time pushed her baby carriage across the line and said, "I'm going for a stroll with my friends today to take a look at West Berlin." You know, to us, it's just crossing a street, but to them, it's getting out of a prison.

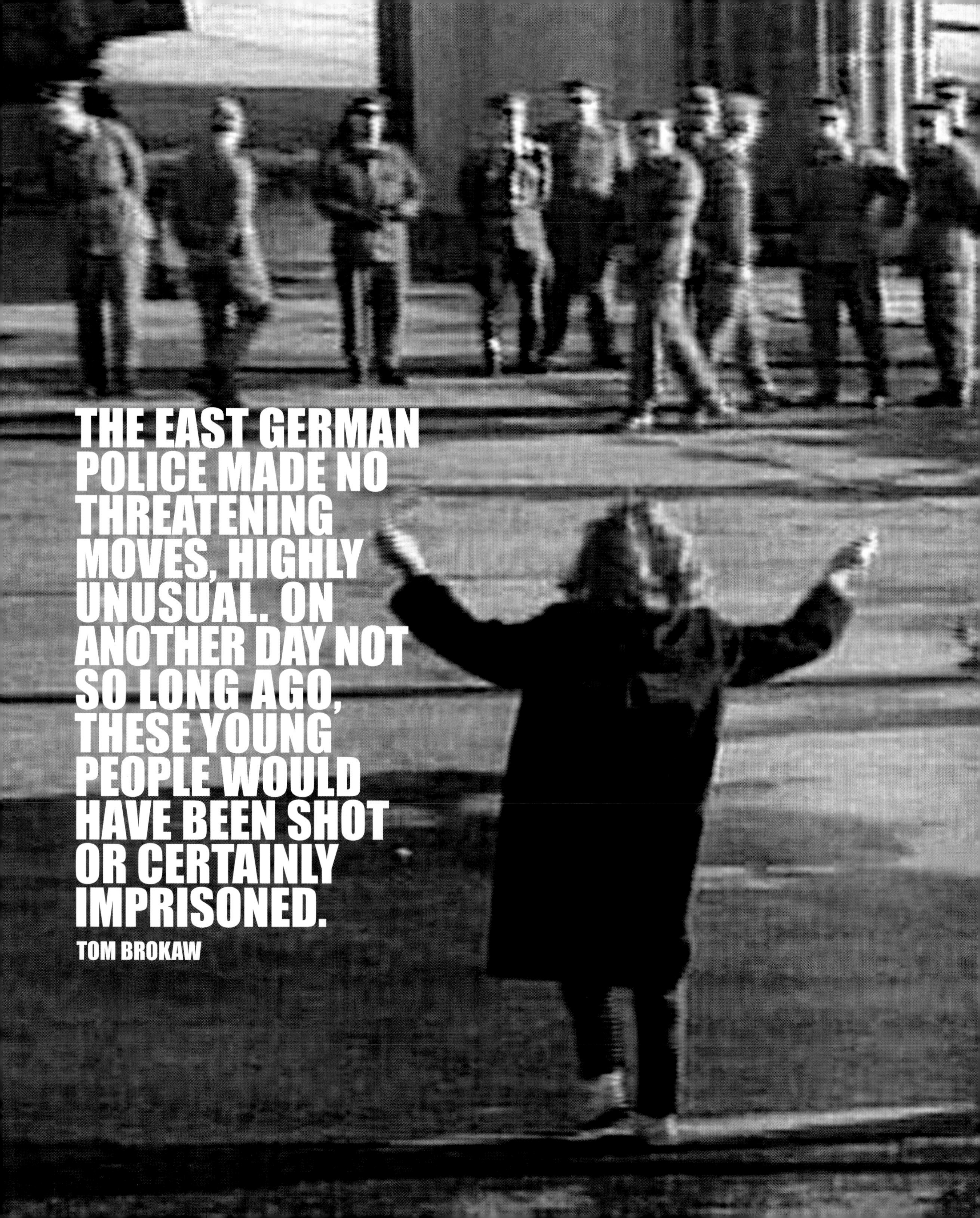

THE EAST GERMAN POLICE MADE NO THREATENING MOVES, HIGHLY UNUSUAL. ON ANOTHER DAY NOT SO LONG AGO, THESE YOUNG PEOPLE WOULD HAVE BEEN SHOT OR CERTAINLY IMPRISONED.

TOM BROKAW

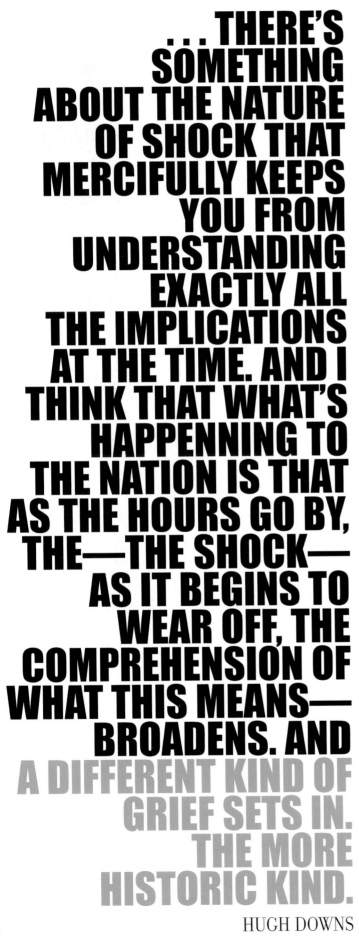

. . . THERE'S SOMETHING ABOUT THE NATURE OF SHOCK THAT MERCIFULLY KEEPS YOU FROM UNDERSTANDING EXACTLY ALL THE IMPLICATIONS AT THE TIME. AND I THINK THAT WHAT'S HAPPENNING TO THE NATION IS THAT AS THE HOURS GO BY, THE—THE SHOCK— AS IT BEGINS TO WEAR OFF, THE COMPREHENSION OF WHAT THIS MEANS— BROADENS. AND A DIFFERENT KIND OF GRIEF SETS IN. THE MORE HISTORIC KIND.

HUGH DOWNS

Jacqueline; Texas Governor John Connally; and Connally's wife, Idanell. The governor was seriously wounded but survived. Kennedy died soon after at nearby Parkland Hospital.

The killer, Lee Harvey Oswald, was arrested later that afternoon but was himself assassinated two days later by a shady Dallas nightclub owner, Jack Ruby, during a jail transfer. Only NBC was covering the transfer live at the moment Ruby pulled the trigger, with reporting from the scene by correspondent Tom Pettit.

Countless exposés, tell-alls, confessionals, and lurid revelations later, the once-gleaming JFK mystique has long since lost much of its luster. But at the time, much of the country had become enthralled with the notion of the Kennedys' Washington as a kind of American Camelot.

Whatever the reality, the Kennedyesque sense of youthful vigor was beguiling and an especially striking contrast to the sedate, aging Eisenhower. Kennedy had faced down the Soviets in the Cuban missile crisis, brashly proclaimed that the United States would put a man on the moon and bring him back before 1970, and stirred young Americans with his call to public service, later embodied in the Peace Corps.

Kennedy had managed to tap a vein of optimism that had somehow survived in the hearts of postwar baby boomers in their teens, a generation raised with the ever-present threat of nuclear war and Communist oppression. He had given them a sense of possibility, a sense that they could actually help forge a better future for themselves, for their families, and for the world.

And then . . . Dallas.

As news of the assassination spread, shock fused with horror, horror became despair, and despair melted into a dazed, surreal sense of grief.

"Today is Saturday, November 23, 1963, the day after the assassination of President John F. Kennedy," said a grim Hugh Downs. "The nation and the world today mourn the forty-six-year-old chief executive whose life was ended by a sniper's bullet as he rode through the streets of Dallas, Texas. I'm Hugh Downs. This is *Today*, a special three-hour program on the death of John Kennedy and the succession of Lyndon Baines Johnson to the greatest responsibility in the world. Jack Lescoulie and Frank Blair are with me today. And together, we'll report on a tragedy that has stunned and saddened men everywhere."

All three networks later abandoned the idea of distinct programs in favor of continuous, commercial-free coverage of the national tragedy.

In the aftermath of the assassination, television both discovered and demonstrated what it alone could do as a mass medium. It allowed the entire nation to share the same experience—the same grief and confusion and numbness—at the same time. Though geographically dispersed, racially divided, culturally fragmented, politically polarized, and split by age, religion, and glaring disparities of wealth, for those four days in November, Americans watching television with their families in their separate apartments and suburban homes and rural farmhouses became one with each other.

Television, and *Today* along with it, would be called to perform this service again and again—occasionally at moments of triumph, hope, and inspiration, but too often in times of more tragedy.

November 22, 1963: Hands reach out to greet President and Mrs. John F. Kennedy upon their arrival at the airport in Dallas, Texas.

November 22, 1963: The limousine carrying mortally wounded President John F. Kennedy races toward the hospital seconds after he was shot in Dallas.

November 23, 1963: Hugh Downs reporting the day after the assassination of President John F. Kennedy.

Left Photo, November 24, 1963: Mrs. John F. Kennedy looks straight ahead toward the casket of her slain husband.

JACK LESCOULIE: Well—as we were talking earlier about it—you and Frank Blair and I, you—there are particular instances wherein a person can tell exactly where they were when they happened. Pearl Harbor was one. And you will carry that particular scar to your grave. You will know where you heard the news about Pearl Harbor.

You would know certainly where you heard the news when President Roosevelt died. And certainly you knew exactly where you were yesterday and where you heard the news and how you heard it. Everybody just a little bit different.

It seemed to me that—the shock of it in New York slowed everything down. Traffic seemed to slow just—and—and not move. Every window in every car—as you passed and drove on the street had the radio playing. Most of them—watching every single minute of the reaction. Wondering.

People were—were very quiet when they talked. Trunk lines jammed in the telephone company. You couldn't get a call even to your home. People wanting to tell everyone else. Wanting to—to almost share this bad news—with the reaction. I'm sure if you tried to call NBC yesterday it was almost impossible.

HUGH DOWNS: I first thought it was the local switchboards, but actually the telephone company was so—set upon. You know what Adlai Stevenson said? That it's beyond instant comprehension. That's something that's coming home to me now more than in the initial shock. Because there's something about the nature of shock that mercifully keeps you from understanding exactly all the implications at the time.

And I think that what's happening to the nation is that as the hours go by, the—the shock—as it begins to wear off, the comprehension of what this means—broadens. And a different kind of grief sets in. The more historic kind.

FRANK McGEE: To Dallas, Texas, and Tom Pettit.

TOM PETTIT: There is Lee Oswald—[Gunshot] he's been shot. He's been shot. Lee Oswald has been shot. There's a man with a gun. And it's absolute panic. Absolute panic. Here in the basement of the Dallas Police Headquarters.

Detectives have their guns drawn. Oswald has been shot. There is no question about it. Oswald has been shot. Pandemonium has broken loose here in the—basement of Dallas Police Headquarters.

Now whether the bullet literally hit Oswald or not we are not su— absolutely positive. But there has been a gunshot. Oswald reached for his stomach doubled up. It will be impossible to determine whether he was hit or not. Did you see whether or not he was hit? He was hit, wasn't he?

FRANK JOHNSON: He grabbed himself on his side and—fell to the ground—

MALE VOICE: Right on the side.

TOM PETTIT: That was my understanding.

FRANK JOHNSON: —with a cry.

TOM PETTIT: We were, what? Four feet away—

FRANK JOHNSON: I was five in front of him—

MALE VOICE: Shot—

FRANK JOHNSON: —when he was shot.

TOM PETTIT: What is your name?

FRANK JOHNSON: Frank Johnson.

TOM PETTIT: And you're with?

FRANK JOHNSON: UPI.

TOM PETTIT: He did grab his stomach. I saw him—

Photo Above, November 23, 1963: Jack Lescoulie and Hugh Downs during a special three-hour program about the death of John Kennedy and the succession of Lyndon Baines Johnson.

November 24, 1963: Tom Pettit reporting on Lee Harvey Oswald from the Dallas Police Headquarters.

Right Photos, Sequence beginning with Oswald moving through crowd to be transferred to the Dallas County Jail. At about 11:15, Oswald is shot at point-blank range in the stomach.

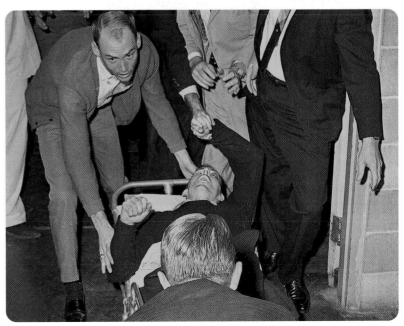

On an April evening barely five years later, the Reverend Dr. Martin Luther King Jr. was shot as he stood on a balcony at the Lorraine Motel in Memphis. In town to help rally support for a sanitation workers' strike, King died shortly after the shooting. Television coverage was spotty at first but intensified as his death was confirmed, and then as several days of rioting began in cities all across the country. King's killer, escaped convict James Earl Ray, was captured in London on June 8.

Three days before Ray was taken into custody, however, the national psyche suffered yet another blow when Robert Kennedy, the assassinated president's younger brother and senator from New York, was murdered during his own campaign for the Democratic presidential nomination.

It was a little past midnight on June 5, 1968, and Kennedy had just won the California primary. After thanking supporters gathered in a ballroom at Los Angeles' Ambassador Hotel, Kennedy and his staff were slipping out through a pantry area when the assassin, Sirhan Sirhan, walked up and fired several shots, striking Kennedy and six others.

As they did in 1963, all the networks shifted to uninterrupted news coverage of the story, and again pulled a disoriented nation together. With Kennedy hospitalized through the night, a clearly shaken *Today* cast the next morning tried to focus on the surreal task at hand.

"The senator," reported NBC correspondent Sander Vanocur, "is still in surgery in Good Samaritan Hospital to remove a .22 caliber bullet from his brain.... The senator [still] had consciousness," Vanocur noted, "after he was shot." The entire chaotic scene had been captured on film by news crews. Viewers saw the footage replayed all too often.

Regular programming resumed that evening on most stations. Kennedy died overnight, and his body was flown to New York City, where it lay in state at St. Patrick's Cathedral before being taken by train to Washington. The funeral, on June 7, was televised live.

Musician John Lennon was no politician like the Kennedys, and he certainly was not a towering civil rights icon like Dr. King. However, when he was killed by disturbed fan Mark David Chapman on the night of December 8, 1980, his death shocked the world. Lennon's music, particularly his work with the Beatles, had been an evolutionary force in popular culture, and the phenomenon of the Beatles, minutely chronicled in every communications medium, challenged traditional definitions of news.

In the overnight hours immediately following Lennon's murder, *Today* producers discarded the show planned for later that morning and began scrambling to pull together a program that would be devoted almost entirely to the Lennon story.

"The top story of the day in New York and around the world, for that matter," *Today* anchor Tom Brokaw told viewers, "former Beatle John Lennon shot and killed in New York last night. We have a live camera at the scene this morning. Lennon was shot at about 11 P.M. New York time just outside his home in the Dakota Apartments facing Central Park West. He was rushed to a nearby hospital but he was pronounced dead on arrival. Police blocked off the street as hundreds of his fans gathered to pay homage to the man responsible for much of the Beatles' success."

Violence returned to politics all too quickly. Three months after Lennon's murder and just two months into his presidency, President Ronald Reagan was shot and seriously wounded as he left a Washington hotel. The gunman, John W. Hinckley Jr., was a deranged twenty-five-year-old obsessed with actress Jodie Foster. Besides striking Reagan, Hinckley's shots also hit a Secret Service agent, a Washington, D.C., police officer, and Reagan press secretary James Brady, who suffered a terrible head wound.

Sacramento, May 16, 1968: Senator Robert F. Kennedy is held onto by an aide as he stands on a seat while campaigning in a motorcade.

December 9, 1980: Jane Pauley during *Today*'s special coverage of the murder of former Beatle John Lennon the night before.

December 8, 1980: Yoko Ono is aided by police as she leaves Roosevelt Hospital in New York late Monday night, after the death of her husband, John Lennon.

Today was off the air when the shooting took place; the next morning, the entire show originated from Washington, with Brokaw and Jane Pauley anchoring follow-up coverage.

"We are in Washington, D.C., this morning for obvious reasons," Brokaw said, "as we continue NBC News coverage of the attempted assassination of President Reagan and the wounding of three people next to him."

Sometimes, though, tragedy strikes live and in real time, as on October 6, 1981. "We want to bring you a late-breaking news story now," Tom Brokaw said urgently, just before the 7:24 station break. "In Cairo today, there was the annual military parade. President Sadat was attending. We are told that there was a single gunshot followed by a burst of automatic weapons' fire, and then all live Egyptian television coverage was cut off right after the shooting. And it has not returned. However, an Egyptian radio announcer is quoted as saying that President Sadat is safe. That's all we know at this time."

Sadat, in fact, had been seriously wounded, as Brokaw quickly learned and relayed to viewers. *Today* stayed on the air for hours that day, updating the story as more information became available. Eventually, *Today* reported the news that Sadat had died from his wounds.

Occasionally, nature manages to synchronize her rampages with *Today*'s broadcast clock. January 17, 1994: "Back now, eight o'clock Eastern time here in New York. I'm Bryant Gumbel here with Katie Couric. We are reporting and updating an ongoing story in Southern California where what seems to be a major earthquake has now struck the Southern California area. We don't know the intensity of it. We don't know the epicenter of it."

"We know it lasted about sixty seconds," Couric added. "There were several strong aftershocks afterwards, and several areas of Los Angeles have been . . . are blacked out at this moment in time."

The epicenter turned out to be Northridge, a suburb in the northern reaches of the L.A. metropolitan sprawl. It hit at 4:31 A.M. local time and its magnitude was 6.8 on the Richter scale. Eventually, the death toll attributed to the Northridge quake reached sixty-one.

Today's coverage continued until noon, Eastern time, evolving as time ticked on. It began with telephone reports from L.A.-based NBC producers and correspondents. Then a security guard at a Beverly Hills Porsche dealership phoned in an account. The network tapped into local feeds of the network's KNBC in Los Angeles and conducted interviews with officials at the National Earthquake Center in Golden, Colorado. Finally, as the sun rose and reporters and camera crews got out onto the streets, there were live shots and taped footage of the devastation.

Television news managers didn't exactly get a "heads-up," either, from Saddam Hussein just before his Iraqi armies invaded and began pillaging Kuwait on August 2, 1990. They got somewhat more information from U.S. officials leading the coalition of forces charged with freeing Kuwait, but very little free access when the air campaign started on January 17, 1991, followed by the 100-hour ground war on February 24.

Restricted access notwithstanding, one of *Today*'s most valuable contributions to public understanding of the Persian Gulf region came a month after the Gulf War ended. Starting March 20, 1991, the show set aside substantial blocks of time for a series on the religion of Islam. It ran three days in a row

Photo Above and Center, October 6, 1981, 8:00 A.M.: Tom Brokaw reporting on the assassination of Egyptian President Anwar Sadat during a parade on the anniversary of the October 1973 War.

Photo Below, January 17, 1994, 8:00 A.M.: Katie Couric and Bryant Gumbel updating the earthquake in Southern California.

Right Photo, January 18, 1994: An aerial view of a home destroyed during the earthquake in the Pacific Palisades section of Los Angeles.

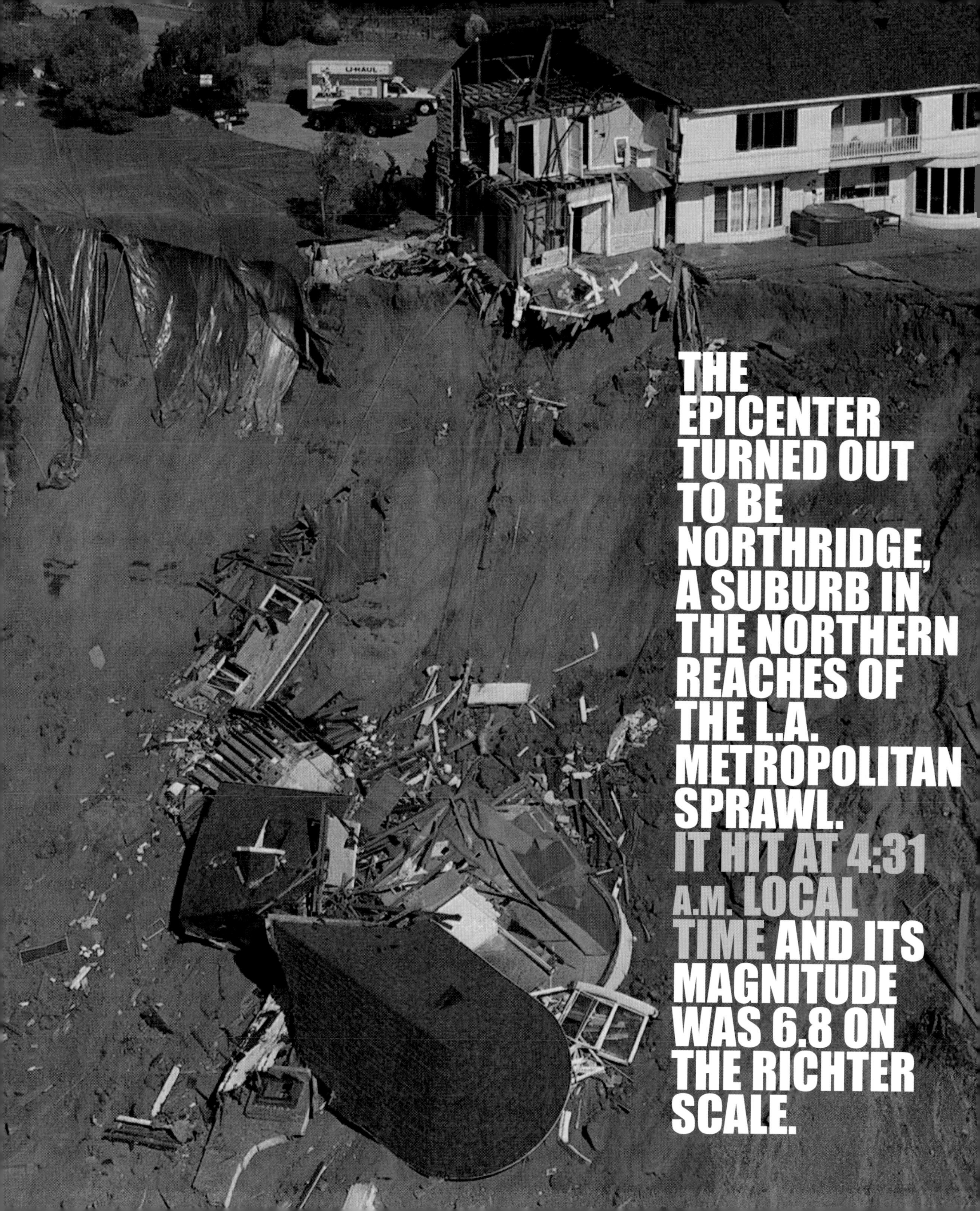

THE EPICENTER TURNED OUT TO BE NORTHRIDGE, A SUBURB IN THE NORTHERN REACHES OF THE L.A. METROPOLITAN SPRAWL. IT HIT AT 4:31 A.M. LOCAL TIME AND ITS MAGNITUDE WAS 6.8 ON THE RICHTER SCALE.

AFTER SEEING ISAIAH MURDERED, SCOTT SAID, HE LAY STILL ON THE LIBRARY FLOOR, PLAYING DEAD AND "PRAYING TO GOD TO GIVE ME COURAGE AND TO KEEP PROTECTION OVER US."

and explored everything from the role of women to the true meaning of the much-bandied-about term *jihad*.

Today has covered invasions, earthquakes, hurricanes, floods, tornadoes, explosions, droughts, famines, peacekeeping missions, genocides, catastrophes of all sorts. With every advance in technology—from communications satellites to slimmed-down cameras, microphones, and portable transmitters—*Today* coverage has become more immediate, more vital, and, in many instances, more heart-breaking.

April 22, 1999, Littleton, Colorado, co-anchor Katie Couric: "Eighteen-year-old Isaiah Shoels was to have graduated from Columbine [High School] next month. Instead, he was killed Tuesday, shot in the face while crouched under a table in the school library. Michael Shoels is Isaiah's father. . . ."

In a quiet, live interview of remarkable intensity, Couric delicately drew out the feelings of the grief-stricken Shoels and, seated next to him, student Craig Scott. Not only had Scott narrowly escaped injury and death in the library at Columbine High School, but he had witnessed his friend Isaiah Shoels being shot. Scott's sister, Rachel, was killed in another part of the school.

The segment was terribly sad, but it also contained a moment of exceptional warmth and poignance. It came during Scott's description of what had happened that day. After seeing Isaiah murdered, Scott said, he lay still on the library floor, playing dead and "praying to God to give me courage and to keep protection over us." At that precise point in the interview, Michael Shoels edged over and took Scott's hand in his. Setting aside his own grief, anger, and bitterness, the parent in Shoels saw a traumatized young man in need and reached out to console, steady, and comfort him.

KATIE COURIC, co-host (in Littleton, Colorado): Mr. Shoels, thank you so much for being here. We are so terribly sorry about your son.

MICHAEL SHOELS (son killed at Columbine High School): Okay.

COURIC: I understand from everyone at the school that Isaiah was extremely well-loved by the students, a very popular young man. Can you tell me a little about him?

MR. SHOELS: Well, Isaiah was very outgoing. He was a—you know, he was—he had a lot, you know, he had a lot to live for, you know what I'm saying? And I really do feel that he was taken out a little bit too early. I mean, behind a, you know—this situation is getting bad. It's getting bad.

KATIE COURIC: Eyewitnesses say your son was singled out because . . .

MICHAEL SHOELS: Yes, he was.

KATIE COURIC: . . . he was an African American?

MICHAEL SHOELS: Yes. That's what happened. I mean, that's not a way to go. It's—it's bad you have to go in a situation like that.

KATIE COURIC: What have people told you, Mr. Shoels, about what happened to Isaiah?

MICHAEL SHOELS: They—some of his friends are saying that he was supposed to have been going to lunch. And he decided to go to the, you know, the library, instead, you know, because he had a paper to do. And they said when—when they came in, they was—they was actually hunting him, you know. They was looking for him especially, and that's wrong.

KATIE COURIC: You think he had two strikes against him?

MICHAEL SHOELS: That was most definitely it. I mean, it's no ifs, ands, or buts about it. That's what happened.

KATIE COURIC: Because he was not only black . . .

MICHAEL SHOELS: Yes.

KATIE COURIC: . . . but he was an athlete.

MICHAEL SHOELS: Yes.

. . . .

KATIE COURIC: . . . this Trenchcoat Mafia. What had he told you?

MICHAEL SHOELS: Well, he—you know, we was—he always used to tell me that it was these certain—this certain group always target him and his sisters. And you know, by us being, you know, we're new in this neighborhood. I thought there was just, you know, they was just feeling inferior. But that wasn't the situation. It was true. And, you know, I hate—the reason I'm doing this is because I should have listened to my son and my children. I should have listened to them. Because . . .

KATIE COURIC: What do you think you should have done, Mr. Shoels?

MICHAEL SHOELS: I should have went to the authorities when this stuff was going on, because they had told me time and time. But I felt as though they were strong enough to overcome it, because I trained my children to live with every- and anyone. I mean, it's—it's no reason why anyone should be targeted out behind—behind what their achievements were or what their skin color was.

KATIE COURIC: How was he targeted? Was he harassed or did they say, "We're going to get you"? What sort of things did he tell you?

MICHAEL SHOELS: Well, he always used to tell me that they would, you know, they would—they would target him out and, you know, they—they would pick at him. And, you know, I would—you know, I would say, "Well, son, you know, you just have to overcome that. You would have to overcome that. But, you know, if you need me, just come to me, you know. If it gets that bad to where you can't handle it, come to me," and he never made it.

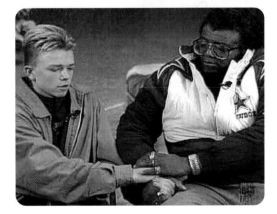

April 22, 1999: Katie Couric interviews Michael Shoels, the father of Isaiah, who was shot at Columbine High School. Student Craig Scott witnessed the shooting.

Craig Scott and Michael Shoels hold hands at the end of the interview, finding support in each other in the wake of their tragedy.

Not every historic moment, of course, is a tragic one. On July 20, 1969, NBC devoted all its airtime to continuous live coverage of the *Apollo 11* mission, climaxing with the thrilling live images of Neil Armstrong becoming the first human to walk on the moon.

A decade later, the Camp David accords brought the possibility of peace to the world's most troubled region: "In a dramatic appearance at the White House last night," *Today* anchor Brokaw reported on September 18, 1978, "Presidents Carter and Sadat and Israeli Prime Minister Menachem Begin announced that after thirteen days at Camp David, they have achieved a framework for peace in the Middle East."

In South Africa, who could have believed that a minority white government and black opposition groups in South Africa would find a way to end the apartheid system that oppressed the millions of its black citizens? Yet Nelson Mandela, a black man who had just been installed as the democratically elected president of South Africa, was interviewed live on *Today* by anchor Bryant Gumbel on June 24, 1994.

Only four years earlier, Mandela had been released from a government prison where he'd spent twenty-seven years for his actions as leader of the African National Congress. Now he was the leader of his country, live from Cape Town and on the air across America with Gumbel anchoring from *Today*'s newly christened, street-level Studio 1A in New York's Rockefeller Plaza. "Live from Cape Town this morning, we are pleased to welcome President Nelson Mandela," Gumbel began. "Mr. President, good morning."

Perhaps more memorable than Gumbel's interview, however, was the opportunity given to visitors on the street outside the studio to participate in the questioning.

"We're continuing live from Cape Town with President Nelson Mandela," Gumbel announced after a commercial break, "who has graciously agreed to take some questions from our outside audience. Mr. President, our first questioner is Jackie from Cleveland, Ohio."

Jackie, obviously thrilled to be communicating directly with the new president, asked about Mandela's plans to improve the education of black South Africans.

"We propose to build more and decent schools for our children," he replied. "We also propose to have free quality education and that for the first ten years, education will be free."

Other events qualified as historic simply because they marked extra-ordinary firsts:

On August 9, 1974, President Richard Nixon made history by resigning his office in disgrace after damning revelations in the Watergate scandal left him no support and essentially no choice. A special extended edition of *Today*, anchored by Barbara Walters and Jim Hartz, included live coverage of the president's farewell to his staff and his departure from the White House by helicopter.

On November 14, 1995, *Today* viewers awoke to hear this startling and historic, not to mention irritating, bit of news from anchor Bryant Gumbel:

"The U.S. government is officially broke this morning and preparing to shut down. A late-night meeting at the White House failed to resolve the budget impasse that has left the country without extensions of either the debt ceiling or spending authority. Although federal employees are going to work as usual this morning, 800,000 nonessential workers may be sent home later today."

And on the morning of November 8, 2000, *Today* found itself in the peculiar position of being unable to report the results of the previous day's presidential election. "Let's recap for a moment," said co-anchor Matt Lauer. "We still don't know who the forty-third president will be. The race hinges on Florida and its twenty-five electoral votes. The vote count there gives a razor-thin margin to Governor George Bush. A recount has been ordered. Meanwhile, as of now, Vice President Al Gore has won the popular vote. Clearly," Lauer said with remarkable understatement, "it's been a long and interesting night."

More remarkable, perhaps, were the prescient comments made two days earlier on *Today* by NBC's Washington bureau chief, Tim Russert. Asked by Lauer where curious citizens should focus their attention as the election returns came in, Russert replied, "Florida, Florida, Florida. I honestly believe, Matt, [that] as goes Florida [so] will go the nation. If I'm mistaken, I'll be the first to admit it. But I think that is the critical state. And we should have a pretty good sense of how that's going because the polls close at seven o'clock."

Russert was right about Florida but wrong about seven o'clock. In fact, all the television news organizations, including NBC, made pretty much of a mess of election-night reporting in 2000. The networks' own backup systems failed to catch faulty exit-poll data that had been collected and distributed by the since disbanded Voter News Service consortium. The result was an embarrassing series of on-air flip-flops by all TV news outlets about who had won Florida when and by how much.

Weeks of challenges, recounts, lawsuits in state and federal courts, rulings by state executives and appellate judges—not to mention intense political strategizing by both parties—kept the nation in suspense until December 12. After hearing oral arguments from representatives of Bush and Gore—a session recorded on audiotape and then, in yet another historic development, broadcast almost immediately—a divided U.S. Supreme Court issued a still-controversial decision ending the Florida recounts and, in effect, awarding the presidency to Bush.

Television pumped energy and immediacy into all these historic events and more. But the medium—*Today* included—seems to find the best in itself at times of gravest crisis, when viewers are feeling the most vulnerable, lost and

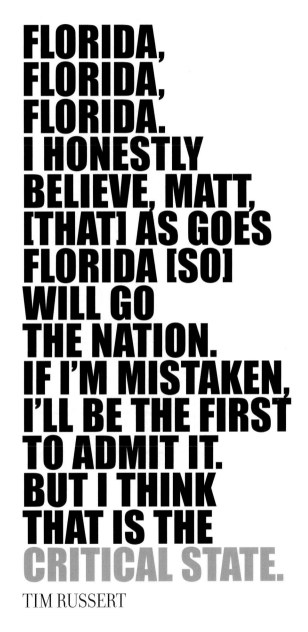

FLORIDA, FLORIDA, FLORIDA. I HONESTLY BELIEVE, MATT, [THAT] AS GOES FLORIDA [SO] WILL GO THE NATION. IF I'M MISTAKEN, I'LL BE THE FIRST TO ADMIT IT. BUT I THINK THAT IS THE CRITICAL STATE.

TIM RUSSERT

November 8, 2000: Matt Lauer reporting on the as-yet-undecided presidential election.

The decision rides on Florida's twenty-five electoral votes.

Tim Russert, NBC's Washington bureau chief, focuses on the importance of Florida.

THIS IS THE MORNING PAPER THIS MORNING, THE DAILY OKLAHOMAN. IT SPEAKS OF A MORNING OF TERROR, AND, INDEED, THAT'S WHAT WE'VE HAD. . . .

BRYANT GUMBEL

Upper Left, April 20, 1995: Bryant Gumbel in front of the remains of the Federal Building in Oklahoma City.

Upper Center, April 19, 1995: An Oklahoma City fireman walks near damaged cars on the north side of the Alfred Murrah Federal Building in Oklahoma City after a truck bomb blast.

This evidence photo of Oklahoma City bombing suspect Timothy McVeigh was taken April 19, 1995, just hours after the Oklahoma City bombing, at the Noble County Jail in Perry, Oklahoma.

shaken to their core. And nothing has produced more of those moments in our lifetime than terrorism.

April 20, 1995, *Today* anchor Bryant Gumbel: "Rescue workers are still sifting through the rubble of the Alfred P. Murrah Federal Building this morning looking for survivors and clues. They have been at this throughout the night, continuing a gruesome job at a nonstop pace since the bomb went off. That was almost twenty hours ago. Its repercussions will be felt for some time to come. . . .

"You can see the federal building right behind me, or what's left of it. Nine stories with a hole blown in the north wall. This is the morning paper this morning, the *Daily Oklahoman*. It speaks of a morning of terror, and, indeed, that's what we've had. . . . Let us begin with the latest numbers. Now, we will tell you, we'll be updating these numbers throughout the morning and they will be changing; but right now this is how it stands: Thirty-six dead. That's a number that most authorities feel is certain to rise. The injured, and this includes all those also who had slight injuries, are at least four hundred; and still at least two hundred are unaccounted for."

The final death toll was 168. Two years later, Timothy McVeigh was convicted of conspiracy and murder for the truck bombing; he was executed by lethal injection on June 11, 2001, in Terre Haute, Indiana.

In his live broadcast the morning after the blast, Gumbel called it "the worst terrorist bombing to ever hit the United States." However, it was by no means the first act of terrorism to strike Americans at home and abroad, even in the modern era. In truth, terrorist acts against Americans have been occurring with depressing frequency almost since *Today*'s birth. In 1954, five U.S. congressmen were wounded on the floor of the House of Representatives by gunfire unleashed from a visitors' gallery by four extremists advocating Puerto Rican independence.

Even in the context of Middle East issues, terrorism against the United States stretches back more than twenty years, at least to the 1979 seizure of American hostages at the U.S. embassy in Tehran. They spent more than a year in captivity.

With the exception of the Oklahoma City tragedy, apparently a wholly homegrown horror, the 1980s and '90s sometimes seemed like an endless procession of terrorist attacks against Americans and U.S. facilities, mostly overseas.

On April 18, 1983, an explosion destroyed the U.S. embassy in West Beirut, Lebanon, killing sixty-three people, seventeen of them Americans. Six months

later, a devastating truck bomb killed 241 U.S. Marines at their headquarters at the Beirut airport. Less than a year after that, yet another bomb killed twenty-four people at an annex to the U.S. embassy in East Beirut.

In 1985, TWA Flight 847 was hijacked on its way from Athens to Rome, flown at gunpoint to Beirut, and held for seventeen days while TV cameras watched. One American sailor on the plane was beaten, shot dead, and dumped onto the runway. Live *Today* coverage included an interview with Roger Testrake, brother of the plane's pilot, John.

That same year, a cruise ship was hijacked at sea; a disabled American vacationer, Leon Klinghofer, was killed and his body thrown overboard by terrorists linked to the Palestine Liberation Organization.

In December 1988, Libyan terrorists planted a bomb on Pan Am Flight 103; it exploded over Lockerbie, Scotland, killing 259 people in the plane and another eleven on the ground.

And in 1993, the terror struck home. A truck bomb exploded in an underground parking area at the World Trade Center in downtown New York City, killing six and injuring scores. A team of Islamist extremists was eventually captured, tried, and convicted of the crime.

Then more targets overseas: 1995, a U.S. military barracks at Riyadh, Saudi Arabia, seven killed by two bombs; 1996, Dhahran, Saudi Arabia, nineteen Americans killed in a bomb blast; 1998, U.S. embassies in Tanzania and Kenya bombed, more than 250 dead; 2000, seventeen U.S. sailors killed when the U.S.S. *Cole*, refueling at anchor in the harbor at Aden, Yemen, is rammed by terrorists in a rubber boat full of explosives.

DESPITE ALL THESE ATTACKS AGAINST THE UNITED STATES, ALL THE PEOPLE DEAD AND WOUNDED, IT STILL CAME AS A SHOCK.

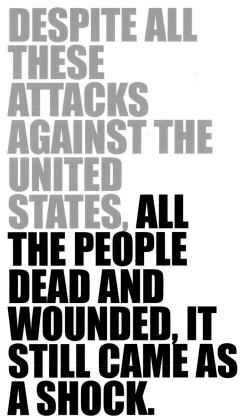

May 4, 1995: An unidentified member of the FEMA Urban Search and Rescue Task Force from Orange County, California, tries to compose himself at Tinker Elementary in Oklahoma City.

September 11, 2001: Live coverage of the World Trade Center towers during the attack.

Despite all these attacks against the United States, all the people dead and wounded, *Today* co-anchor Matt Lauer's report still came as a shock. September 11, 2001; "We're back at nine o'clock Eastern time on this Tuesday morning. And we're back with dramatic pictures of an accident that has happened just a short time ago. You're looking at the World Trade Center in lower Manhattan, where just a few minutes ago, we're told, that a plane—some reports are that it was a small commuter plane—crashed into the upper floors of one of the Twin Towers. You can see fire and flames, or smoke, billowing from that tower. There is a gaping hole on the north side of the building. That's the side you're seeing to the left-hand side of your screen right now. And other damage to the west side of that building, which is to the right side of your screen."

"This is the World Trade Center that was the center of a terrorist bombing some years ago," Lauer reminded viewers, "so the questions have to be asked: Was this purely an accident or could this have been an intentional act?"

To the horror of viewers and broadcasters alike—unmistakable even in the printed transcript of that morning's broadcast—the answer to Lauer's question became all too apparent as the minutes ticked away and live telephoned accounts of witnesses began to pour in. *Today* co-anchor Katie Couric: ". . . and also another eyewitness, Elliott Walker, who is actually a producer here on the *Today* show. Elliott, can you hear me?"

Walker: "Yes. Hi, Katie."

Couric: "Hi, Elliott. Tell me where you are and what you saw."

Walker: "Well, I live in this area. I returned to my apartment. But I was walking down the sidewalk delivering my young daughter to school. And we heard a very loud sound, the kind of sound you hear when a plane is, you know, going fast past you—*Nnnnnn*—followed by an enormous crash and an immediate explosion. I don't think we could feel shock waves, but we—we sort of felt like we did.

"And we were in a position where we could see the Trade Center almost immediately between the other buildings, and an enormous fireball that must have been 300 feet across was visible immediately, a secondary explosion, I think, and then plumes of smoke. I must be . . . there must have been a three-block cloud of . . . of white smoke. Now, from where I was on the street a moment ago, you can, in fact, see smoke leaving the building on three sides. It seems to be coming out on at least four or five floors. The area is filled with hundreds of dozens of pieces of paper that are just sort of floating like confetti. The area is swarmed with emergency vehicles and sirens."

Couric continued questioning Walker, but then something else, something almost inconceivable, happened, and Walker interrupted her:

Walker: "Oh, my goodness . . ."

For half a second, it didn't register:

Couric: "I mean, do you know if there were many people in the building?"

Walker: "Oh . . . another one just hit. Something else just hit, a very large plane just flew directly over my building . . ."

Today weatherman Al Roker also saw it: "Oh, my . . ."

Walker: ". . . and there's been another collision. Can you see it?"

Couric: "Yes."

Lauer: "Yes."

Couric: "Oh, my . . ."

Walker: "Something else has just . . ."

Lauer: "You know what . . ."

Walker: ". . . and that looked more like a 747."

Lauer: ". . . we just saw a plane circling the building. We just saw a plane circling the building, a second ago on the shot right before that."

Walker: "I think there may have been another impact. Can you tell? I just heard another very loud bang and a very large plane that might have been a DC-9 or a 747 just flew past my window, and I think it may have hit the Trade Center again."

The searing images spilled onto the screen, one after another. The anchors' voices stayed measured, constricted. They were, as everyone was at that point, uncertain of the facts, but there was no doubt about the need to stay composed, to carry viewers through whatever this terrible thing turned out to be.

The news only became worse. NBC correspondent Jim Miklaszewski, reporting live from the Pentagon: "Katie, I don't want to alarm anybody right now, but apparently there . . . it felt, just a few moments ago, like there was an explosion of some kind here at the Pentagon. We haven't been able to see or . . . or hear anything after the initial blast. I just stepped out in the hallway. Security guards were herding people out of the building, and I saw just a moment ago as I looked outside, a number of construction workers who have been working here have taken flight."

The images and their awful significance were seared into viewers' memories, and the steady professionalism of television news people reporting the events for all networks, including the staff of *Today*, earned national acclaim.

Barely a month later, the terrorism story seemed to take yet another bizarre and frightening turn. Envelopes containing the bio-toxin anthrax had arrived in the mail of some congressmen in Washington and media organizations in Florida and New York. The contents of one envelope, addressed to NBC's Tom Brokaw, infected an assistant in his office.

Brokaw had become part of the news story, and on October 15, he came to the *Today* studios for an interview with Matt Lauer. After asking Brokaw about the sequence of events and the health of his assistant, Lauer probed the sensitive subject of network security. "As two NBC employees," Lauer said, "we cover this story, we know about the aftermath of the attacks on September 11. Do you think that the systems here were vigilant enough, given the circumstances we're dealing with?"

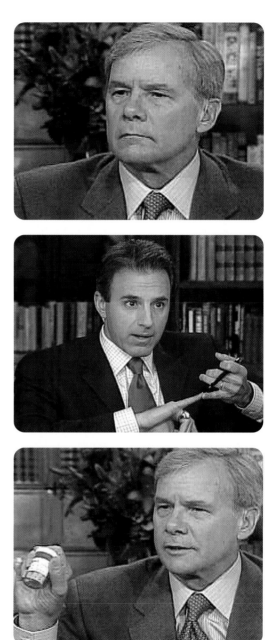

October 15, 2001: Matt Lauer interviews Tom Brokaw about an envelope filled with anthrax sent to Brokaw.

Tom Brokaw comments on his chance of infection: "I may have been exposed. I'm not sure, but I'm confident about the fact that Cipro's going to get me through this."

LIVE
CHOPPER 4

I DON'T DIMINISH THE FACT THAT THERE HAS BEEN BOTH EMOTIONAL AND PSYCHOLOGICAL SCARRING THAT HAS GONE ON HERE, AND WE'RE GOING TO HAVE TO WORK TO HEAL THOSE AS WELL.

TOM BROKAW

September 11, 2001: Live coverage on *Today* of the World Trade Center towers during the attack.

Right Photo, World Trade Center after the second plane hit.

Brokaw seemed uncomfortable discussing it at first: "I don't want to—I do think it is now, Matt, and I think that the—I'd love to turn the clock back, as I have two thousand times over the weekend."

Brokaw praised his assistant's courage and persistence, and then wondered about the long-term effects on everyone at NBC. "I don't diminish the fact," he said, "that there has been both emotional and psychological scarring that has gone on here, and we're going to have to work to heal those as well."

Scarring of a more literal sort figured prominently in an extraordinary story Couric reported on the air on March 12, 2002, six months after the Trade Center and Pentagon attacks. "There was a small group of people gravely injured on that day who are struggling to recover," Couric said. "One of those victims is forty-one-year-old Lauren Manning. Burned over nearly eighty-five percent of her body, she was one of seventeen victims taken to the burn unit of New York Presbyterian Hospital. Six of those people later died. But much to everyone's surprise, Lauren Manning lived."

As thousands of letters of support, mostly from strangers, began to arrive at the hospital, her husband, Greg, began e-mailing updates on her condition. He signed them, "Love, Greg and Lauren," even though doctors kept Lauren in a drug-induced coma for a month to spare her some of the excruciating pain of her injuries and early therapy.

Greg compiled his e-mails in a book that tells the story of his wife's literally painstaking recovery, including the moment she emerged from her coma and, later, the first time she saw her son, Tyler, who was just ten months old when his mother was engulfed by a ferocious fireball in the lobby of the World Trade Center.

There was no denying the powerful emotions of the Mannings' story and no effort to do so. Couric handled the interviews and narration with exceptional delicacy. Beyond that, though, the story struck a universal chord and conveyed something transcendent about the pointlessness of violence and the resilience of the human spirit.

Lauren Manning's survival had nothing to do with how she was injured. Whether it was the result of a terrorist attack or a house fire made not the slightest difference. All that mattered was luck, medical care, support from those close to her, the force of her will, and the strength of her heart. Anyone who watched her story on *Today* that morning came away inspired and enlightened.

...I DID NOT WANT TO DIE. I PRAYED TO GOD. I SCREAMED TO GOD TO LET ME LIVE FOR TYLER AND MY HUSBAND. THAT'S WHAT I WANTED TO DO. I JUST WANTED TO LIVE.

LAUREN MANNING

Greg and Lauren Manning in a snapshot before September 11.

KATIE COURIC: . . . Monday we mark the six-month anniversary of the World Trade Center attacks. We remember those who perished and we're thankful for those who escaped. But there was a small group of people gravely injured on that day who are struggling to recover.

One of those victims is forty-two-year-old Lauren Manning, burned over nearly 85 percent of her body. She was one of seventeen victims taken to the burn unit of New York Presbyterian Hospital. Six of those people later died. But much to everyone's surprise, Lauren Manning lived. Once you get to know her, it's not surprising at all. Lauren's husband Greg writes about her courage and determination in a new book called *Love, Greg and Lauren*. This is their story.

LAUREN MANNING: I mean, it was seemingly just—a very perfect life. I mean, I was very in love and am with my husband. And we were blessed to have—our son. And—I just felt so fortunate in so many ways.

GREG MANNING: We'd had a beautiful summer. We had a beautiful son. We had a beautiful life. You know we were having a great time.

KATIE COURIC: These are snapshots of Greg and Lauren Manning's life before. Married for nearly two years. A baby son, Tyler, ten months old. High-powered jobs on Wall Street, both of their offices at the World Trade Center. The morning of September 11, a phone call at home made Lauren late for her job at Cantor Fitzgerald.

You got to work, at least to the lobby of the World Trade Center, just before nine o'clock?

LAUREN MANNING: Just before the plane must have struck. I got out of the cab and there was this piercing loud whistle. And I was almost saying to myself, what is that? Should I go in? I proceeded to walk through the doors and there was this whir of debris flying. And seconds later, this fireball came and just hit me from behind. It kind of flung me toward the doors as it pushed me out, and I just floundered across the highway to a grassy median area where I laid down and rolled to try to put the fire out.

COURIC: A bond salesman came up to you and helped you.

LAUREN MANNING: Wonderful man came.

KATIE COURIC: Helped get the fire off you.

LAUREN MANNING: Yes.

KATIE COURIC: Put the fire out and stayed with you until an ambulance came and picked you up?

LAUREN MANNING: He did. He stayed with me and held my hand for as long as it took. He even moved me about twenty feet down because as I looked up, I thought from my perspective, the building was going to fall. Little did I know that that would happen at that time.

KATIE COURIC: Greg's office was in the other tower. A director at Euro Brokers, he was still at home caring for Tyler.

Meanwhile, Greg, you're at home. You're listening to a radio show and suddenly . . .

GREG MANNING: Yes.

KATIE COURIC: . . . you hear a plane has crashed into the World Trade Center.

GREG MANNING: Right. And I ran out to our terrace and see One World Trade Center with a huge black hole in, and all this black smoke billowing out. And I—my first thought is that it's just a direct hit on Cantor Fitzgerald. And so all of a sudden I'm thinking, you know, that she's somehow there and she hasn't made it. And then I got the phone call.

KATIE COURIC: And the phone call said . . .

GREG MANNING: "Mr. Manning, we're with your wife. She's been badly burned, but she's going to be all right. We got her on an ambulance."

And I said, "Where are you taking her?" The phone cut off. Twenty minutes later I got a phone call from St. Vincent's. "Mr. Manning, we have your wife here."

KATIE COURIC: You rushed to St. Vincent's.

GREG MANNING: It was eight blocks from our apartment. I walked over there. I found Lauren on the tenth floor. She was lying in bed. Her face looked like she had a deep tan. She was draped in sheets. And the first thing she said to me was, "Get me to a burn unit."

KATIE COURIC: Lauren, I know you said to your husband, "Greg, I was on fire. I ran out. I prayed to die. Then I decided to live for Tyler and for you."

LAUREN MANNING: It was a fleeting moment, because I did not want to die. I prayed to God. I screamed to God to let me live for Tyler and my husband. That's what I wanted to do. I just wanted to live.

KATIE COURIC: Hours later, Lauren was transferred to New York Presbyterian Hospital's burn unit, where she was placed in a medically induced coma for more than a month. Can you explain why you were put in a drug-induced coma?

LAUREN MANNING: I was put into the coma in order for the surgeons to begin working on my body, and certainly to—from the perspective of a human being that's been that badly burned, deal with the pain. But while I was in that comatose or sedated state, I was living in this other world. I have a very vivid recollection of fighting to find my way back, that I had somehow been taken to another country and struggling to come back to my family.

KATIE COURIC: I know when Lauren was first taken to the burn unit, you were told her chances of survival were less than 50 percent.

GREG MANNING: Yes.

KATIE COURIC: Later you found out they were far less than that.

GREG MANNING: Well, since Lauren was burned over $82\frac{1}{2}$ percent of her body, that means she had a $17\frac{1}{2}$ percent chance of making it. It was very hard to hear. And I kept finding things that reassured me that she had whatever it was she needed to overcome this.

KATIE COURIC: During this period, you would play her music.

GREG MANNING: Right.

KATIE COURIC: You would read Lauren poetry, poems like Robert Burns's "My Love Is Like a Red, Red Rose."

GREG MANNING: "My love is like a red, red rose, that's newly sprung in June. My love is like the melody, that's sweetly played in tune. As fair thou art my bonnie lass, so deep in love am I: And I will love you still, my dear, till all the seas run dry."

KATIE COURIC: Did you hear the poems?

LAUREN MANNING: I knew someone was there. I do believe I did.

KATIE COURIC: In fact, many were there for Lauren Manning. Thousands of letters and cards poured into the hospital for Lauren and the other burn victims. So many people praying for her survival.

You started e-mailing people and giving updates on how Lauren was doing.

GREG MANNING: The first thing I really said was, "Thank you for all your support and prayers," because they were coming from everywhere, from everyone who had ever known Lauren, was reaching out and just saying, you know, "We love her and tell her we're with her."

KATIE COURIC: And you signed all the e-mails, "Love, Greg and Lauren."

GREG MANNING: The first time I signed it, I wrote, "Love, Greg." And it just didn't look right. I just thought, She's going to make it. These are from her, too. And I put her name there. I wanted all of those people to have connected to her, to have felt like they had taken every step with her.

March 12, 2002: In the aftermath of September 11, Katie Couric interviews Lauren and Greg Manning.

Since the attacks of September 11, thwarting terrorism has become the top priority of the American government. Subsequent U.S. military action in Afghanistan clearly resulted from that policy. The U.S. invasion of Iraq in 2003 was also positioned by the Bush administration as part of its antiterrorism efforts, although that assertion remains the subject of bitter debate.

There is no doubt, however, that news outlets, including *Today*, covered the military campaign against Saddam Hussein's brutal regime with greater immediacy than any conflict before it.

Today's format was restructured around war coverage and its airtime expanded substantially, with continuing coverage supplied live in all time zones. The anchor team was geographically split: Couric worked from NBC studios in New York and Lauer from facilities near American military command headquarters in Qatar. Ann Curry reported from U.S. naval ships in the Persian Gulf and a variety of locations in Kuwait and Iraq.

Despite concerns about physical and ethical hazards, NBC and other news organizations large and small jumped at the Pentagon's offer to allow correspondents and TV production staff to accompany and, with some restrictions, report live on the actions of specific military units. The practice was called embedding, and it brought reporters and viewers alike into frighteningly close proximity to combat.

The danger was real; more than a dozen journalists died during the operation, including thirty-nine-year-old *Weekend Today* co-anchor David Bloom. On April 6, Bloom suffered a pulmonary embolism while traveling with and reporting on the Army's Third Infantry Division. While not directly combat-related, his death may well have resulted from a dislodged blood clot that formed during his long hours of cramped—and quite vivid—reporting from a specially adapted armored military vehicle.

MORE THAN A DOZEN JOURNALISTS DIED DURING THE OPERATION, INCLUDING 39-YEAR-OLD WEEKEND TODAY ANCHOR DAVID BLOOM.

. . . TODAY COVERED THE MILITARY CAMPAIGN AGAINST SADDAM HUSSEIN'S REGIME WITH GREATER IMMEDIACY THAN ANY CONFLICT BEFORE IT.

POLITICS

CIVIL RIGHTS MOVEMENT
ROSA PARKS
LITTLE ROCK
WATTS RIOT 1965
BLACK PANTHER PARTY
REVEREND DR. MARTIN LUTHER KING
O. J. SIMPSON TRIAL
VIETNAM
CHICAGO CONVENTION
ASSASSINATION OF ROBERT KENNEDY
NIXON'S RESIGNATION
CLINTON-LEWINSKY
PRESIDENT CLINTON'S IMPEACHMENT

Start talking politics in any location outside the I-495 interstate that rings Washington, D.C., and there's a good chance people will start scrambling for the exits.

But politics is much more than tiresome politicians, offensive campaign ads, and hustling ward heelers. At its core, politics is about power—the power to get things done and effect change. Sometimes, too, politics winds up being about the abuse of power.

Not long after its debut in 1952, *Today* began to focus on a political movement that was coalescing around the idea that black Americans, many of whom had served and sacrificed for their country overseas in World War II, had waited long enough for equality at home. The movement drew encouragement from the 1948 directive of then-President Harry S. Truman ordering the racial integration of the armed services. But it was galvanized in 1954 and 1955 by U.S. Supreme Court rulings requiring an end to segregated public schools "with all deliberate speed." The civil rights movement began to gather speed itself, developing and refining tactics for challenging the barriers to racial equality.

On December 1, 1955, Rosa Parks, a forty-two-year-old black seamstress and part-time civil rights activist in Montgomery, Alabama, defied a local ordinance requiring blacks to give up seats on municipal buses to white passengers. Her arrest became the catalyst for a year-long, city-wide bus boycott that demonstrated the economic muscle of the city's black community and raised the profile of a young boycott organizer, the Reverend Dr. Martin Luther King Jr.

It also confirmed the effectiveness of King's belief in nonviolent protest as the path to real change: On November 13, 1956, the Supreme Court upheld a lower-court decision that the segregationist practices of Montgomery's bus system were unconstitutional.

With the movement now attracting national attention, events in Little Rock, Arkansas, the following year triggered an extraordinary response from *Today*. On September 4, 1957, nine black students arrived for their first day of school at Little Rock's previously all-white Central High School. Although integration of the school had been approved earlier by the local school board, Arkansas National Guard troops under the control of Governor Orval Faubus refused to let the children enter the building.

On September 10, *Today* aired a live interview between Faubus and NBC's Frank McGee from the governor's mansion in Little Rock. McGee set up the situation succinctly in the accepted vernacular of the day: "Governor Faubus challenged the power of the federal government when he ordered his National Guardsmen to turn nine Negro students away from a white high school in Little Rock," he reported.

"Sir," McGee said, turning to the governor, "with two hundred armed National Guardsmen to do the job, why did you not permit the Negro students to enter the school and let the guardsmen proceed to contain the violence?"

Faubus's attempt to explain his actions was utterly unpersuasive, and it dismayed *Today*'s host, Dave Garroway, who shared his feelings with the audience. "An interview I shall never forget was just conducted by Frank

February 24, 1956: Rosa Parks arrives at circuit court to be arraigned in the racial bus boycott, in Montgomery, Alabama.

September 10, 1957: Frank McGee interviews Governor Orval Faubus from his mansion in Little Rock.

Governor Faubus attempts to explain his actions.

Photo Right, September 9, 1957: Richard Richardson, 17, and Harold Smith, 17, two of the six black students, attempt to enter Central High School in Little Rock, Arkansas, amidst jeering white faces.

Photo Right Below, September 9, 1957: Defiant white students block the doors of the school, denying access to six black students.

GOVERNOR FAUBUS CHALLENGED THE POWER OF THE FEDERAL GOVERNMENT WHEN HE ORDERED HIS NATIONAL GUARDSMEN TO TURN NINE NEGRO STUDENTS AWAY FROM A WHITE HIGH SCHOOL IN LITTLE ROCK.

FRANK McGEE

WE ARE CONFRONTED AS A PEOPLE WITH OUR GRAVEST TEST OF NATIONAL CONSCIENCE AND NATIONAL UNITY.

DAVE GARROWAY

September 1957: Dave Garroway expresses dismay at Governor Faubus's remarks.

October 9, 1960: The Rev. Dr. Martin Luther King Jr. under arrest by Atlanta Police Captain R. E. Little, left rear, passes through a picket line in front of a downtown department store.

McGee with the governor of Arkansas, Orval Faubus," Garroway said. "On this cool September morning, 1957, it is a fair question to ask yourself, I believe: Is this the United States of America? Is this our home? Is this where we live? Is this the country that we knew? And I don't have an answer to that question."

An answer of sorts was supplied ten days later by Federal District Judge Ronald Davies, who ordered integration at Central High to proceed, saying that Faubus's goal all along had been to deny the students entrance, not to keep the peace.

A frenzied mob unrestrained by local police on September 23 kept Davies's order from being obeyed, but two days later, with the National Guard now under federal control and one thousand U.S. paratroopers from the 101st Airborne Division on hand, segregation at Central High came to an end.

Today's coverage, however, was just beginning. One week after black students peacefully entered Central High, the show devoted an entire hour to deeper questions raised by the events in Little Rock. Garroway opened the hour this way.

"We are confronted as a people with our gravest test of national conscience and national unity," he said. "For the next hour, we'll try to explore some of the many complex issues which comprise this bitter debate over integration, which, in practice, means Negro children going to the same school as equals with whites."

In the hour that followed, *Today* allowed the advocates of integration and the defenders of segregation to make their case to Americans coast to coast. Viewers at home could then measure what they saw and heard against what they felt in their own hearts—and decide which side they were on.

As the battle for civil rights accelerated, news organizations began making the story a top priority, and developments began to unfold across the American South at a furious pace. In February of 1960, black college students began a highly disciplined campaign of sit-ins at whites-only facilities, starting with the lunch counter at a Woolworth's store in Greensboro, North Carolina. The next year, integrated teams of civil rights activists launched the so-called Freedom Rides, targeting segregation in public accommodations. Voter registration campaigns soon followed. And the summer of 1963 saw the triumphant March on Washington, where a crowd 250,000 strong heard Dr. King, at the height of his oratorical power and with the Lincoln Memorial over his shoulder, deliver his glorious "I Have a Dream" speech.

Though the movement's tactics remained steadfastly nonviolent, its actions were provocative enough to spark violent and sometimes lethal responses. The 1961 Freedom Riders were frequently beaten when they disembarked at bus terminals and crossed color lines to use facilities. NAACP leader Medgar Evers was murdered outside his home in Jackson, Mississippi, on June 12, 1963. On September 15, 1963, a bomb planted at the Sixteenth Street Baptist Church in Birmingham, Alabama, killed four girls attending Sunday school. In August of 1964, the bodies of three murdered civil rights workers were found in an earthen dam in Mississippi.

And on March 7, 1965—Bloody Sunday, as it came to be called—six hundred defenseless demonstrators leaving Selma, Alabama, on a fifty-mile march to the state capitol in Montgomery were savagely attacked by local police and state troopers after crossing the Edmund Pettus Bridge on their way out of town.

The brutality ultimately backfired, however. Graphic TV news coverage of cops on horseback flailing with billy clubs and masked troopers firing tear-gas canisters at praying protestors outraged the nation. A new march was scheduled, this time under federal protection, and by the time the group arrived in Montgomery on March 25, its numbers had swelled to 25,000.

Most significant of all, propelled by the media coverage of the events in Alabama, President Lyndon Johnson was able to push through Congress a sweeping Voting Rights Act with little overt opposition. He signed it into law in the U.S. Capitol rotunda on August 8.

The violence against civil rights demonstrators, however, was having another kind of impact. The incidents fed a long-simmering anger among African Americans over the heavy-handed approach police had historically taken with them.

Unrest was not exclusive to the South. In the middle of a searing summer heat wave in 1965, a drunk-driving arrest by police in Los Angeles touched off six lethal days of rioting and looting in Watts, a predominantly black enclave. Radical black activists found increasing support for their argument that blacks could not depend on the police to protect them.

Against this backdrop, a *Today* report that aired on July 26, 1966, attempted to demystify a new term causing concern in more traditional civil rights circles: black power. The extended segment included the perspectives of black leaders from communities as disparate as Harlem, Watts, Cleveland, Chicago, Baltimore, and Grenada, Mississippi, and it underscored the sense of militancy that was spreading within the movement.

Later that year, in Oakland, Huey P. Newton and Bobby Seale organized the nation's first chapter of the Black Panther Party. Activists in many more cities soon followed their lead—convinced that only blacks were capable of addressing the unique political, social, and economic problems of African Americans, no matter how sincere and well-meaning whites might be. The civil rights movement was splintering.

The harder-line approach embraced by some elements of the African-American community coincided with the broadening horizons of the Rev. Dr. Martin Luther King Jr. In 1964, Dr. King was awarded the Nobel Peace Prize, and, building on his now international status, he began to speak out about the United States' escalating military actions in Vietnam.

THE BRUTALITY ULTIMATELY BACKFIRED, HOWEVER. GRAPHIC TV NEWS COVERAGE OF COPS ON HORSEBACK FLAILING WITH BILLY CLUBS AND MASKED TROOPERS FIRING TEAR-GAS CANISTERS AT PRAYING PROTESTORS OUTRAGED THE NATION.

The Klu Klux Klan conducting a meeting.

August 1968: A scene depicting police directing a line of protesters.

May 28, 1971: Black Panther Bobby Seale, after serving twenty-one months in prison.

On April 18, 1966, *Today* aired a lengthy interview between host Hugh Downs and Dr. King, who explained the rationale behind his expanding perspective:

"The church," King told Downs, "being the moral guardian of the community, had to take a basic, forthright stand on the issue of civil rights. . . . I see the church as the conscience of the community, the conscience of the nation, the conscience of the state. And consequently, the church must be involved in all of the vital issues of the day, whether it's in the area of civil rights or whether it's dealing with the whole question of war and peace. I think the church has in many instances been all too silent on the issue of the war," King said. "There have been too many instances where individual clergymen and the church in general gave a kind of moral sanction to war as if it was a holy venture. And it is my strong feeling that we've got to make it clear that war itself is the enemy of mankind."

However justified his widening vision might have been, broad support for civil rights began to ebb. Black-power rhetoric grew angrier, and violence swept through African-American communities in Newark and Detroit in the summer of 1967.

King would not live to see either the fulfillment of his civil rights dreams at home or the end of the war abroad that had come to concern him. On April 4, 1968, he was killed in Memphis by a single rifle shot fired by James Earl Ray. His murder ignited violent disturbances in dozens of cities from Boston to Kansas City, Chicago, and Detroit. In the nation's capital, neighborhoods burned, and U.S. troops patrolled the streets.

April 1968: Chet Huntley of NBC News covers the assassination of the Reverend Dr. Martin Luther King.

HUGH DOWNS: I want to ask you in a moment about poverty and about war and peace. But right now, I—I'd like your opinion on whether you think the civil rights movement would have gotten as far as it has to date without the active participation of the clergy?

DR. KING: No, I really don't think so. I feel that the Negro himself must initiate many moves to end the long night of oppression, segregation, and discrimination. But I don't think the problem itself can be totally solved until there is a kind of grand alliance, or what I call the coalition of conscience working together. And the Negro cannot solve this problem by himself. He's 10 percent of the population. He needs allies over and over again in the white community. And I think we've definitely gotten further with this kind of cooperation from the church.

HUGH DOWNS: When it comes to the issue of war and peace, how far do you think a clergyman should go in the matter of asserting leadership? I have in mind particularly now the conflict in Vietnam. What can the clergyman do? What should he do?

DR. KING: I think the clergyman first must in his messages and through his congregation seek to get to the idea—ideational roots of war, so to speak, and seek to take a general stand against war itself. There have been too many instances where individual clergymen and the church in general gave a kind of moral sanction to war as if it was a holy venture.

And it is my strong feeling that we've got to make it clear that war itself is the enemy of mankind. And as President Kennedy said, "Unless we put an end to war, war will put an end to mankind." Along with this, I think we've got to deal with specific wars and speak to the nation and the world honestly about them.

And this is where I'm very happy that the National Council of Churches, for instance, Pope Paul and many of the Jewish rabbis of the country, have come out in very vocal and forthright terms calling for a negotiated settlement in this situation, calling for the recognition of Red China in order to ease tensions in southeast Asia, calling for a cessation of the bombings in the North and other things that are vital and necessary, I think—to bring about peace in that very turbulent situation.

HUGH DOWNS: There's been a lot of discussion in magazines and among theologians of a concept that says God is dead. What would be your answer to people who say God is dead?

DR. KING: . . . The other thing is—that is very important for me to say at this point, is that I feel that there is a greater and more dangerous type of atheism that we must be concerned about than the argument about God is dead. That's theoretical atheism to a degree. But I'm concerned about practical atheism, and that is, living as if there is no God. But it is my conviction that anyone who feels that life has meaning and that there are value structures in the universe—and anyone who has an ultimate concern believes in God.

The only atheist in my mind is a person who says that there are no values in the universe, and I do find people living as if there is no God, as if there are no values. And I'm more concerned about this kind of practical atheism than I'm concerned about the theol—theoretical atheism that will come and go.

This is not a new idea. Ever since the days of Nietzsche, there has been—discussion of the idea of God being dead. And certainly in many, many instances the name of God has appeared in the obituary column of philosophical journals and the ideas of our world. But in spite of this—God, the great reality, the principle of creation—that creative force for good in the universe always ends up breathing again.

HUGH DOWNS: Thank you, Dr. King.

DR. KING: Thank you.

Today
April 18, 1966
Hugh Downs
and the Reverend Dr. Martin Luther King Jr.

AND IT IS MY STRONG FEELING THAT WE'VE GOT TO MAKE IT CLEAR THAT WAR ITSELF IS THE ENEMY OF MANKIND.

REVEREND DR. MARTIN LUTHER KING JR.

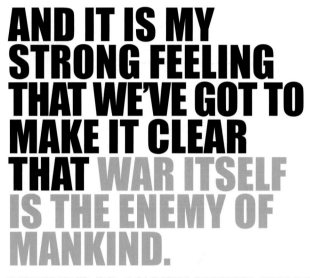

... THE POST-VERDICT REACTIONS SAY AN AWFUL LOT MORE ABOUT WHAT THE RACES ARE PREDISPOSED TO BELIEVE ABOUT EACH OTHER THAN ABOUT MR. SIMPSON'S REAL GUILT OR INNOCENCE?

BRYANT GUMBEL

June 15, 1995: Defendant O. J. Simpson grimaces as he tries on one of the leather gloves prosecutors said he wore the night his ex-wife Nicole Brown Simpson and Ronald Goldman were murdered, during Simpson's double-murder trial in Los Angeles.

Tuesday, October 3, 1995: O. J. Simpson clenches his fists in victory after the jury found him not guilty.

The early chapters of the civil rights struggle were written in the South, where the brazen grotesqueries of officially sanctioned racism offered targets that few felt comfortable defending. But the subtler manifestations of racial discrimination and prejudice, in the South and North alike, would prove more persistent—in part because they festered in the shadows of people's hearts and minds, and in part because, filtered through their personal and cultural experiences, blacks and whites sometimes simply saw things differently.

Just how different those perceptions can be—and how divided the country remains even now—was strikingly revealed some thirty years later in the aftermath of the criminal trial of O. J. Simpson, a black man who was one of football's all-time great competitors.

Simpson's ex-wife, Nicole, and one of her friends, Ronald Goldman, both white, were brutally murdered on June 12, 1994, and Simpson was soon arrested and charged with the homicides. The case became a media/celebrity spectacle and a societal obsession. His 1995 trial was televised live in its entirety on cable, and even the broadcast networks carried the trial live at moments of high interest. Race took center stage during the trial when defense lawyers exposed racist language used by a white police investigator, Detective Mark Fuhrman.

The brief reading of the verdict on October 3 aired live on dozens of channels at once, making it one of the most-watched events in the history of the medium. But more remarkable was the stark difference between the reactions of blacks and the reactions of whites to the not-guilty verdict. NBC cameras at the Howard University Law School in Washington showed black students cheering the result; whites at a bakery in Chicago were appalled.

Footage of the contrasting reactions was shown again on *Today* two days later as anchor Bryant Gumbel began an interview with two national newspaper columnists—the *Chicago Tribune*'s Clarence Page, who is black, and Frank Rich of the *New York Times*, who is white.

"Would you both allow," Gumbel asked, "that the post-verdict reactions say an awful lot more about what the races are predisposed to believe about each other than about Mr. Simpson's real guilt or innocence?"

Rich readily agreed, noting that America was in a period "where the signs of racial polarization are all out there. This trial just tapped into it," he said.

Actually, Page added, the dialogue between the races "broke down in the sixties. . . . We were too optimistic. White people in America, especially right now, look at how far we have come, and we have come a long way since the sixties and the fifties. But blacks are looking at how far we have to go . . . We need to get past our denial and start talking again about the racism that's still there."

The Vietnam War was conducted by the military, of course. Millions upon millions of men and women fought on all sides; 1.4 million were killed, including 58,000 Americans; and more than two million were wounded. But the Vietnam War was created by politics, challenged by politics, and finally, forced to an end by politics.

In the early 1960s, the battle between Soviet- and Chinese-backed Vietnamese nationalists in North Vietnam and a succession of U.S.-supported leaders in the South was positioned as a stand-fast struggle between communism and democracy. U.S. policy endorsed the metaphor of dominoes: If the North were allowed to take the South by force, the remaining non-Communist countries of southern Asia would topple, one after the other, like dominoes. In the most extreme scenario, Japan, the Philippines, and even India and Australia would be at risk.

In the 1950s and early '60s, Presidents Eisenhower and Kennedy sent civilian advisors and American military-training specialists to help South Vietnam develop a fighting force to counter the regular army of North Vietnam and its allied Viet Cong guerrilla rebels in the South. By 1963, the U.S. military presence in Vietnam had crept up to about 15,000, but the matter wasn't on many radar screens in the United States.

In the summer of 1964, however, an election year pitting President Lyndon Johnson against the hawkish Republican conservative Senator Barry Goldwater, Vietnam suddenly exploded into the public consciousness. On August 2 and again on August 4, two U.S. destroyers on patrol off the coast of Vietnam in the Gulf of Tonkin were allegedly attacked by North Vietnamese torpedo boats. Johnson ordered a massive military retaliation and asked Congress to authorize whatever actions he deemed necessary.

International tensions soared. NBC's Pauline Frederick told *Today* audiences on August 6 that even the nonaligned members of the United Nations were concerned that the conflict might intensify and spread.

Serious questions have since been raised about the official account of the first so-called attack in the Gulf of Tonkin, and the second attack seems never to have happened at all. Whatever actually occurred, the incident produced two immediate results: First, during the August 5 retaliatory strikes ordered by Johnson, two Navy jets were shot down. The pilot of one, Lieutenant Edward Alvarez Jr., became the first American prisoner of war in Vietnam. He spent eight and a half years locked up in North Vietnam. Then on August 7, a compliant Congress gave Johnson the Gulf of Tonkin Resolution he wanted, which he then used to justify an unprecedented military buildup in Vietnam.

By 1968, the U.S. military presence stood at nearly 550,000 personnel. But the increase in troop strength and combat operations brought with it increased scrutiny by the press, increased questioning of national policy, and increased casualties. From 1961 through 1965, before combat troops arrived, an average of 1,900 U.S. soldiers had died each year in Vietnam and another 7,300 had been wounded. In 1968, the U.S. death toll was 14,600, with 87,000 more wounded.

The year 1968—strewn with violent protests, assassinations, and riots at home—was one of the most traumatic in U.S. history. For the Vietnam War,

...1.4 MILLION WERE KILLED, INCLUDING 58,000 AMERICANS; AND MORE THAN TWO MILLION WERE WOUNDED.

Today image from Vietnam.

Antiwar protests often grew violent, as in this *Today* scene.

it was the turning point. Although the fighting, bombing, and dying would continue for years, the beginning of the end of America's involvement came on January 30 with the Tet Offensive.

In the midst of local observances of the Tet religious holiday, North Vietnam launched a ferocious coordinated offensive against the South's biggest cities. For a time, they even held the grounds of the U.S. Embassy in Saigon. "The Tet Offensive," explained co-anchor Katie Couric in a 1993 in-depth series looking back at the year 1968, "destroyed any illusions that the war in Vietnam would be won soon. The fierce fighting was a stunning blow to a public already deeply divided over the war."

In fact, the Johnson administration had led the American public to believe that the United States was well on the way to winning the war. Just two months earlier, top U.S. military commanders in Vietnam had returned to the States to bolster support despite the proliferating antiwar protests on college campuses. "I've never been more encouraged during my entire almost four years in this country," General William Westmoreland was quoted as saying in November of 1967. "I think we're making real progress."

Such reassurances sounded hollow at best as the Tet Offensive got under way. In the end, the campaign was a military defeat for the North, which suffered enormous casualties and failed to achieve its goal of seizing the South. But the political impact of Tet was just the oppposite. Graphic war coverage, airing mainly on network nightly newscasts, only added to the public's growing discomfort with U.S. policies, especially in light of the Johnson administration's sunny pronouncements.

Among the most distressing footage shown on TV was the summary execution of a bound Viet Cong prisoner, Bai Lop, on a Saigon street on February 1, 1968. NBC News cameraman Vo Suu was the only person filming when Nguyen Ngoc Loan, a general in the South Vietnamese national police force, fired a single pistol shot at point-blank range into Lop's head. (A still photograph made at the same time by the Associated Press's Eddie Adams won a Pulitzer Prize.)

After Tet, events seemed to unfold at breathtaking speed. On March 12, antiwar Democratic Senator Eugene McCarthy ran a startlingly strong second to Johnson in the New Hampshire primary. On March 16, New York Senator Robert Kennedy entered the race for president.

And on March 31, at the end of a nationally televised address, Johnson stunned viewers with this declaration: "With America's sons in the fields far away, with America's future under challenge right here at home, with our hopes and the world's hopes for peace in the balance every day, I do not believe that I should devote an hour or a day of my time to any personal partisan causes or to any duties other than the awesome duties of this office, the presidency of your country. Accordingly, I shall not seek, and I will not accept, the nomination of my party for another term as your president."

Days later, the Rev. Dr. Martin Luther King Jr. was assassinated in Memphis. A month after that, Robert Kennedy was slain in Los Angeles.

Then, in August, the Democratic Party and the antiwar movement fatefully converged in Chicago. Democrats came to anoint Vice President Hubert

Right Photo, August 1968: Chicago police arrest a man at Grant Park during demonstrations that disrupted the Democratic National Convention.

1968: Lyndon Baines Johnson announces that he will not seek renomination for president.

February 1, 1968: Eddie Adams's Pulitzer Prize–winning photo of the South Vietnamese National Police Chief Brigadier General Nguyen Ngoc Loan executing a Viet Cong officer with a single pistol shot in the head in Saigon.

June 5, 1968: Robert Kennedy the night of his assassination in Los Angeles.

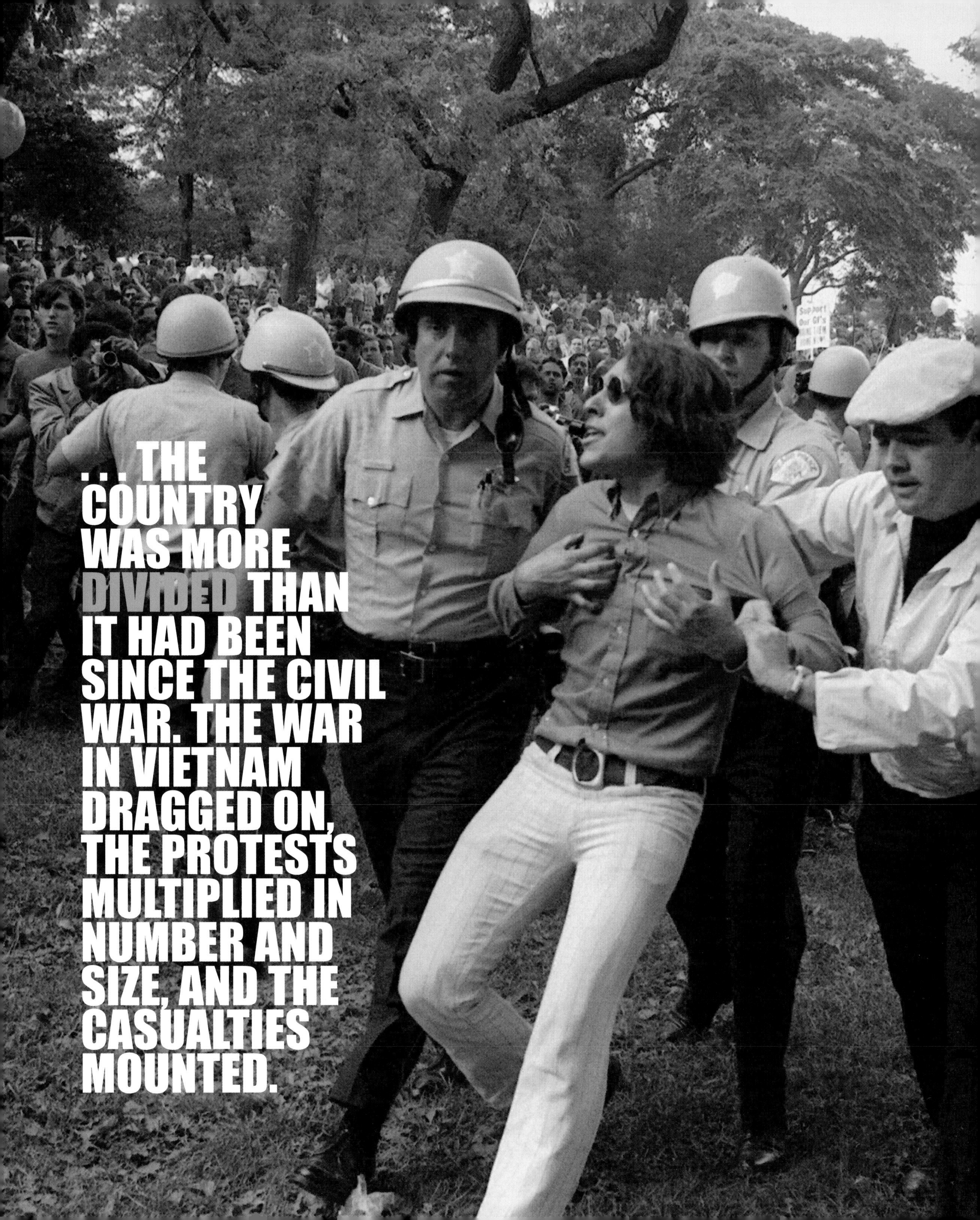

. . . THE COUNTRY WAS MORE DIVIDED THAN IT HAD BEEN SINCE THE CIVIL WAR. THE WAR IN VIETNAM DRAGGED ON, THE PROTESTS MULTIPLIED IN NUMBER AND SIZE, AND THE CASUALTIES MOUNTED.

AS A TAPED MONTAGE OF STREET VIOLENCE SCENES PLAYED ON SCREEN, VIEWERS HEARD FRANK SINATRA'S "MY KIND OF TOWN (CHICAGO IS)" PLAYING ON THE SOUNDTRACK.

August 1968: Joe Garagiola during *Today*'s coverage of the Democratic National Convention in Chicago.

August 1968: Violence during the Democratic Convention.

Humphrey as their presidential candidate. Protestors, riding the rising tide of opposition to the war, came to make a point.

But Chicago's old-school autocratic mayor, Richard J. Daley, was determined to maintain tight control of his city during the convention; however, in ugly incidents broadcast nationwide, demonstrators and reporters alike were beaten that week on the streets of Chicago and, occasionally, on the convention floor. A special study group of the National Commission on the Causes and Prevention of Violence later issued a report—the so-called Walker Report—labeling the events in Chicago a "police riot."

Today originated from Chicago during the convention, and many staff members witnessed or found themselves caught up in some of the violence inside and outside the International Amphitheater, where the convention took place. The closing credits of the final *Today* broadcast from Chicago summed up their experiences, with a bitterly ironic twist. As a taped montage of street violence scenes played on screen, viewers heard Frank Sinatra's "My Kind of Town (Chicago Is)" playing on the soundtrack.

By the end of 1968, the Democrats had lost the White House to Republican Richard Nixon, and the country was more divided than it had been since the Civil War. The war in Vietnam dragged on, the protests multiplied in number and size, and the casualties mounted. Publication of the Pentagon Papers, starting June 13, 1971, in the *New York Times*, exposed more government deceptions about the war.

A peace treaty signed in 1973 allowed the U.S. to pull out the last of its troops on March 29, and two years later, South Vietnam officially surrendered to the North.

The bitter divisions created by the war have been slow to heal, even with the passage of time and the cycling of generations. A week of special *Today* broadcasts in 1985, airing ten years after the fall of Saigon, examined a vast array of Vietnam War–related issues and, in deepening Americans' understanding of those difficult times, surely helped.

Anchor Bryant Gumbel was on location in Vietnam for the week; Jane Pauley anchored stateside. Reports spread across the five days included interviews with key government officials, both American and Vietnamese; military analysts; veterans; former protestors; and draft evaders. Stories touched on everything from the military and political lessons of the war to the effects of the herbicide Agent Orange on American veterans, Vietnam's environment, and the health of its people; the plight of mixed-race children of American soldiers and Vietnamese women; Vietnam's current economy; the role of women in Vietnamese society and much more.

But the most moving moments of the week may well have aired the first day, April 29. Pauley was live at the Vietnam Veterans Memorial on the mall in Washington, D.C., a place of extraordinary emotional power. One of her segments focused on a newly published book, *Dear America: Letters Home From Vietnam*, and as part of the report, some veterans and family members read portions of the letters aloud. The effect was profoundly moving. Among the excerpts read on the air that morning:

"Vietnam has my feelings on a seesaw," one soldier wrote from his military camp. "There are a few kids who hang around, some with no parents. I feel so sorry for them. I do things to make them laugh, and they call me *Dinky Dow*, which means 'Crazy.' I hope that's one reason why we're here, to secure a future for them. It seems to be the only justification I can think of for things that I've done."

"You know, I actually enjoy this tour," another soldier wrote to his girlfriend, "as long as I am busy enough to keep my thoughts from wandering back to you. But that is never for very long. It is almost strange that the one who has always made me so happy can now make me sad, because I miss you so much, darling one."

The wounds of Vietnam—physical, political, psychological, societal—still run deep. But in its broadcasts that week, and particularly in the segment on the letters, *Today* made at least some small contribution to the process of healing.

Soldier during the Vietnam War in footage aired in a *Today* special about the year 1968.

1968: A military burial during the Vietnam War.

August 9, 1974: NBC's Tom Brokaw on *Today* outside the White House on the day of Nixon's resignation.

President Nixon delivers his resignation speech with the parting words: "To have served in this office is to have felt a very personal sense of kinship with each and every American. And leaving it, I do so with this prayer: May God's grace be with you in all the days ahead."

August 9, 1974: *Today*'s Jim Hartz reports on Nixon's resignation.

The notion of political dirty tricks, especially in the rough-and-tumble context of campaigns, certainly didn't begin with the Watergate scandal. But during the Nixon administration, the practice mutated from sometimes elaborate pranks on the campaign trail into burglary, bribery, perjury, conspiracy, illegal wiretapping, and obstruction of justice in the Oval Office itself.

The scandal took its name from the Watergate office, hotel, and apartment complex just blocks from the White House in Washington, D.C. In 1972, the Watergate was home to, among other things, the headquarters of the Democratic National Committee, and in the wee hours of June 17, five men broke into the DNC offices to try to plant eavesdropping and wiretapping devices. Instead, they were arrested by police.

Found among their possessions was a phone number scrawled on a piece of paper. *Washington Post* reporters recognized it as a White House telephone exchange, and that slender thread of information became the launching point for one of the most celebrated investigations in the annals of American journalism.

The newspaper's pursuit of the story—all but alone at first—has long since been enshrined in nonfiction literature (*All the President's Men*, by *Post* reporters Carl Bernstein and Bob Woodward) and on the big screen. (Robert Redford and Dustin Hoffman played Woodward and Bernstein, respectively.) Other news organizations eventually started chasing the story too, as it got bigger and bigger and led higher and higher in the administration. NBC's legal correspondent at the time, Carl Stern, interviewed Watergate prosecutor Leon Jaworski for *Today* on January 18, 1974. Jaworski was trying to discover who was responsible for a suspicious eighteen-and-a-half-minute blank spot in an audiotape recording of a key White House conversation.

In one of Watergate's more bizarre moments, *Today*'s Barbara Walters snagged Martha Mitchell—the estranged wife of one of Nixon's closest and oldest associates, John Mitchell—for an interview that aired on March 12, 1974. Mrs. Mitchell had already established a reputation for outlandish, unpredictable comments, and the *Today* segment was no exception. She claimed that her husband, who had resigned as attorney general to become head of the Nixon re-election effort, was being set up as a fall guy for Watergate, although she offered no details. She had no explanation for why her husband had left her and didn't know where their daughter was. She complained that the media were making her look crazy, and she denied being an alcoholic.

Just five months later, the tone was far more somber as Walters and Jim Hartz anchored *Today*'s extended live coverage of Nixon's resignation as president, his farewell address to the White House staff, and the departure of the Nixon family from Washington. "Good morning," Hartz began. "This is *Today* in Washington, Friday the ninth of August, and at the White House, President Nixon and his family are preparing to leave for private life in California as the nation awaits the swearing in of Vice President Gerald Ford as the thirty-eighth president of the United States. That ceremony will come at noon, Eastern time, which is the effective hour of the resignation

announced by Mr. Nixon last night. He called his departure from office a move in the best interest of the nation, and he expressed hope for a healing of the Watergate wounds under Mr. Ford."

In the years that followed, just about all the familiar names in the real-life Watergate drama—John Dean, Charles Colson, G. Gordon Liddy, John Ehrlichman, Richard Kleindienst—turned up on *Today*, usually to promote a book.

One key Watergate figure with no book to hustle, however, was Judge John Sirica, whose rulings on executive privilege and Nixon's secret tapes played a major role in the scandal. Sirica appeared on *Today* on June 17, 1982, the tenth anniversary of the original break-in. In his interview that day, he called Watergate the greatest political scandal in U.S. history.

It would not be the last.

July 24, 1973: John D. Ehrlichman, Nixon's former domestic affairs advisor, is sworn in during hearings on the Watergate conspiracy.

The Nixon White House tape recorder.

IRAN-CONTRA

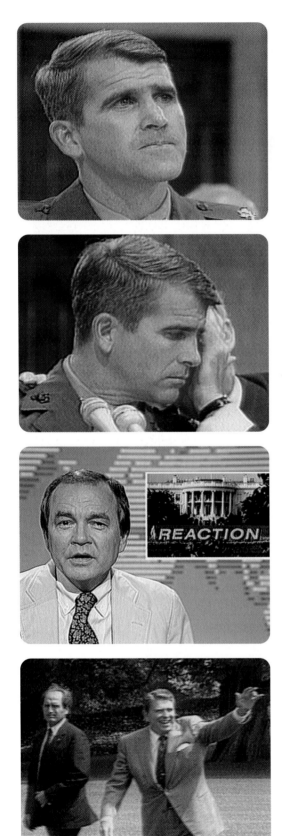

Summer 1987: Oliver North during his Iran-contra testimony.

John Palmer reports on Iran-contra for *Today*.

President Reagan denied that he ever knew that covert activities were being financed by profits from the Iran arms sales.

In Watergate, the president and his men abused the power of their positions for partisan political gain, to punish their perceived enemies, and to try to hide their crimes. In the Clinton-Lewinsky scandal twenty-five years later, the principal sins were marital infidelity, betrayal of trust, and legal evasions arising from both.

Between them lay the Iran-contra affair, in which officials at the highest and most sensitive levels of the executive branch broke criminal and civil laws and systematically ignored the fundamental mandates of the Constitution. They sought neither partisan advantage nor personal gratification but, rather, specific policy objectives denied them through legitimate means. Many regard Iran-contra, therefore, as the worst subversion of the American democratic system of all.

For most Americans, the Iran-contra affair was synonymous with the name of Oliver North, a Marine lieutenant colonel whose blunt-spoken televised testimony riveted the nation in the summer of 1987.

"The joint congressional committee investigating the Iran-contra affair is expected to hear from three witnesses today," *Today* news anchor John Palmer reported on July 14. "Former National Security Advisor Robert McFarlane will return to the witness chair . . . to rebut some of the testimony given by Oliver North. . . . But the first order of business this morning: one last opportunity for the committee to question Oliver North."

As a national security aide in the Reagan White House, North had been a key operative in a complex illicit international conspiracy, and he seemed wholly untroubled by it. Acting on specific authorization of his superiors—including, he believed, the president—North arranged for the sale of U.S. military equipment to Iran through middlemen. That alone violated an existing trade embargo. Besides paying these arms dealers for the weapons, Iran also agreed to persuade terrorists in Lebanon to release westerners, including Americans, they had taken hostage. That twist violated stated government policy of not negotiating with terrorists.

And on top of everything else, the arms-sale profits that weren't devoured by the middlemen were made available to the contra rebels of Nicaragua, a group dedicated to overthrowing the country's duly recognized Sandinista government—violating a specific congressional ban on aid to the contras.

By October, the committee's staff had begun drafting its final report, and the political sniping kicked into high gear. "Two Republican congressmen say a draft report on the findings of the Iran-contra committee is filled with anti-administration innuendo," Palmer told *Today* viewers on October 1. "They also say the draft implies that President Reagan knew that money from arms sales to Iran was being diverted to Nicaragua's rebels."

A separate criminal investigation of Iran-contra by Independent Counsel Lawrence Walsh found nothing to justify prosecuting the president. However, Walsh's final report, dated August 4, 1993, notes that "President Reagan created the conditions which made possible the crimes committed by others by his secret deviations from announced national policy as to Iran and hostages and by his open determination to keep the contras together 'body and soul' despite a statutory ban on contra aid."

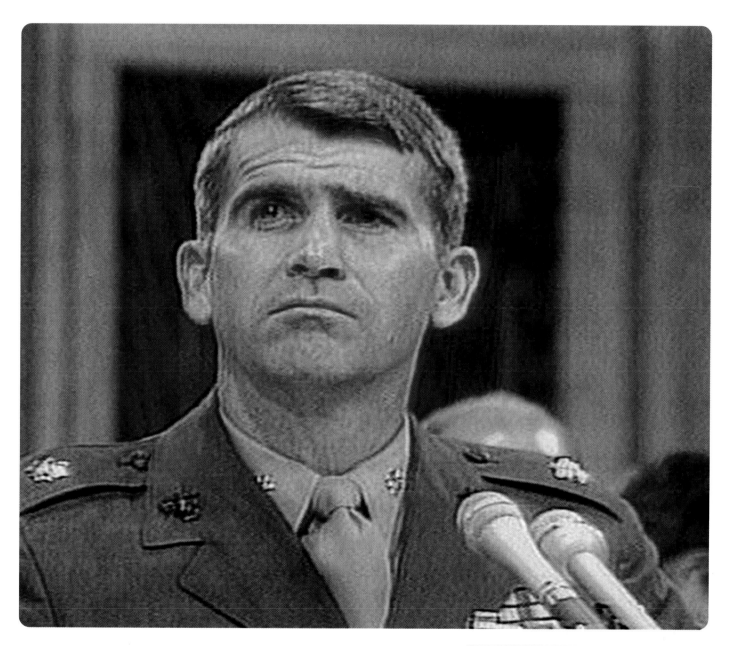

The investigation produced fourteen indictments, seven guilty pleas, and four convictions at trial on charges ranging from perjury to destruction of evidence to tax evasion. Two of the convictions—North's and that of former national security advisor Admiral John Poindexter—were later reversed because they had received grants of immunity before giving their congressional testimony. An appeals court panel said that their televised admissions might have contributed to their criminal convictions.

Two other indicted senior administration officials, including former Secretary of Defense Casper Weinberger, were pardoned before trial by then-President George Bush, who had been Reagan's vice president during Iran-contra and had since succeeded him in the Oval Office. The Bush pardons for his former colleagues raised serious questions, given that Walsh's report took note of the vice president's conflicting statements and delaying tactics during the course of the investigation. "The criminal investigation of Bush," the report concluded, "was regrettably incomplete."

1987: Oliver North during his televised testimony. Scene during Iran-contra hearings.

October 13, 1992: Katie Couric interviews Barbara Bush until a surprise visit from George Bush. At that point, the interview switches focus to President Bush.

KATIE COURIC: On the flipside, some observers, some Democrats say that you have not leveled about your knowledge of Iran-contra.

GEORGE BUSH: Glad you asked that, and I knew you would. You know how many questions we've answered on Iran-contra? Take a guess. You're not the—I'm—I'm the interviewer. I remember you told Barbara off a minute ago. But four thousand. Four hundred and fifty by me. Some under oath. Some to the news media. Thirty-five hundred questions by staff. And to bring this up in a desperate attempt to level it with the—with the failure to tell the truth on the draft, I'm sorry, I think they're totally different. So, there it is.

KATIE COURIC: But those—those questions were asked, Mr. President, were they not, prior to Casper Weinberger and George Schultz coming forward—

GEORGE BUSH: Well, what's the—

KATIE COURIC: —and talking about your knowledge—

PRESIDENT BUSH: —ask me. Now this might be a good chance to ask me the question you wanna ask. Which is it?

KATIE COURIC: Do you have any knowledge of the Iran-contra arms for hostages deal while you were in office—

PRESIDENT BUSH: Well, I've—I've testified—

KATIE COURIC: —as Vice President—

PRESIDENT BUSH: —450 times under oath, some of 'em; in our staff, 3,500. Yes. But nobody's accused me of not doing it. In terms of the contra part of it, absolutely not. And no one has suggested I did. Diversion of arms for support for the contras, no. And no one's challenged that. What was challenged, I think—I'll help you with the question. What was challenged—

KATIE COURIC: Oh, thank you, Mr. President.

PRESIDENT BUSH: Well—well—

KATIE COURIC: Go ahead. No, go—no, no, no—

PRESIDENT BUSH: —ask me that—

KATIE COURIC: I want you to go ahead.

PRESIDENT BUSH: You—you already—you already asked that—

KATIE COURIC: Clarify what—clarify what you think . . .

PRESIDENT BUSH: Well, what was asked was whether—whether—I knew the—that—that Casper Weinberger and Schultz, how strongly they opposed it. And I said to that there were two key meetings where I—where—where they almost got into a—a shouting match, I'm told, that I did not attend, but I said all along that—that I knew about the arms going. And I supported the President—I—I gave speeches about it. So, it's—it's—it's a crazy thing to try to equate this with telling the truth on the draft.

KATIE COURIC: Howard Teicher, who was an official with the National Security Council—

PRESIDENT BUSH: Yeah.

KATIE COURIC: —came on our program a few weeks ago and said he fully briefed you—

PRESIDENT BUSH: He did.

KATIE COURIC: —about everything—

PRESIDENT BUSH: I don't remember Howard doing it, but I remember—but—but not about the contra part of it. He didn't say that. Please be careful. He did not say that.

KATIE COURIC: He said that you knew the details and that you were, as we understand it, in the loop.

PRESIDENT BUSH: Katie, Katie, you're saying something he didn't say.

KATIE COURIC: Okay.

PRESIDENT BUSH: You're saying that he said I knew about the funds being diverted to the contras. I did not. And no one including the—in—

KATIE COURIC: But you knew about the arms for hostages.

PRESIDENT BUSH: Yes, and I've said so all along. Given speeches on it. But to equate this with whether you've told the truth on the draft, I'm sorry, I—I've been under oath on this. And it's—it's strange. Strange.

KATIE COURIC: Let me ask you, if I could, Mr. President, about the justice department investigation—

PRESIDENT BUSH: No, I—

KATIE COURIC: —of William Sessions, the head of the FBI—

PRESIDENT BUSH: I know—

KATIE COURIC: —Can you confirm—

PRESIDENT BUSH: No.

KATIE COURIC: —there is a justice department investigation—

PRESIDENT BUSH: I cannot. I just read it in the paper this morning. I just read—

KATIE COURIC: No knowledge of any kind of justice—

PRESIDENT BUSH: No, no. Nothing I know about.

KATIE COURIC: All right. Well, I can say they're making a move toward the Oval Office.

PRESIDENT BUSH: —out—we're out—

KATIE COURIC: Mr. President, thank you very much. What do you expect to hear in tonight's vice presidential debate before you go?

BARBARA BUSH: Come on, Katie.

PRESIDENT BUSH: What time do we break for the hour here? I'd like to be on for another half hour.

KATIE COURIC: You've got fifteen more minutes, if you'd like to stay with us.

PRESIDENT BUSH: I—I'd like another segment here—

KATIE COURIC: What—what are you expecting?

PRESIDENT BUSH: I think Dan Quayle will go—I love these polls. Ninety-two percent of the people or eighty-three think Gore will be the winner; sixteen Quayle. He'll—he'll—he'll do fine. He has taken a real pounding out there, and just so grossly unfair. Do you remember the p—you remember the pounding he took on going in to the National Guard? I do.

He served his country, and all the terrible pounding he got for influence, which indeed was not true going into the Guard. And now we have the guy running for president who wanted to stay out of everything. And oh, we gotta look back. It was twenty years ago. We gotta heal the wounds. Come on, let's have some fairness. Dan Quayle will do great in this debate.

BARBARA BUSH: Come on, we gotta go.

KATIE COURIC: Thank you so much for talking—

PRESIDENT BUSH: He'll be great.

KATIE COURIC: —with—Mrs. Bush, thank you again. Mr. President, could you join us again next week by any chance?

PRESIDENT BUSH: Katie—

KATIE COURIC: Nothing like a live request.

PRESIDENT BUSH: Well—

KATIE COURIC: Would you join us next week?

(The president departed with a wry smile and a promise to think about it.)

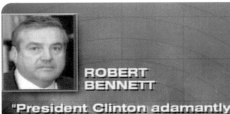

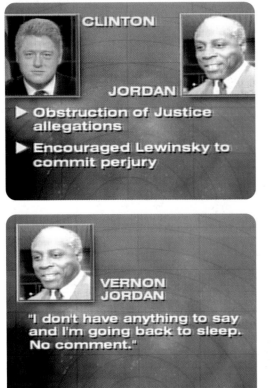

ROBERT BENNETT

"President Clinton adamantly denies that he ever, ever had anything to do with this woman. She is under oath saying she didn't do anything. I smell a rat here."

CLINTON

JORDAN

▶ Obstruction of Justice allegations

▶ Encouraged Lewinsky to commit perjury

VERNON JORDAN

"I don't have anything to say and I'm going back to sleep. No comment."

January 21, 1998: Graphics on *Today* as the Clinton-Lewinsky relationship emerged as a public scandal.

At the start of 1998, most Americans probably had no more than a general awareness of an ongoing investigation by Independent Counsel Kenneth Starr into Whitewater, a failed Arkansas real-estate development connected to President Bill Clinton and First Lady Hillary Rodham Clinton. The land deal had gone sour years earlier, when Clinton was governor of the state. The drawn-out investigation had produced relatively little beyond charges that it was politically motivated.

Little wonder, given that context, that a story posted on the *Washington Post*'s web site the morning of January 21 hit like a rocket. (A few days earlier, *Newsweek* magazine had delayed publishing a similar story to allow reporters more time to verify the information.) Reporting for *Today* from the White House, NBC's David Bloom told viewers what was happening:

"NBC News has confirmed," Bloom said, "that Kenneth Starr, the independent counsel, is investigating allegations that President Clinton and his longtime friend Vernon Jordan pressured a twenty-four-year-old former White House intern to lie about whether she had an affair with the president."

The allegations suggested the possibility of obstruction of justice. "Namely, that the two men may have encouraged Monica Lewinsky . . . to commit perjury. . . . I should point out," Bloom concluded, "*The Washington Post* broke most of the story early this morning, and that these are as yet unproven allegations against the president."

Thus began a cycle of charges and countercharges, denials and evasions, political calculations, leaks, some mistakes, blush-inducing revelations, and sometimes frenzied coverage that dominated the news for a solid year.

NBC News and *Today* pushed the story hard, sometimes generating news in the process. One of the early headline makers was Matt Lauer's January 27 interview with Mrs. Clinton. It had been scheduled long before the Lewinsky story broke and was to have focused on the issue of child care.

The first lady showed up as promised, and she and Lauer eventually got around to child care—but not before he had conducted a respectful but aggressive and remarkably direct interview about the scandalous accusations. "There has been a question on the minds of a lot of people in this country, Mrs. Clinton, lately," he began, "and that is, what is the exact nature of the relationship between your husband and Monica Lewinsky? Has he described the relationship in detail to you?"

The interview ran almost twenty minutes. It was tense and compelling. Lauer tried to get Mrs. Clinton to say what she knew, what the president had told her, and which reported incidents might be true; Mrs. Clinton was supportive of her husband, unruffled despite the personal nature of the discussion, and shrewdly circumspect.

"I think the important thing now is to stand as firmly as I can," she repeated, "and say that, you know, that the president has denied these allegations on all counts, unequivocally, and we'll see how this plays out. . . . Everybody says to me, 'How can you be so calm?' or 'How can you just, you know, look like you're not upset?' And I guess I've just been through it so many times. I mean, Bill and I have been accused of everything, including murder, by some of the very same people who are behind these allegations."

Several questions and answers later, Lauer followed up Mrs. Clinton's comment

about their accusers. "You have said, I understand, to some close friends, that this is the last great battle," Lauer said, "and that one side or the other is going down here."

"Well, I don't know if I've been that dramatic," she replied, "but I do believe that this is a battle. . . . This is the great story here, for anybody willing to find it and write about it and explain it, [sic] is this vast right-wing conspiracy that has been conspiring against my husband since the day he announced for president. A few journalists have kind of caught on to it and explained it, but it has not yet been fully revealed to the American public. And, actually, you know, in a bizarre sort of way, this may do it."

And it might have—her right-wing-conspiracy assertion was not without foundation—except that the president, in fact, had lied about Lewinsky. Whether he did so under oath is debatable, but he certainly lied about it to his staff, his friends, the American people, and, for a time, to his wife.

The truth—or, at least, something a lot closer to it—emerged many months and much legal and political maneuvering later in a televised prime-time

Deccember 19, 1998: Holding hands with first lady Hillary Rodham Clinton, President Clinton prepares to speak at the White House following the historic impeachment vote by the House of Representatives.

Monica Lewinsky and President Clinton before the scandal broke.

... YOU KNOW, THAT THE PRESIDENT HAS DENIED THESE ALLEGATIONS ON ALL COUNTS, UNEQUIVOCALLY AND WE'LL SEE HOW THIS PLAYS OUT.

HILLARY RODHAM CLINTON

February 12, 1999: Ann Curry reports on the expected result of Clinton's trial in the Senate.

President Clinton strides across the White House lawn.

address by Clinton on August 17. The next morning on *Today*, Lauer asked *Newsweek* columnist Jonathan Alter and former Clinton press secretary Dee Dee Myers to assess the speech—and the damage.

"Well, in all honesty, Matt, I was a little disappointed," Myers said. "I think the president missed an oppportunity to rise above it in a way, to really come to the nation to apologize in a slightly more heartfelt way and to leave it at that."

Alter concurred. "You can see his anger being projected from where it should be—at himself—onto other people. Whatever their excesses, whatever Ken Starr may have done wrong in the investigation, whatever the press may have done wrong, this starts with Clinton in a fundamental act of irrationality," Alter said. "At the core of this is why he did something that was so stupid, especially by a man who we know is so smart."

Clinton might well have handled his confession with more grace, but that probably would not have altered the fate that awaited him. After all, opinion polls already suggested that ordinary Americans thought Clinton was doing a decent job as president, even though they were appalled by his conduct. But his political adversaries smelled blood in the water and history in the making. They would make history, but they wouldn't get blood.

On Saturday, December 20, 1998, the House of Representatives passed two articles of impeachment against Clinton, one charging him with grand jury perjury and one with obstruction of justice.

The next morning, Sunday's *Today* opened with a tape of Saturday's announcement of the House vote tally, and then Jack Ford, the show's co-host at the time, summed up the moment: "With those words, an elected president was impeached for the first time in U.S. history, leaving Bill Clinton and the nation uncertain about their futures today. . . ."

And they would remain uncertain for nearly two months. The impeachment trial began January 7, 1999, in the United States Senate with Supreme Court Chief Justice William Rehnquist presiding. It ended on February 12 with Clinton's acquittal. Early that morning, *Today* news anchor Ann Curry read the headline-to-be: "The Senate is preparing to make history this morning with a verdict in the trial of President Clinton," Curry said as she introduced NBC's Joe Johns from Capitol Hill.

"The framers of the Constitution," Johns reported, "made it hard to try, convict, and remove a president from office—so hard that it has never been done, and members of the Senate do not expect it to happen today." It did not.

Clinton was shamed but still president, spared because enough senators decided that lying to cover up an extramarital affair—even lying under oath— did not constitute "high crimes and misdemeanors," the Constitution's standard for removal from office.

MATT LAUER: . . . There has been a question on the minds of a lot of people in this country, Mrs. Clinton, lately, and that is what is the exact nature of the relationship between your husband and Monica Lewinsky? Has he described that relationship in detail to you?

MRS. CLINTON: Well, we've talked at great length. And I think as this matter unfolds, the entire country will have more information. But we're right in the middle of a rather vigorous feeding frenzy right now. People are saying all kinds of things, putting out rumor and innuendo. And I have learned over the last many years being involved in politics, and especially since my husband first started running for president, that the best thing to do in these cases is just to be patient, take a deep breath, and the truth will come out. But there's nothing we can do to fight this firestorm of allegations that are out there.

MATT LAUER: But he has described to the American people what this relationship was not . . .

MRS. CLINTON: That's right.

MATT LAUER: . . . in his words.

MRS. CLINTON: That's right.

MATT LAUER: Has he described to you what it was?

MRS. CLINTON: Yes. And we'll—and we'll find that out as time goes by, Matt. But I think the important thing now is to stand as firmly as I can and say that, you know, that the president has denied these allegations on all counts, unequivocally, and we'll—we'll see how this plays out. I guess—everybody says to me, "How can you be so calm?" or "How can you just, you know, look like you're not upset?" And I guess I've just been through it so many times. I mean, Bill and I have been accused of everything, including murder, by some of the very same people who are behind these allegations. So from my perspective, this is part of the continuing political campaign against my husband.

MATT LAUER: To the best of your knowledge, Mrs. Clinton, has your husband ever given or received gifts from or to Monica Lewinsky?

MRS. CLINTON: I'm not going to comment on any specific allegation, because I've learned we need to put all of this into context, and it will be put into context. And anyone who knows my husband knows that he is an extremely generous person to people he knows, to strangers, to anybody who is around him. And I think that, you know, his behavior, his treatment of people will certainly explain all of this.

· ·

MATT LAUER: We're talking about Kenneth Starr, so let's . . .

MRS. CLINTON: . . . well, we're talking about—but it's the whole operation. It's—it's not just one person, it's an entire operation.

MATT LAUER: Did he go outside of his rights, in your opinion, to expand this investigation? After all, he got permission to expand the investigation from a three-judge panel.

MRS. CLINTON: The same three-judge panel that removed Robert Fiske and appointed him. The same three-judge panel that is headed by someone who is appointed by Jesse Helms and Lauch Faircloth.

MATT LAUER: Also, Judge Reno approved . . .

MRS. CLINTON: Well, of course . . .

MATT LAUER: . . . this expansion of an investigation

MRS. CLINTON: . . . well, you're—of course she is, because she doesn't want to appear as though she's interfering with an investigation. I don't—look, I—I'm not going to take all that on, because I've learned that we just have to ride this out. It's just a very unfortunate turn of events that we are using the criminal justice system to try to achieve political ends in this country. And—and, you know, when I'm here today, I'm not

YOU KNOW, WE'VE BEEN MARRIED FOR 22 YEARS, MATT, AND I HAVE LEARNED A LONG TIME AGO THAT THE ONLY PEOPLE WHO COUNT IN ANY MARRIAGE ARE THE TWO THAT ARE IN IT.

HILLARY RODHAM CLINTON

only here because I love and believe my husband, I'm also here because I love and believe in my country. And if I were just a citizen out there, maybe because I know about the law and I have some idea, some of the motivations here, I would be very disturbed by this turn of events.

MATT LAUER: When—when—the last time we visited a subject like this involving your family was 1992, and the name Gennifer Flowers was in the news . . .

MRS. CLINTON: Mm-hmm.

MATT LAUER: . . . and you said at the time of the interview, a very famous quote, "I'm not some Tammy Wynette standing by my man."

MRS. CLINTON: Mm-hmm.

MATT LAUER: In the same interview, your husband had admitted that he had, quote, "caused pain in your marriage."

MRS. CLINTON: Mm-hmm.

MATT LAUER: Six years later you are still standing by this man, your husband . . .

MRS. CLINTON: Mm-hmm.

MATT LAUER: . . . through some difficult charges. If he were to be asked today, Mrs. Clinton, do you think he would admit that he again has caused pain in this marriage?

MRS. CLINTON: No. Absolutely not, and he shouldn't. You know, we've been married for twenty-two years, Matt, and I have learned a long time ago that the only people who count in any marriage are the two that are in it. We know everything there is to know about each other, and we understand and accept and love each other. And I just think that a lot of this is deliberately designed to sensationalize charges against my husband, because everything else they've tried has failed. And I also believe that it's part of an effort, very frankly, to undo the results of two elections.

MATT LAUER: Le—let me talk about your role. There have been reports that you've taken charge at the White House and decided to be the chief defender of your husband, of the president, and deflect these charges. How much of a role are you taking in this, do you think you should take?

MRS. CLINTON: Well, I certainly am going to defend my husband. And I'm certainly going to offer advice. But I am by no means running any kind of strategy or being his chief defender. He's got very capable lawyers and very capable people inside the White House, and a lot of very good friends outside the White House.

MATT LAUER: But you're probably the most credible defender of the president at this time.

MRS. CLINTON: Well, I probably know him better than anybody alive in the world, so I would hope that I'd be the most credible defender.

MATT LAUER: James Carville, who you know . . .

MRS. CLINTON: Great human being.

MATT LAUER: I'm sure you like him, especially at this time. He has said that this is war between the president and Kenneth Starr. You have said, I understand, to some close friends that this is the last great battle, and that one side or the other is going down here.

MRS. CLINTON: Well, I don't know if I've been that dramatic. That would sound like a good line from a movie. But I do believe that this is a battle. I mean, look at the very people who are involved in this, they have popped up in other settings. This is the great story here, for anybody willing to find it and write about it and explain it, is this vast right-wing conspiracy that has been conspiring against my husband since the day he announced for president. A few journalists have kind of caught on to it and explained it, but it has not yet been fully revealed to the American public. And, actually, you know, in a bizarre sort of way, this may do it.

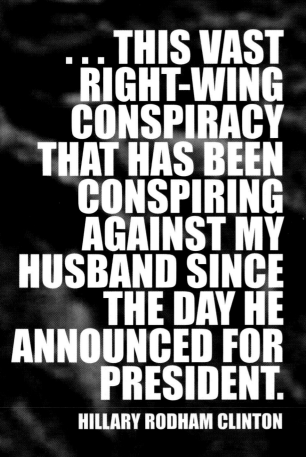

. . . THIS VAST RIGHT-WING CONSPIRACY THAT HAS BEEN CONSPIRING AGAINST MY HUSBAND SINCE THE DAY HE ANNOUNCED FOR PRESIDENT.

HILLARY RODHAM CLINTON

LIFE ISSUES

WOMEN'S PROGRESS
DR. SALLY RIDE
ANITA HILL CONTROVERSY
ENVIRONMENTAL AWARENESS
EARTH DAY
THREE MILE ISLAND
LOVE CANAL
CHERNOBYL DISASTER
COMPUTER REVOLUTION
MAN ON THE MOON
APOLLO 11 MISSION
CHALLENGER DISASTER
FIRST LIVE KIDNEY TRANSPLANT
AIDS/HIV
COLON CANCER COVERAGE

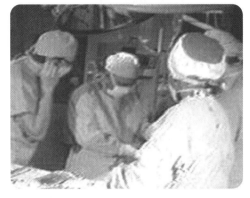

Estelle Parsons, top,
Helen O'Connell with Dave Garroway,
and Betsy Palmer with Frank Blair, bottom,
all served as *Today* Girls in the early years.

If there is one unfailing certainty in life, it's that the pace of change is constantly accelerating.

The fifty-plus years since *Today* first appeared have witnessed the most sweeping changes in human history. There have been mind-boggling leaps in science and technology, in medicine, and in how humans understand their place in the world's complex ecosystem. Maybe most important of all, though, have been the changes in how men and women think about and relate to each other.

On March 3, 1952, a *Today* newscast closed with one of those stories intended to leave viewers smiling at the goofy things people do sometimes. It seems that the good people of Aurora, Illinois, had celebrated leap year by doing something completely crazy on February 29. They let the women run the town!

That *Today* would offer this item as a small amusement to its viewers was hardly surprising. The notion of women as comically out of place in the political arena—and most every place else except the home—was widely held at the mid-point of the twentieth century, at least by men. At the time *Today* premiered, remember, American women had been able to vote for their president for only the last thirty-two of the 176 years since the founding fathers had signed the Declaration of Independence.

During World War II, things had been different; with the men off fighting the good fight against fascism, necessity became the mother of female employment. America needed its women to work, and some seven million did—two million of them in industrial jobs. But after the war, women once again found themselves pigeonholed by constricting stereotypes. Among them:

—Only women can bear children, and only women are emotionally suited to rear and nurture them. Working outside the home runs counter to these biological imperatives.

—Women, the fairer sex, are also the weaker sex, pound for pound. They need, deserve, and want protection from the grind of daily employment. A single woman might take a job for a while to support herself, but only until she snags a man to marry and provide for her and their offspring.

Early *Today* mirrored what it supposed were the beliefs of its audience about gender roles, and it had no reason to doubt them. But as those attitudes evolved over time, the show changed with them, albeit slowly.

However substantive the contributions of women were behind the scenes in the early years of *Today*, when they were put in front of the cameras, their function became more ornamental, although there were occasional exceptions.

Estelle Parsons, who went on to an award-winning career as an actress, was a *Today* production assistant before the show even premiered. During her two-year stint on staff, Parsons booked guests, wrote background materials for the on-air cast and conducted off-air interviews for later broadcast, many with a focus on politics.

Parsons eventually began appearing on camera. "Dave [Garroway] came to me," Parsons told Katie Couric on *Today*'s fiftieth anniversary broadcast,

"and said, 'You wrote this book review. Why don't you do it on the air?'"
Parsons said she never thought Garroway was suggesting an equality of the
sexes, however. "I think he was just trying to make a good show."

Garroway's definition of "a good show" may have expanded to make room
for a woman in the cast, but when their participation was formalized after
Parsons left in 1955, women became girls: "Today Girls." The first to
arrive—fresh and fresh-faced from a year-long, worldwide promotional tour
as Miss America 1954—was Lee Ann Meriwether. She was clever, quick, young,
and very pretty. In one early segment, Meriwether stood next to the show's
big weather map and bantered breezily with Garroway as he chalked forecast
temperatures on the board. Summing up the fair weather expected across
most of the country, he declared, "What a nice day" and headed off to another
part of the studio. As he walked, he linked Meriwether with the lovely day
ahead: "Wonder if she brings 'em with her?" he mused dreamily. "One look
from her today, and it turns better."

From 1955 to 1964, nine women served as "Today Girls." Meriwether, former
band singer Helen O'Connell, and Pat Fontaine each stayed for more than a
year. The rest came and went within months, including Florence Henderson,
who bore the nickname "Bubbles." It may have been meant affectionately,
and it may have fit her on-air personality, but there was also something
vaguely condescending about it—as there was about much of the interaction
between the Today men and their Today Girls.

The women persevered, though, carving out an on-air niche comparable to
what newspapers of the era called the society or women's beat. Their realm
was domesticity: fashion, cooking, shopping, home care and entertaining,
and being or becoming a wife and mother.

Lee Ann Meriwether with Frank Blair and Jack Lescoulie,
above, Florence Henderson, and Pat Fontaine with Hugh
Downs, below, served as Today Girls in the early years.

Today
1956
Frank Blair,
Pauline Frederick, and Marjorie King

DAVE GARROWAY: Let us—drop up and see who's there with Frank.

FRANK BLAIR: Yes. Dave, one of—my guests needs no introduction I think, NBC's own Pauline Frederick.

PAULINE FREDERICK: Thank you, Frank.

FRANK BLAIR: The only woman network news commentator in the country, and her guest and mine, I'm glad to say, is Marjorie King of station KNBC San Francisco. Both Pauline and Marjorie have been honored by *McCall's* magazine's annual awards presented to the outstanding women in radio and television. And to both of these ladies, *Today*'s heartiest congratulations to you.

PAULINE FREDERICK: Thank you, Frank.

MARJORIE KING: Thank you, Frank.

FRANK BLAIR: Now, Pauline, you were honored for your ingenious and energetic news coverage, and your courage to say what you believe.

PAULINE FREDERICK: Well, it's a very nice recognition, Frank, in this particular field where there aren't too many women doing news.

FRANK BLAIR: That's true. And—I know that one thing—that often tests this frankness of yours is the difficulty women reporters experience in news coverage. Do you really find difficulty?

PAULINE FREDERICK: I don't find any particular difficulty, but not many other women have the opportunity.

FRANK BLAIR: And also because you're so capable of it.

PAULINE FREDERICK: Thank you.

FRANK BLAIR: We think so anyway. And congratulations on your assignment at the conventions. You're to be anchorman on NBC's radio network, and I think it's a great idea having—a woman anchorman for a change.

PAULINE FREDERICK: I'm very excited about it.

FRANK BLAIR: Marj—

PAULINE FREDERICK: . . . the endurance to go through it.

FRANK BLAIR: I'm sure you will. Marjorie, I'd like to talk to you for a minute. Tell me about this business of yours finding positions for women over forty?

MARJORIE KING: Well, this first job finding office for women over forty created in San Francisco. We discovered—it's going to fill a great need, and in fact, we're getting requests from all over the country, Frank, to go . . . and do likewise. And I have a wonderful idea. You see this folder here?

FRANK BLAIR: Yes.

MARJORIE KING: It's called Careers Unlimited for Women.

FRANK BLAIR: Good.

MARJORIE KING: We sent it to all the governors of the forty-eight states and—on the way back to San Francisco—I think it would be nice if we made arrangements with United Airlines and just dropped them in all the states. Then they'd know how to make—a job finding office also for women over forty.

FRANK BLAIR: Maybe we can. That's a good idea.

1956: Frank Blair interviews NBC's Pauline Frederick, top left and top right, and Marjorie King of KNBC on *Today*.

By the time *Today* Girl Maureen O'Sullivan left in 1964, however, change was in the wind. Betty Friedan's *The Feminine Mystique*, published in 1963, had struck a responsive chord among women who felt they had been denied choices in life, that their only option was to try to live up to an idealized image of a wife and mother. The book is generally credited with setting the stage for the modern feminist movement. The progress of that movement and the career of Barbara Walters would follow parallel trajectories.

Walters began contributing to *Today* in 1961 as a freelance writer hired by producer Fred Freed; his successor, Robert "Shad" Northshield, quickly expanded her role. Bright, appealing, and assertive, Walters soon began appearing on the air to introduce her filmed reports.

"Last week," *Today*'s Frank Blair drolly told viewers on August 29, 1961, "we forced our staff writer Barbara Walters to go to Paris for the fashion openings."

A chatty Walters played along: "Oh, Frank, it was awful. First of all, every day I had to go and look at fashion shows. And then I had to have lunch at Maxim's and drink champagne. And then I had to smell all the perfume at Dior's. I mean, it was soooo trying."

The following year, though, Walters pushed the envelope a bit, and in the unlikeliest of settings: the new Playboy Club in New York City. For a pre–New Year's Eve story, Walters went through a shortened version of the training course required of the club's "bunnies"—waitresses outfitted in strapless one-piece bathing suits with built-in bust lifts, fishnet stockings, high heels, a floating collar and cuffs, rabbit-ear headgear and a ball of white

Maureen O'Sullivan with Hugh Downs. O'Sullivan served as *Today* Girl in the early years.

November 21, 1966: Betty Friedan, feminist and author of *The Feminine Mystique*, gives a talk in New York.

. . . AND AT THE END OF THE REPORT, TODAY HOST HUGH DOWNS TOLD HER THAT "YOU MAKE A VERY CUTE BUNNY."

fluff at the rump. The footage showed Walters and other servers wearing the mandatory costume and waiting on club customers.

Highlights from this report invariably turn up on *Today* anniversary shows because Walters looks so silly stuffed into the costume and asking waitresses about such serving techniques as the "bunny dip" and the "bunny perch." Walters even admitted feeling flattered when a doorman at the club mistook her for one of the regular servers, and at the end of the report, *Today* host Hugh Downs told her that "You make a very cute bunny."

But her willingness to let herself look ridiculous was slyly subversive; it forced at least some viewers to wonder about the mindset responsible for stripping women down, jacking up certain body parts, slapping a poof of cotton on their behinds, and branding them bunnies.

Walters tried twice to get the *Today* Girl spot when it opened up, losing out to Pat Fontaine in 1962 and to Maureen O'Sullivan in the spring of 1964. But when O'Sullivan left in the fall of 1964, Walters—this time armed with Downs's endorsement—became the show's tenth and last *Today* Girl, with an important distinction: She also retained her status as reporter and writer.

The change came just as the women's movement in America was gathering momentum. The 1964 Civil Rights Act banning racial discrimination in hiring outlawed sex discrimination as well. In 1966, the National Organization for Women (NOW) was formed to press for equal treatment of women in all areas of society.

Nineteen sixty-six also proved to be a breakthrough year for Walters, and the vehicle for it was a *Today* feature on former President Dwight Eisenhower and his wife, Mamie. Pegged to the couple's fiftieth wedding anniversary, the piece was filmed at the Eisenhowers' farm in Gettysburg, Pennsylvania, and broadcast on July 1. In a lengthy interview, the affectionate Eisenhowers shared personal details of their lives together, including the effects of long wartime separations and the deaths of loved ones.

But there was more on the mind of the former president, who also had commanded all allied forces in World War II, than familial wistfulness: "I miss the feeling of being in the center of things and being a party to decisions that I know are going to be important," Eisenhower admitted. "Once you've been in a position of considerable authority, and I certainly have since 1941, to feel that you have very little influence whatsoever. . . . You might say it's a relief, but also sometimes it's a disappointment, too."

It was an extraordinary moment, offering insight not only into the humanity of a national icon but into the allure of power itself. Walters had taken what might otherwise have been little more than a celebrity anniversary story and churned it into something meatier. Two months later, she shed the Girl title and became a full-time *Today* panelist.

A feminist breakthrough for the show itself came less than four months after Walters's promotion. *Today* devoted most of the show on January 10, 1967, to a series of reports collectively titled "Women: The Discriminated-Against Majority." The centerpiece of the broadcast was a group interview Walters conducted with four working women, including one who was married and had a child.

1962: Barbara Walters dressed up as a bunny at The Playboy Bunny Club in New York City for a pre–New Year's Eve story.

November 14, 1959: Dwight D. and Mamie Eisenhower during his presidency.

The following year, the federal Equal Employment Opportunity Commission banned separate "help wanted" ads for men and women, although legal challenges delayed enforcement until 1973.

The late sixties and early seventies saw Walters's work grow more and more substantive, as carefully cultivated connections to the Johnson and Nixon administrations produced major *Today* interviews with President and Mrs. Nixon; Dean Rusk, secretary of state under Presidents Kennedy and Johnson; Henry Kissinger, who served Nixon in several senior capacities; and Nixon's chief of staff, H. R. Haldeman.

The women's movement was becoming similarly robust. A 1969 best-seller published by the Boston Women's Health Collective, *Our Bodies, Ourselves*, pushed the subjects of women's health, physiology, and sexuality into the mainstream. The nonpartisan National Women's Political Caucus, founded in 1971, began backing candidates, especially women, who supported women's issues. *Ms.* magazine made its first appearance in 1971. In 1972, Title IX of the Education Amendments banned sex discrimination at schools receiving federal funds, setting up a massive expansion of women's college sports. In its 1973 *Roe v. Wade* decision, the Supreme Court made early-term abortions a legal option for pregnant women.

But even as Walters was scoring interview coups, her progress on the *Today* set hit a roadblock in the form of Frank McGee, Downs's successor as *Today* host. As an NBC correspondent, McGee had earned acclaim for his coverage of civil rights, the space program, and the war in Vietnam. But, not unlike a lot of professional men of his era, he had a blind spot when it came to sharing the spotlight with women.

In a recent *Today* interview with Katie Couric, Walters said that McGee's contract actually prohibited her from asking a question in live studio interviews until McGee had asked three. Walters explained, "It went all the way up to the president of NBC, who said, 'That's the way it should be. Barbara cannot come in until the fourth question.'"

McGee died of complications from bone cancer on April 17, 1974, having hosted his last *Today* show just a few days before. On April 22, Walters became the first woman ever named to the position of *Today* co-host, a testament to her hard work, her determination, and a clause in her contract guaranteeing her the title upon McGee's departure from the show.

Walters left *Today* and NBC in 1976 for a million-dollar salary at ABC, an industry first. After an initial high-profile misfire co-anchoring the network's evening newscast with Harry Reasoner, she moved into prime time and, later, daytime as well, and has thrived in both.

In the years that followed, women moved into many areas of American life formerly denied to them. In September 1981, Sandra Day O'Connor became the first woman confirmed as an associate justice of the U.S. Supreme Court. Three years later, Democrat Geraldine Ferraro ran for vice president as Walter Mondale's running mate, the first woman to appear at the top of a major party ticket.

Meanwhile, coverage of women's issues became ever more tightly woven into the fabric of *Today*. History was being made by women so frequently that Jane Pauley asked Dr. Sally Ride, an astrophysicist about to become the

Barbara Walters interviews Henry Kissinger.

August 30, 1975: Gloria Steinem, editor of *Ms.* magazine, presents Jimmy Carter a copy of the magazine which features his mother, "Miss Lillian," on the cover.

1981: Sandra Day O'Connor becomes the first woman justice on the U.S. Supreme Court.

first American woman in space, whether additional stress accompanied the responsibility. "For the rest of your life," Pauley said in their May 12, 1983, *Today* interview, "you are going to be one of the most celebrated women in the world. Have you come to terms with that yet?"

No, Ride said. She was trying to stay focused on her work and let history take care of itself after the flight.

"You wouldn't rather be the second woman in space, would you?" said Pauley, pressing the matter.

"I want to go into space as soon as I can," Ride replied. "But there are aspects of being the first woman in space that I'm probably not going to enjoy."

Pauley—knowing the swaggering, all-male, test-pilot roots of the space program—asked Ride if there was "anybody here at NASA who is still unconvinced that women have a place in the space program?"

Ride's response was revealing: "Let me put it this way," she said. "I think that everyone who's been associated with the women astronauts is convinced that they can do the job as well as men. But there are people at NASA—not necessarily here in Houston, but maybe in Washington—that need some convincing."

Ride rode into space aboard the shuttle *Challenger* on June 18, 1983, and returned safely to Earth.

In the summer of 1986, *Today* shifted the focus to women and culture—specifically, the status of women in the movie industry. "Women in Film," a four-part series by NBC's Jim Brown, looked not just at actresses but women producers, cinematographers, editors, and directors. Among those interviewed was Dede Allen, whose film editing credits include *Bonnie and Clyde*, *The Hustler*, *Reds*, *The Breakfast Club*, *The Addams Family*, and *John Q.*

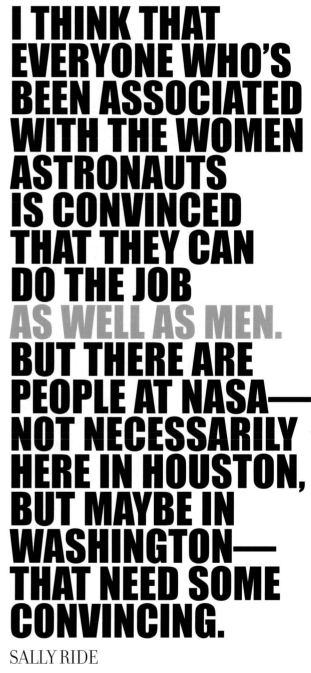

I THINK THAT EVERYONE WHO'S BEEN ASSOCIATED WITH THE WOMEN ASTRONAUTS IS CONVINCED THAT THEY CAN DO THE JOB AS WELL AS MEN. BUT THERE ARE PEOPLE AT NASA— NOT NECESSARILY HERE IN HOUSTON, BUT MAYBE IN WASHINGTON— THAT NEED SOME CONVINCING.

SALLY RIDE

June 18, 1983: Sally Ride becomes the first American woman in space.

October 8, 1991: Katie Couric interviews Anita Hill for *Today*.

"I came out of a period," Allen told Brown, "when you didn't get jobs because they said, 'Well, they will get married and they will have children and then they won't be able to work.'" Things changed for Allen, just as coverage of women's issues continued to change.

President George Bush's 1991 nomination of Clarence Thomas to the U.S. Supreme Court, for example, ignited a ferocious controversy after an Oklahoma law professor, Anita Hill, accused Thomas of having sexually harassed her when they worked together earlier in their careers. *Today* co-anchor Couric conducted a key interview with Hill at the time.

Changing attitudes toward feminism itself—or, at least, changing perceptions of it—emerged in a provocative 1994 *Today* segment with substitute co-host Elizabeth Vargas and Bonnie Fuller, then-editor of a new magazine, *Marie Claire*.

In its first issue, the magazine published the results of a public opinion survey suggesting that many women now felt alienated from feminism.

"I think it's probably because the movement has become identified with causes that they don't see are relevant to their own lives," Fuller told Vargas, "and, in fact, that perhaps frighten them."

According to the survey, substantial numbers of women believed that feminists had different priorities from mainstream women and that the movement pitted the interests of women against those of men.

Vargas, however, offered another possible explanation for the poll's negative findings. Is it possible, she wondered, that women actually still embrace the ideals and goals of feminism but recoil from a label that has become politically tainted?

"That's right," Fuller replied. "For all those reasons that we've been discussing, feminism unfortunately has become a dirty word."

Maybe so. But *Today*'s definition and coverage of women's issues has only expanded with time. In a segment last December, for example, a group of active older women talked with news anchor Ann Curry about things they would like to have done differently when they were younger. Resisting gender stereotypes was a common theme. Actress Marion Seldes, seventy-five, wished she had been bolder. "I was too obedient," she said. "I thought that the way to be successful was to please. It took me a long, long time, and now I'm free."

Fay Gold, sixty-nine, owner of a gallery in Atlanta, condemned the hypocrisy of her youth. "At age twenty, in the year that I grew up in, there were too many secrets," Gold said. "There was a lot of sneaking around and lots of secrets. Because I was following what I wanted to do, but you couldn't tell anybody. Where now, the kids move out and move in with a guy or . . . you know, it's a natural thing."

More heartening was the sense of possibility and expectation that the women expressed about their futures, age notwithstanding.

"All my growing-up years, I heard melodies in my head," said Sister Elise, a nun and former teacher. "I spent forty-four years in our two schools, but what I really wanted to do was to compose, to write these melodies down. But I had to wait until these last few years. Now I'm eighty-one, and this is the flowering of my musical life."

KATIE COURIC: On "Close Up" this morning, the Clarence Thomas nomination. As we've reported, the Senate is to vote tonight on whether Thomas should get a lifetime appointment to the Supreme Court. But a charge that Thomas sexually harassed one of his employees a decade ago has fueled new, last-minute debate over the nomination. Anita Hill, now a professor of law at Oklahoma University, is the woman who says Thomas harassed her. She's with us—with us now from Oklahoma City. Professor Hill, good morning.

ANITA HILL: Good morning.

KATIE COURIC: As it stands right now, the Senate will be voting tonight. In your view, should that vote take place?

ANITA HILL: Well, I think that's a decision for the Senate to—to make. They must determine whether or not they have—each member has fully had an opportunity to take into account what is in the FBI report, what is in my statement, and has answered all of the questions that they might have about this situation.

KATIE COURIC: Professor Hill, let's backtrack for a minute. Can you tell me what happened ten years ago? How you were sexually harassed?

ANITA HILL: That's in the FBI statement. And I really don't want to get into the details of what is in that FBI report and in my affidavit.

KATIE COURIC: You claimed, Professor Hill, that this was not a single incident. Can you give me an idea of how many times you were the subject or on the receiving end of what you would call sexually harassing comments or behavior?

ANITA HILL: In fact, that is also in the affidavit. I cannot say how many times this occurred. I can tell you that it occurred during different periods of time. So that there were periods of time when there was no such activity. And then, there were other periods when it picked up again.

KATIE COURIC: So you're not describing one incident. You're describing a type of behavior that you saw more than once, in fact.

ANITA HILL: Yes.

KATIE COURIC: Okay. Some people are wondering, if you had these negative experiences, why you followed Clarence Thomas from the Department of Education to the EEOC?

ANITA HILL: Well, I have responded to that question. But I'm really happy to respond again. It was during a period where the activity had ceased. There had been some activity. It had ceased for some weeks and perhaps even months. And I assumed that the activity had ended permanently. And that we were going to be able to continue with the professional relationship. I liked the substance of the work that I was doing. I wanted to do civil rights work at that time. And I enjoyed the substance of the work. And I saw this as one of my only real opportunities to engage in civil rights work. And so, one might look back and say it was poor judgment on my part. But I, at the time, it was the judgment that I used. In addition, I had only worked with Clarence Thomas for approximately nine months at that time. I had quit another job to go to work with him. And I did not believe that I could explain to an employer why I had left a job so quickly, two jobs really in two years. And I also did not—was not sure exactly how he would receive my leaving. And whether or not he would support me in finding a new position. There are a lot of reasons that went into the decision. I did not, I could not, I did not have the option of staying in education. That would have meant that I would have no job.

KATIE COURIC: As you know, Professor Hill, much has been made of the timing of this. Whether this whole thing is politically motivated. Do you believe you were following the proper channels and dealing with the appropriate people in making these charges known?

ANITA HILL: I do believe that. That—I don't know the Washington system.

Today
October 9, 1991
Katie Couric
and Anita Hill

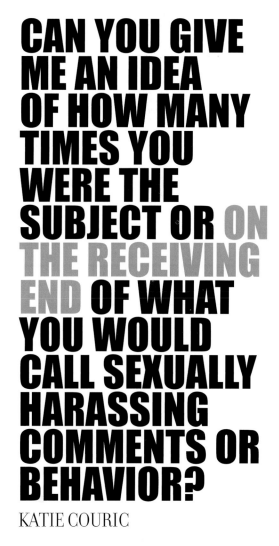

CAN YOU GIVE ME AN IDEA OF HOW MANY TIMES YOU WERE THE SUBJECT OR ON THE RECEIVING END OF WHAT YOU WOULD CALL SEXUALLY HARASSING COMMENTS OR BEHAVIOR?

KATIE COURIC

WE MUST REALIZE THAT NO ADVANCE WE MAKE IS UNATTAINABLE BY OTHERS, THAT NO ADVANTAGE IN THIS RACE CAN BE MORE THAN TEMPORARY.

PRESIDENT HARRY S. TRUMAN

November 1, 1952: The first U.S. hydrogen bomb test is shown in the Pacific at Eniwetok Atoll, Marshall Islands.

Photo Right, April 22, 1970: Dennis Hayes, head of Environmental Teach-In, Inc., the Washington organization coordinating activities for Earth Day, is shown at the group's Washington, D.C., office.

Today was born in 1952. So was the hydrogen bomb.

Today's birth occurred on national television on January 14 and in full public view in a glass-windowed studio in midtown Manhattan. The bomb's debut, cloaked in military secrecy, came nine and a half months later on a remote Pacific atoll named Eniwetok.

On the first *Today* broadcast, host Dave Garroway told viewers they were watching a show made possible by the most advanced news-gathering resources available. *Today* would be, he vowed, a force for good. "We hope," he said, "to keep you more free, more informed. Because I believe, as I hope you do, that an informed people tends to be a free people."

In the last State of the Union message of his presidency, dated January 7, 1953, President Harry S. Truman warned of a possible holocaust:

"In the thermonuclear tests at Eniwetok," he wrote, "we have entered another stage in the world-shaking development of atomic energy. . . . We must realize that no advance we make is unattainable by others, that no advantage in this race can be more than temporary. The war of the future would be one in which man could extinguish millions of lives at one blow, demolish the great cities of the world, wipe out the cultural achievements of the past—and destroy the very structure of a civilization that has been slowly and painfully built up through hundreds of generations. Such a war is not a possible policy for rational men."

Garroway saw science and technology as tools to impart knowledge leading to wisdom, freedom, and, ultimately, happiness. Truman knew they also could bring humanity to utter ruin. In the years that followed, people began to appreciate both perspectives.

On one hand, the breakthroughs of science and the engines of technology carried Americans to the moon and back, cracked the genetic code of living things, invented dazzling new means of communication, and supplied at least some segments of society with an endless stream of devices that made work easier and play more fun.

On the other hand, progress was punctuated with frightening reminders that a blind reliance on science could be dangerous. It turned out that none of the Earth's systems—biological, industrial, natural, artificial—functioned without affecting all the others. Rachel Carson's *Silent Spring*, published in 1962, sounded one of the earliest alarms and is generally credited with launching the modern environmental movement. Carson found indications that DDT, a powerful insecticide used to control mosquitoes and the diseases they spread, was harming other animals as well.

Not long after, groups like the Sierra Club and the Environmental Defense Fund began leading successful campaigns to ban DDT and prevent massive power-plant projects that would have flooded parts of the Grand Canyon, among others.

By 1970, the need to rein in pollution, clean up the air and water, and preserve irreplaceable areas of natural beauty was widely accepted. April 22 was designated as the first-ever Earth Day, and *Today* built a wide-ranging week's worth of programs around the nationwide observances.

"This is second part of our five-part series on the environment," host Hugh Downs

told viewers on April 21. "It turns out that the faithful internal combustion engine is responsible for approximately 60 percent of our air pollution. . . ."

Twenty-fours hours later, the celebratory moment arrived. "It's April 22, Earth Day. There are Earth Day demonstrations in practically every community around the country," Downs declared. "Today, we want to talk about the social implications of our environmental struggle."

The groundswell of public support for environmental principles quickly translated into action: In 1972, the Clean Water Act, the Marine Mammals Protection Act, the Environmental Pesticide Control Act, and the Ocean Dumping Act all became federal law. Still, huge gaps remained. The discovery in 1978 of toxic-chemical contamination around the community of Love Canal near Niagara Falls, New York, led two years later to passage of legislation creating a so-called superfund to pay for cleaning up dangerous waste sites and compensating their victims.

In the spring of 1979, Americans were both fascinated and terrified by an environmental crisis that threatened to escalate into an environmental calamity just outside Middletown, Pennsylvania. "The Three Mile Island nuclear plant is still, this morning, leaking small amounts of radioactivity," *Today* co-host Jane Pauley told viewers on March 30. Two days earlier, plant managers had discovered that the nuclear core was partially melted. "Officials have said the levels are not dangerous for the population," she said.

Days later, however, the situation was still unresolved, and NBC's Don Oliver took *Today* viewers to the Idaho National Engineering Lab, where scientists and technicians were using simulations to test various procedures for bringing the Pennsylvania reactor under control.

The Three Mile Island incident shook public confidence in nuclear-generated electricity, and plans for scores of nuclear facilities were canceled. Just a few years later, Americans realized that environmental disasters aren't necessarily contained by national borders. "Official Soviet reports this morning still say only two people died in that nuclear disaster in the Ukraine," *Today* news anchor John Palmer reported on April 30, 1986. "But unofficial reports tell of hundreds or even thousands of casualties. It is believed the reactor fire is still burning and radiation levels are high in countries bordering the Soviet Union. Radiation has contaminated both milk and rainwater in Sweden."

Even today, precise information about the havoc wreaked by the Chernobyl disaster doesn't exist. More than 130,000 people were evacuated from the immediate area within a few weeks, a response regarded as woefully inadequate. A United Nations report in 2000 put the immediate death toll at about forty, with another 1,800 children having contracted thyroid cancer through radiation exposure. But the Soviet government failed to identify and keep track of the thousands of civilian and military decontamination workers brought in to clean up the site under deadly conditions with minimal protective gear. Their fate is impossible to quantify.

Beyond the human toll, Soviet-controlled news agencies acknowledged three years later that close to 40 percent of the land area in the republic of Belarus and 14 percent of Ukraine had been radioactively contaminated.

1986: The Chernobyl nuclear power station is shown at top, before the accident and, below, after the explosion and fire that destroyed one reactor and released radioactive particles into the atmosphere.

At the Three Mile Island power plant near Middletown, Pennsylvania.

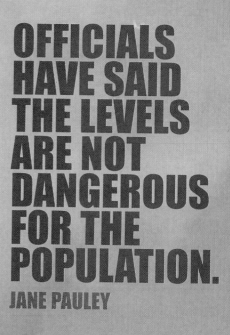

OFFICIALS HAVE SAID THE LEVELS ARE NOT DANGEROUS FOR THE POPULATION.

JANE PAULEY

It may be difficult to grasp just how untechnological the world was in 1952. Of course, there was no such thing as a personal computer, a mouse, a modem, or the Internet. Also still awaiting discovery at the time of *Today*'s birth were touch-tone telephones, radial tires, Astroturf, birth-control pills, Doppler radar, audio- and videocassettes, compact discs, the Walkman, in-line roller skates, nondairy creamer, and the minivan.

There were no communications satellites, weather satellites, spy satellites, or satellites of any kind. There was no space travel and no NASA. There was a rocket program run by and for the military, although U.S. test rockets seemed to explode unexpectedly with some regularity.

Getting into space suddenly became a priority for the United States on October 4, 1957, when the Soviet Union successfully launched the world's first space satellite, *Sputnik 1*. It beeped, too, beaming back to earth electronic signals that left Americans unsettled about something looking down on them from "up there"—something the Russians put there.

Sputnik jump-started the American space program; Cold War fears demanded it. A few months later, the U.S. successfully launched its own satellite, *Explorer 1*, and the space race was on, propelled primarily by strategic military concerns.

The Soviets scored another first on April 12, 1961, when cosmonaut Yuri Gagarin became the first human being to enter space and orbit the earth. Less than month later, American Alan Shepard followed in a *Mercury* capsule, flying just high enough and long enough to qualify as the first American in space. On February 20, 1962, John Glenn stayed longer and flew farther, becoming the first American to circle the globe in space.

The American space program then split into two branches. One, using unmanned satellites and interspace probes, concentrated on scientific inquiry, direct military needs, and commercial development. The other pursued a goal that stirred the collective imagination of the nation and, later, the world. As President John F. Kennedy put it in a special address to Congress in 1961, "I believe that this nation should commit itself to achieving the goal, before this decade is out, of landing a man on the moon and returning him safely to earth."

The *Apollo* program, which met the challenge, proved to be the farthest-reaching, most expensive, and most complicated technological and engineering endeavor in the history of human existence. Still, imagination and romanticism notwithstanding, some doubted its value, even at the peak of the excitement.

Morning coverage of the July 16, 1969, launch of *Apollo 11*—the first moon-landing mission—was handled by NBC's principal news anchor team, Chet Huntley and David Brinkley, with reporting from Frank McGee, Roy Neal, and others. Huntley repeatedly mentioned the expense of the space program and the question of priorities, given the abundance of serious problems yet to be solved on Earth.

In a *Today* interview with NBC's Roy Neal on the tenth anniversary of *Apollo 11*'s successful moon landing, astronaut Buzz Aldrin questioned the wisdom of continuing to make space exploration a priority. "We're worried about nuclear waste, energy, environment pollution. They're tough to grapple with. They're not quite simple as saying we'll put a man on the moon and bring

AMERICAN ALAN SHEPARD FOLLOWED IN A MERCURY CAPSULE, FLYING JUST HIGH ENOUGH AND LONG ENOUGH TO QUALIFY AS THE FIRST AMERICAN IN SPACE.

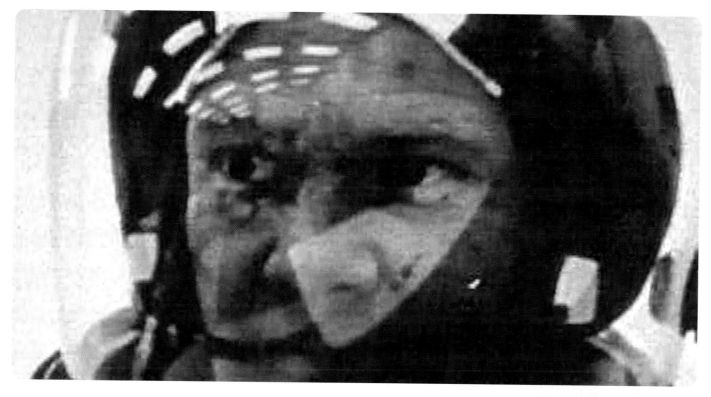

him back to regain national prestige," said Aldrin, the *Apollo 11* crew member who followed Neil Armstrong onto the moon's surface. "I really hesitate to use the word, but all of us—the government, the people, the media—we got caught up in a lie as to why we're going to the moon. In my way of thinking, we went there to get men there and bring them back. And to the extent that people were thinking we went there for science or all these other additional benefits, that waters down the whole effort."

By the twentieth anniversary, though, Aldrin was mellowing. In a *Today* interview on July 20, 1989, he acknowledged the importance of demonstrating to the world the superiority of American technology, which *Apollo 11* did. In the future, he added, the U.S. and Russia ought to collaborate on space projects.

Five years later, Aldrin seemed to have come full circle—or full orbit. He said that the mere fact that men had walked on the moon had changed people's lives. He said that being able to compare the Earth to the moon reinforced people's appreciation for their home planet. And he said that fifteen years of sobriety had left him a much better person than he had been when he was drinking.

Today has been punctuating its news coverage with human touches like that for more than fifty years. When tragedy struck the space program in 1986, the show naturally devoted its entire broadcast to the *Challenger* disaster: the search for wreckage and remains, the investigation into causes, the possible effects of the accident on the space program, the memorial services for crew members, and the president's expression of sorrow, sympathy, and prayers.

But it also made time for some human grace notes in its coverage, including a profile of mission commander Francis "Dick" Scobee. The piece closed with a clip from a previous interview in which Scobee acknowledged the technical sophistication of their work but added that "a lot of things can go wrong in space flight."

Seventeen years later, when the shuttle *Columbia* and its crew came to a similar end, the basic pattern and elements of *Today*'s coverage of the tragedy were, alas, all too familiar.

July 20, 1979: From *Today*'s tenth anniversary celebration of the first moon landing.

Photos on Preceding Page and Following Page, the *Apollo II* mission of 1969.

July 16, 1969

Today
July 20, 1979
Buzz Aldrin

Today: Man had landed on the moon. Armstrong followed Aldrin, spent just over two hours on the lunar surface. They planted a flag, collected some rock samples, talked to President Nixon in the White House, then returned to their ship and ultimately to Earth.

Where are they now? Neil Armstrong became a Professor of Aerospace Studies at the University of Cincinnati. Michael Collins is the Undersecretary of the Smithsonian Institution in Washington. He was instrumental in setting up the new Air & Space Museum there.

Edwin Aldrin went back to the Air Force, then into private business. He told NBC correspondent Roy Neal recently he's not sure exactly what was accomplished with the moon landing ten years ago.

BUZZ ALDRIN: We've got challenges in the future and we're in line for gasoline. We're worried about nuclear waste, energy, environment pollution. They're tough to grapple with. They're not quite simple as saying we'll put a man on the moon and bring him back to regain national prestige. I really hesitate to use the word, but all of us—the government, the people, the media—we got caught up in a lie as to why we're going to the moon. In my way of thinking, we went there to get men there and bring them back. And to the extent that people were thinking we went there for science or all these other additional benefits, that waters down the whole effort.

Today
1969
Frank McGee
and Neil Armstrong

FRANK McGEE: Why do you take over manual control in the last phase there? Why not let the whole thing be automatic?

NEIL ARMSTRONG: Well, the—the vehicle is capable of flying—automatically all the way to a touchdown. However—it has no ability to discern a good landing area and pick out craters and rocks. And—so, it will just—go—to some geographic point as best it knows. A man, of course, cannot only steer the vehicle into a desirable landing area that's free of obstructions, but he can also kill any small residual rates or translation when it's over the ground at touchdown which might—might make the vehicle tend to turn over or stub its toe. Although about—five feet altitude, we'll probably—turn the descent engine off and free-fall to the surface. That—that's done so that the—the—descent engine won't be firing at—at—pr—close proximity to the—to the landing spot.

FRANK McGEE: What kind of a physical sensation do you expect at actual touchdown? Have any idea?

NEIL ARMSTRONG: Well, I think it'll be—I hope—I hope it'll be relatively mild. There's no intention to make—a smooth touchdown—that you might—expect in an airplane or a helicopter. We would—prefer to—come in with a several feet-per-second vertical velocity so that we will—collapse—the struts on the—descent stage to a sufficient degree so that that bottom step on the ladder is close enough to get down to the moon and even more important, close enough to get back up on.

Today interviews Buzz Aldrin in 1989, top left, and Neil Armstrong in 1969, top right.

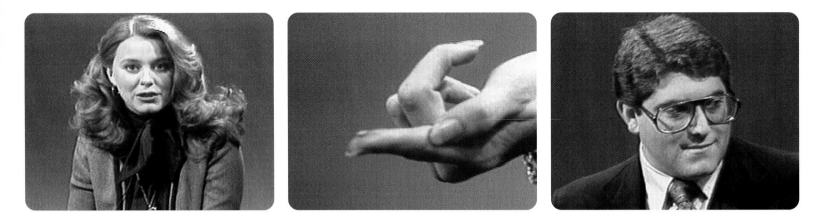

I AM HOLDING IN MY FINGER A TINY LITTLE CHIP THAT HAS CHANGED YOUR LIFE, AND IT'S GOING TO CHANGE A LOT MORE IN THE COMING MONTHS AND YEARS. IT IS A SILICON CHIP. . . .

JANE PAULEY

February 10, 1978: Jane Pauley interviews Roger Shiffman in a demonstration of the new computer revolution.

Today has always shown an affinity for technology and gadgetry. In 1956, host Dave Garroway was ad-libbing a commercial about Saran Wrap, which had come on the market three years earlier, when he suddenly reached toward the camera and peeled a piece of the transparent plastic off the lens. "I've done this whole commercial through a piece of Saran Wrap," he said cheerily.

During the 1960s and early 1970s, science and industry steadily piled up the pieces that would converge to create the home-computer revolution. The first "mouse" appeared in 1964, the microprocessor chip in 1971. Handheld calculators, the first commercially available computer game, and word processing programs came along in 1972. In 1974 and 1975, hobbyist magazines published directions for kits to build personal computers.

One very critical year was 1977. Tandy and Commodore introduced computers with built-in monitor screens, the first of their kind. The Apple and Microsoft companies were both incorporated, and the Apple II home computer became the industry leader.

On June 22, 1977, computers came to *Today*. In a segment running almost ten minutes, Jane Pauley interviewed Texas Instruments' Charles Clough about the development of computer chips containing vastly more capability than mere transistors or even integrated circuits.

A few months later, the chip was back. "I am holding in my finger a tiny little chip that has changed your life," Pauley told viewers on February 10, 1978, "and it's going to change a lot more in the coming months and years. It is a silicon chip, and that's the core of the computer, the brain," she said. "It stores all of the information and processes the information, and we're going to see now how the computer revolution is coming into your home."

The following year, *Today* anchor Tom Brokaw presented a multipart series on how technology might change everyday life in the future: "In the next decade, technology may wire us together into a kind of network nation," he said. "We have shown you this week how we really are moving toward a global village, electronically."

That village came to be known as the Internet.

JANE PAULEY: I am holding in my—my finger a tiny little chip that has changed your life, and it's going to change a lot more in the coming months and years. . . . It's a silicon chip, and that's the core of the computer, the brain. It stores all the information and processes the information, and we're going to see now how the computer revolution is coming into your home with the help of Roger Shiffman, who markets something called the Video Brain. It's a computer for the home, and some experts predict that many—many middle-class-type homes will be having a computer like this in their houses by 1985. First of all, Mr. Shiffman, the Video Brain does a number of things around the house. Could you rattle off a list of some of the things it could do?

ROGER SHIFFMAN: Certainly. Some of the things that we can do with the Video Brain would include such things as computing financial information, whether it's checkbook balancing or financial mortgage calculations to determine payments. It will educate, could teach music as you will see in the demonstration. It will also teach languages, language arts. And at the same time, you have the ability to be entertained by the product.

JANE PAULEY: Play checkers with me?

ROGER SHIFFMAN: Checkers, absolutely.

JANE PAULEY: And pinball?

ROGER SHIFFMAN: Pinball, gladiator games, and a number of other educational areas as well that we will see.

JANE PAULEY: Well, as Tom says, it can't print money, but if it can help balance a checkbook, that's a big step. We're going to see a demonstration though this morning of how a computer can help teach you how to read music. I'll kind of leave that to you.

ROGER SHIFFMAN: All right. Thank you. We've entered a cartridge into the computer now, the Video Brain cartridge is the Music Teacher One. With this cartridge, there are two different areas that you can deal with. We'll look at "Learn a Song." Now, with "Learn a Song," you're looking at music staff, and there's a time bar involved. And right now, we're going to have the computer play a song for us.

JANE PAULEY: Who is likely to use this? So, I assume if I've got a piano in the house, I might learn how to read music on my piano.

ROGER SHIFFMAN: That's correct. But the people who don't have pianos in their homes can utilize the Video Brain and this one simple cartridge to learn to read music. And there are so many homes without pianos that will end up utilizing a Video Brain for all of the other aspects, the other education, the languages, the math tutors, et cetera. But they also have another function here by learning to play music and read music.

JANE PAULEY: How much does it cost today? Is it available for—for home use this very day?

ROGER SHIFFMAN: Uh-huh. It will be available this month. It will be available in a number of markets, and the unit retails for $500 with the—$500 for the entire—

JANE PAULEY: Do you have to—to have a degree in engineering to—to operate the thing?

ROGER SHIFFMAN: Absolutely not. The unit attaches to any standard television system. It works with any color or black-and-white TV in any household, and of course, there's more TVs than bathtubs. So we know that everyone's got a monitor who would utilize it. And it is so simple to operate because of the turnkey system, which means that it prompts the user what to do from beginning to end to get the desired end result.

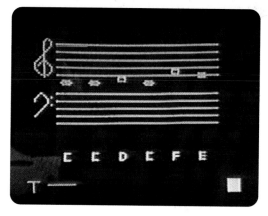

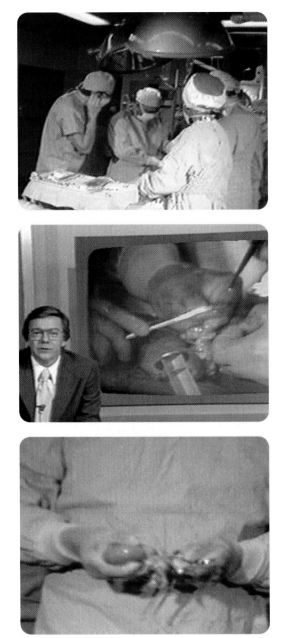

In 1976, *Today* decided to show its viewers what a kidney-transplant procedure was like—live, from the operating room. "Today, for the first time on national television, you will witness a kidney-transplant operation as it actually takes place," co-host Jim Hartz said at the beginning of the February 26 broadcast. "Our live minicam is in the operating room at the Downstate Medical Center in Brooklyn where a kidney transplant is about to be performed . . ."

Today's life span has coincided with a period of astonishing advances in medical science. Within a few years of *Today*'s premiere, vaccines for polio and measles were sparing children and families from untold suffering. The rapid development of imaging systems using magnetism, high-frequency sound waves, flexible tubes of optical fibers and sharper, safer X rays helped physicians see, diagnose, and treat illnesses that had previously been undetectable until too late. And during the show's first fifty-plus years, the fantastical notion of replaceable body parts—not only kidneys, but hearts, lungs, livers, corneas, hips, knees, and more—became a reality.

Today's coverage of medicine and health has included everything from reports of new developments to practical information to cautionary stories to public service of the highest order.

In 1977, *Today* anchor Tom Brokaw looked at a burgeoning movement with a string of successes under its belt: "For years, nonsmokers say they suffered in silence. And then, about five years ago, they said, 'No more,'" Brokaw reported. "In city after city and in most states, nonsmokers pushed for and increasingly won the battle for laws banning smoking in public places."

Dr. Art Ulene, who contributed medical and health-related reports to *Today* for years, reported on everything from working too hard to walking for exercise; menopause, prostate disease, pregnancy, and back pain; and the importance of physical exercise to the elderly. Sometimes, though, medical technology seemed to progress so quickly that people and society were unprepared for the moral and ethical dilemmas that resulted.

"It was in April of 1975 that the Quinlans got the phone call that their daughter, twenty-one-year-old Karen Ann Quinlan, was in a coma," *Today*'s Jane Pauley reported. "In the ensuing two and a half years, the Quinlans have been in and out of court and have been at the hospital virtually every day. . . ." At issue: In the absence of detectable brain functioning, were the machines that maintained their daughter's respiration and heartbeat keeping her alive or prolonging her lifelessness? The Quinlans' situation only grew more vexing, Pauley pointed out, when the respirator was withdrawn and Karen Ann's lungs kept breathing on their own. She died, finally, in June of 1985, never having regained consciousness.

NBC science correspondent Robert Bazell has filed countless reports for *Today*, perhaps none more important than a multipart series on AIDS that aired in the fall of 1985, just a few years after the disease was identified. Segments discussed theories of its origin, means of transmission, symptoms, progression, treatment, and prognosis—and the discrimination experienced by too many of its victims.

The series began, however, by attempting to clarify the rampant misinformation about AIDS. "We start," anchor Bryant Gumbel said on September 9, "with

February 26, 1976:
For the first time on national television, *Today* broadcasts a kidney transplant, live from the operating table. *Today* anchor Jim Hartz reports during the procedure.

BRYANT GUMBEL: On the court, Arthur's calm demeanor belied the fire in his belly. He defeated the pressures of race, made history without the histrionics, and enriched the game with his dignity.

ARTHUR ASHE: I was one of those players who took everything in. I always knew what was going on around me. I'm not sure if it was—just because of my nature or if it was a conditioned way of—a means of survival that I think blacks in the South developed. You were—you always have a special set of antennae out for tr—you're always looking over your shoulder.

BRYANT GUMBEL: Arthur was the perfect ambassador for his court, the ultimate gentleman for a game rooted in civility. But what made him special was his refusal to rest on his on-court excellence. He used that fame for much bigger purposes.

ARTHUR ASHE: Now I'm in Johannesburg, South Africa, in a tennis stadium called Ellis Park.

BRYANT GUMBEL: Arthur fought apartheid in South Africa and he fought racism at home. He taught inner-city youngsters and pushed for tougher academic standards for college athletes. Two heart attacks at an early age weakened his body, but not his will.

ARTHUR ASHE: I've known since the time of my brain operation in September 1988 that I have AIDS.

BRYANT GUMBEL: Arthur was hurt and angry when his privacy was invaded just last year in the name of news and AIDS.

ARTHUR ASHE: I am angry that I was put in the, as I mentioned, unenviable position of having to lie if I wanted to protect my privacy. . . . I—I would have preferred to, as I mentioned yesterday, to have kept it quiet because I'm not sick. You know, the—I'm not incapacitated—and I had some things I'd like to do without having to, you know, see the reaction on—on people's faces in the street or whatever. But now I think, you know, we'll make the best of it. Some good will come out of all this obviously.

BRYANT GUMBEL: He took up that last challenge and fought the disease and its attendant bigotry right to the very end. This past weekend, he planned to speak at an AIDS forum in Connecticut. Too ill to attend, he sent a home video.

ARTHUR ASHE: I'm now quite familiar with—many of the problems—medical and otherwise—that AIDS patients have to go through. There is still a tremendous amount of work to be done with the public to assure them that ordinary contact with people like myself—poses absolutely no danger to them.

DOCTOR: At three fifteen today, Arthur Ashe died of pneumonia and other complications from his battle with AIDS. And I'm very sorry for Arthur and his family.

BRYANT GUMBEL: The emotion of Sunday's news conference spoke volumes about Arthur's impact.

EULOGIST: Arthur was so special because of his quiet courage and selflessness which made a lasting impact on those he touched. Arthur set an example and a standard of personal conduct for all of us who loved him to try and emulate in our lives. The world will never experience another sportsman like Arthur Ashe.

ARTHUR ASHE: I say time is short in a relative way. I mean, ten years from now, no, I probably won't be here. But five years from now? Maybe. But obviously when you see time compressed like that and—and you have so many things you want to do, you have the feeling that, "Gee, I've gotta do everything tomorrow."

Today
February 8, 1993
Bryant Gumbel
pays tribute to Arthur Ashe

ARTHUR WAS HURT AND ANGRY WHEN HIS PRIVACY WAS INVADED JUST LAST YEAR IN THE NAME OF NEWS AND AIDS.

BRYANT GUMBEL

July 5, 1975: Arthur Ashe holds his Wimbledon trophy cup after defeating fellow American Jimmy Connors in the final match of the men's singles championship at Wimbledon, England.

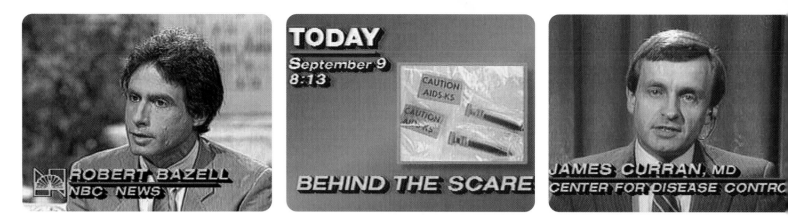

some questions and answers, the myth versus the reality of the most deadly, complex disease in our time." Joining Gumbel were Bazell and Dr. James Curran, then the director of the AIDS branch of the Centers for Disease Control in Atlanta.

Curran noted that virtually all the cases of AIDS in the U.S. to date involved homosexual or bisexual men, intravenous drug users irrespective of sexual orientation, and people who had received transfusions of tainted blood.

In that case, Gumbel asked Bazell, "Why are we seeing so many otherwise intelligent people—undertakers, teachers, medical aides, et cetera—so afraid of contracting it?"

First of all, Bazell said, the disease is both fatal and unfamiliar. "It's something new that's infected humanity for the first time, probably, in the last few decades. So it's scary, for starters."

Bazell pointed to another factor. "I think that a lot of the blame for that rests with us in the media," he said. "The truth is, you get this disease mainly through sexual intercourse and primarily through anal intercourse as practiced by male homosexuals. And we've been reluctant to say those things on the air until now, and I think that that's led to a lot of the panic, a lot of the hysteria."

No medical topic has received more attention on *Today* than colon cancer, and perhaps nothing else the show has done on medicine has provided a greater public service. To date, *Today* co-anchor Katie Couric has been responsible for three separate five-part series on colon cancer, representing a massive commitment of airtime and resources. The reason for the show's extensive coverage is no mystery. For Couric, it's not just business; it's personal.

Her connection to colon cancer was first forged in October 1996, when Jeff Zucker, *Today*'s executive producer at the time and one of Couric's closest colleagues, was diagnosed with the disease. He was treated and recovered, but experienced a recurrence three years later. He underwent treatment again, recovered again, and has been healthy ever since. He left *Today* in December 2000 to become president of NBC Entertainment.

In the time between Zucker's two occurrences, Couric's husband, Jay Monahan, was diagnosed with colon cancer. He fought it for nine months but died in January 1998.

Couric, who had taken time off to be with her husband and their daughters in his final weeks, returned to work on Febuary 24. Seven months later, *Today* aired Couric's first, five-part "Confronting Colon Cancer" series. It explained what the disease is, how it's treated, and how a colonoscopy exam can find and easily remove precancerous polyps before they become dangerous and spread cancer throughout the body.

September 9, 1985: *Today* airs a multipart report on AIDS with NBC science correspondent Robert Bazell.

The second "Confronting Colon Cancer" series aired in March 2000. It began with the story of Mickey Lettieri, who had seen Couric's first series and started wondering about taking the test. His wife, a survivor of cervical cancer, was then able to persuade Lettieri to have a colonoscopy. He did, and doctors found and removed cancerous polyps in the earliest stages of development. Having the exam when he did may well have saved Lettieri's life. Later segments addressed the reluctance of some health insurers to cover the cost of a colonoscopy and described some promising new preventive measures and experimental therapies for treating the disease.

In part two, though, Couric gave viewers an inside look—at herself. "This morning, as we continue our weeklong series on the disease," she said, "we want to tell you about what many consider the most effective test around. It's called a colonoscopy. The idea scares some people; it makes others squeamish. But I assure you, it's not bad. It's worth it. I know. I went for my first colonoscopy a few weeks ago."

Couric first showed viewers what preparing for the test entailed—taking several doses of laxative and then drinking copious amounts of water to clean out the colon. "Hi, everybody. Here we are in my kitchen. It's about eighteen hours-plus before I get my first colonoscopy, and here's my cherry-flavored NewLightly [laxative]. Looking forward to drinking this in the next several hours. . . . Okay now, I haven't eaten anything for three hours because my stomach's supposed to be empty, and I had a light lunch. I had a turkey wrap. . . . Okay, per Dr. Forde's instructions [Dr. Kenneth Forde of New York Presbyterian Hospital], I have purchased some limes at my neighborhood grocery store, because he said if you suck on a lime before and after you drink this stuff, it's much more palatable. So here we go. My first glass. Mm, mm, mm, looking forward to it. Ooh. Here goes nothing. . . . Well, I'm not sure I'd order it at a restaurant."

Couric arrived for her test the next morning, anxious about the possibility of pain. "I heard you're a little light on the sedation," she told Dr. Forde. "I'd like to request plenty o' sedation."

Within minutes, a sedated but still communicative Couric underwent the procedure, photographed from angles that preserved her modesty. Then again, images of the inside of her colon, all six feet of it, were being splashed across the monitor in the examining room, not to mention TV screens all across America.

Afterward, Couric reassured viewers that the procedure had been painless and only minimally uncomfortable: "I just want to reiterate that it really didn't hurt," Couric said. "I felt a teeny bit of cramping, and I'm a big baby. So for me to say that, that's a lot."

Couric's three series (the third came in March 2003)—made that much more accessible by her informality and self-effacing humor—have given people critically important information about colon cancer, humanized the process, and demystified a subject that too many people find uncomfortable even to think about, much less discuss.

Although it would be impossible to quantify, simple logic—and more than a few anecdotal accounts—suggests that these series have saved lives that might otherwise have been lost.

SIMPLE LOGIC—AND MORE THAN A FEW ANECDOTAL ACCOUNTS—SUGGESTS THAT THESE SERIES HAVE SAVED LIVES THAT MIGHT OTHERWISE HAVE BEEN LOST.

March 2000: Katie Couric graces the cover of *Time* magazine for her extraordinary efforts in educating the public during *Today*'s "Confronting Colon Cancer" series.

Today
March 6, 2000
Katie Couric
and Mickey Lettieri

IT'S A DISEASE THAT NOBODY WANTS TO TALK ABOUT, BUT IN FACT, COLON CANCER IS THE SECOND LEADING CANCER KILLER IN THIS COUNTRY FOLLOWING LUNG CANCER. . . .

KATIE COURIC

March 6, 2000: Katie Couric interviews Mickey Lettieri in part 1 of her colon cancer series.

Facing Page, Katie Couric undergoes a colonoscopy, live on *Today*.

AL ROKER: As you'll see, Katie is on the cover of *Time* magazine this week, "Katie's Crusade." And with more on that, let's go inside to Katie.

KATIE COURIC: Thank you very much. This morning, we begin a weeklong series called "Confronting Colon Cancer." It's a disease that nobody wants to talk about, but in fact, colon cancer is the second leading cancer killer in this country following lung cancer, claiming some 56,000 lives every year. That's the bad news. The good news is that colon cancer has a better than 90 percent cure rate if it's caught early. So, we begin this morning with the story of a man who's living proof that early detection can save your life.

MICKEY LETTIERI: I'm a fifty-eight-year-old father of four. I have three and a third grandchildren. We've been married, it's gonna be, thirty-five years. I've got a job as a physical education teacher and I did it for thirty-four years. I never get sick. I had the flu seven, eight years ago. Nothing ever happens to me. I'm the healthiest person I know.

KATIE COURIC: Meet Mickey Lettieri. I did recently because I was so moved by a letter he wrote following the series we did on colon cancer in 1998. You're not really the letter-writing type, is that right?

MICKEY LETTIERI: Oh.

KATIE COURIC: Had you ever written a letter to—

MICKEY LETTIERI: You're my first, kiddo.

KATIE COURIC: Really?

MICKEY LETTIERI: You are my first. "Dear Katie, A short note to say thanks. It was because of your efforts that my wife pushed me into getting a long overdue colonoscopy that probably saved my life. The results of the pathology came back positive, and you could have knocked me over with a feather. I had absolutely no signs or symptoms of any kind. The cancerous polyp was removed during the procedure, and I never even felt a thing. I have become one of your army of staunch supporters. The procedure was not all that bad. We wake up with you every day, and because of you, we will continue to wake up every day. Please continue to spread the word, and thank you, thank you, thank you."

KATIE COURIC: The procedure that saved Mickey's life, a colonoscopy, examines the entire inside of a colon. A lighted scope checks for polyps or other growths. It's more expensive than other methods. There is a very slight risk of perforation. But it is the only screening technique that both detects and removes growths that shouldn't be there. Like so many others, Mickey had avoided getting screened for colon cancer.

MICKEY LETTIERI: There is no way in the world I would ever do that. Zero. Impossible. I can't. Literally cannot have that done.

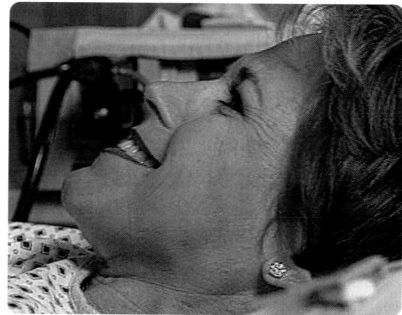
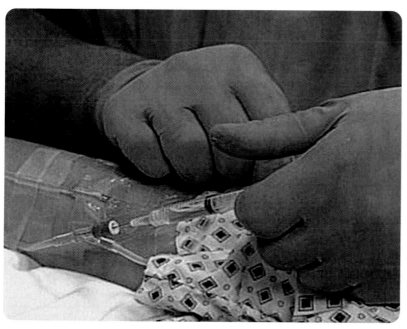
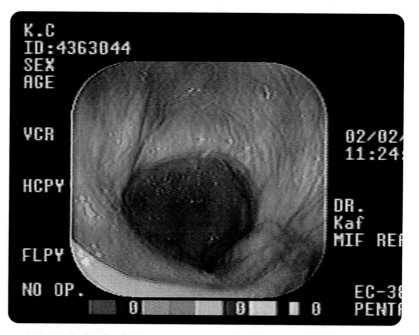

K.C
ID:4363044
SEX
AGE

VCR

HCPY

FLPY

NO OP.

02/02/
11:24:

DR.
Kaf
MIF REA

0   0   0

EC-38
PENTA

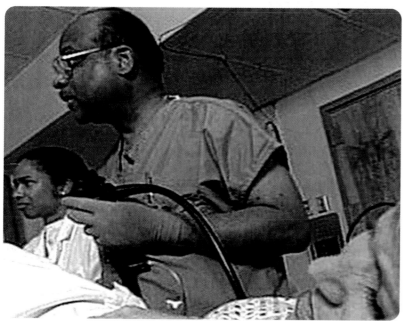
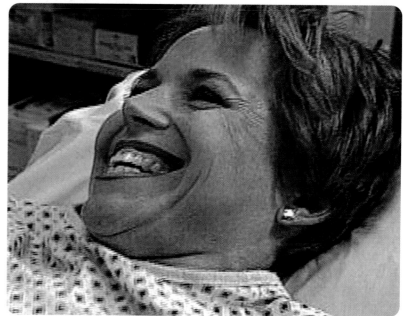

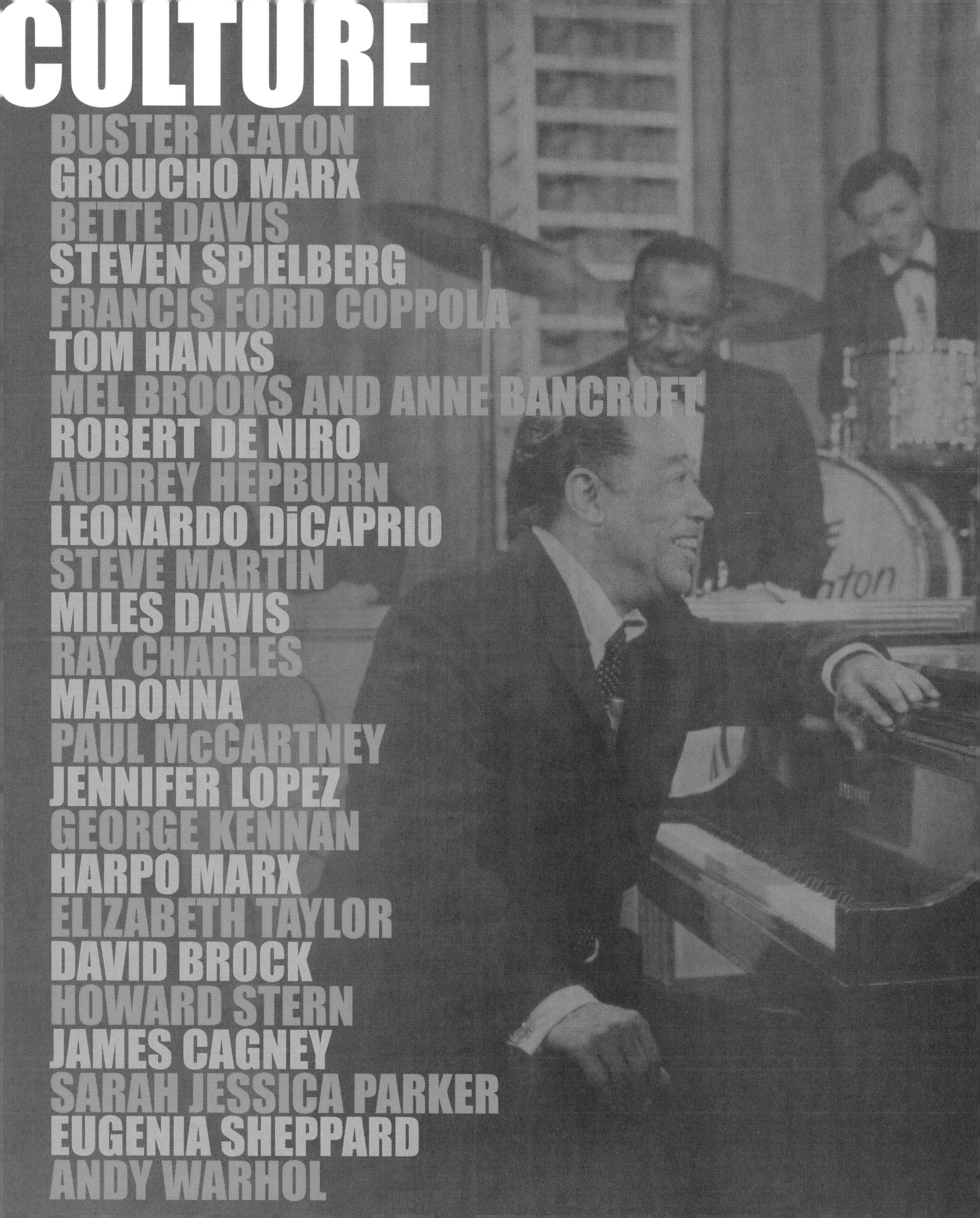

CULTURE

BUSTER KEATON
GROUCHO MARX
BETTE DAVIS
STEVEN SPIELBERG
FRANCIS FORD COPPOLA
TOM HANKS
MEL BROOKS AND ANNE BANCROFT
ROBERT DE NIRO
AUDREY HEPBURN
LEONARDO DiCAPRIO
STEVE MARTIN
MILES DAVIS
RAY CHARLES
MADONNA
PAUL McCARTNEY
JENNIFER LOPEZ
GEORGE KENNAN
HARPO MARX
ELIZABETH TAYLOR
DAVID BROCK
HOWARD STERN
JAMES CAGNEY
SARAH JESSICA PARKER
EUGENIA SHEPPARD
ANDY WARHOL

There was never any doubt that the arts would play a central role on *Today*.

On its very first broadcast, January 14, 1952, host Dave Garroway promised viewers regular reports on movies, books, music, art, and plays. Recorded music played between segments. One of the in-studio guests was an author, Fleur Cowles, who discussed the book she'd just written about Argentina and Eva Peron.

In the years to come, *Today*'s coverage would include everything from interviews and feature stories to reviews, essays, arts controversies in the news, and live performances. The specific focus would shift periodically to accommodate new genres and trends, new performers, variations in popular tastes, and competitive pressures. But culture would always remain essential to the show.

One mid-October morning in 1955, Dave Garroway found himself at the *Today* weather board with no chalk to write temperatures and forecasts. A man standing by the board reached out slowly and, without uttering a sound, handed Garroway a piece of chalk.

It was movie director Alfred Hitchcock, and he turned up several more times on *Today* that morning—an homage to his tradition of slipping unobtrusively into his own movies and a testament to the young show's drawing power.

Another giant of cinema—silent-movie pioneer Buster Keaton—got a lot more screen time on *Today* in the spring of 1963. Keaton got an entire show, actually, after his early work had begun receiving renewed attention and acclaim, some thirty years after alcoholism and meddling studio executives had sent his career and life into a tailspin. Keaton lit up the *Today* set, sharing secrets about his seat-of-the-pants movie-production techniques and regaling the cast with stories of how, when he was a toddler in vaudeville, his father would literally throw him to people in the audience as part of the family's act.

In one bit of prearranged shtick, *Today*'s Jack Lescoulie deliberately mispronounced Keaton's name several times, and Keaton responded by smashing a pie into Lescoulie's face. Host Hugh Downs asked Keaton if he'd please do it again. He did.

Far less calculation was possible later that year when Groucho Marx—his storied movie days behind him and his TV show *You Bet Your Life* off the air—showed up to hawk a book.

"We're in imminent danger of mental derailment here talking to Groucho Marx," Downs said, as Marx's anarchic comedy pretty much demolished any semblance of order. "He has that effect on people."

Marx complimented the then-current *Today* Girl, Pat Fontaine, on her charm, her teeth, and her legs, and agreed to show her his famous crouch-walk—with one condition: "Well, I'll tell you," Marx said. "I'll show you my walk if you'll show me your wiggle."

"I don't wiggle," Fontaine replied.

"Well, there's no point in walking if you don't wiggle," he said.

After several exchanges like that, Fontaine was nearly blushing, even in black and white: "Oh, I wish I was dead or anyplace else or something," she said.

November 8, 1963: Groucho Marx on *Today*, smoking his signature cigar and chasing *Today* Girl Pat Fontaine around the studio.

Photo Right: A scene from one of Buster Keaton's dozens of movies shows why he was nicknamed "Great Stone Face." *Today* devoted an entire show to him in 1963.

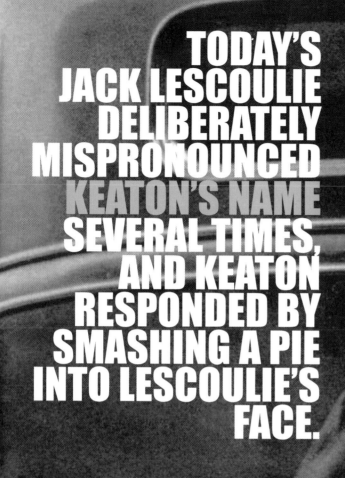

TODAY'S JACK LESCOULIE DELIBERATELY MISPRONOUNCED KEATON'S NAME SEVERAL TIMES, AND KEATON RESPONDED BY SMASHING A PIE INTO LESCOULIE'S FACE.

IFORNIA '34

88 10

HUGH DOWNS: We're in imminent danger of mental derailment here talking to Groucho Marx. He has that effect on people.

GROUCHO MARX: Really?

HUGH DOWNS: And—

GROUCHO MARX: I regard myself as a very simple man. Homegrown.

HUGH DOWNS: You're not a simple man, Groucho.

GROUCHO MARX: No.

HUGH DOWNS: Pat started to ask him a question. I said whatever it is—

GROUCHO MARX: Which one is Pat of you three?

HUGH DOWNS: On the left.

GROUCHO MARX: On the left? Oh. You're charming.

PAT FONTAINE: Thank you.

GROUCHO MARX: You have beautiful teeth.

HUGH DOWNS: Now ask him your question, Pat.

PAT FONTAINE: I kind of wish I hadn't even thought it up.

GROUCHO MARX: Yeah?

PAT FONTAINE: Groucho, how did you get that funny, kooky walk of yours . . . ?

GROUCHO MARX: Well, I'll tell you. I'll show you my walk if you'll show me your wiggle.

PAT FONTAINE: I don't wiggle. . . .

GROUCHO MARX: You don't?

PAT FONTAINE: Uh-uh.

GROUCHO MARX: Well, there's no point in walking if you don't wiggle. But I can tell you a story about that. You want to walk?

PAT FONTAINE: Not particularly. I'd much rather hear your story.

HUGH DOWNS: Yeah. What's the story?

GROUCHO MARX: I'd rather see you walk *(laughter)*.

···

GROUCHO MARX: But I want to tell you about Marilyn Monroe. When we— we did one picture in which she had a bit. She got a hundred dollars for one day's work. You can imagine how long ago this was.

And Lester Cowan, who was producing the picture, he called me up because I was going to do the scene with Marilyn. He called me up and he said, "I wish you'd come over to the studio tomorrow, to my office, because we're going to try out three girls for the part in this picture." I think it was called *Love Happy* or something. Terrible picture.

So, I sat there with Lester. And then the three girls were there. I was introduced to them. And he said, "Now the first girl, walk." And she walked across from one end to the other. And I says, "Very nice." He says, "Now the second girl, walk." And she did it too. And then he—the third one. He says, "Now you walk across." And he says, "Which one do you like the best?" And I says, "You're kidding, aren't you? How can you take anybody except that last girl?" The whole room revolved when she walked. And it was Marilyn Monroe. And she got a hundred dollars. And then, we quit shooting at five. And she got twenty-five dollars extra for going to a couple of gas stations. They were plugging some kind of gas or something, which was part of the picture or something. And she got twenty-five dollars extra for that. They took snapshots of her from six to eight o'clock. She was a wonderful girl, really. A very nice girl.

HUGH DOWNS: I had no idea she started with you, Groucho, in a Marx Brothers picture.

GROUCHO MARX: That was her first picture. It was almost our last.

Today
November 8, 1963
Pat Fontaine, Hugh Downs,
and Groucho Marx

HOW CAN YOU TAKE ANYBODY EXCEPT THAT LAST GIRL? THE WHOLE ROOM REVOLVED WHEN SHE WALKED. AND IT WAS MARILYN MONROE.

GROUCHO MARX

1949: Marilyn Monroe with Groucho in the Marx Brothers film *Love Happy* (United Artists).

I THINK THERE'S A LITTLE LESS MASCULINITY FLOATING AROUND ALL OVER THE WORLD . . .

BETTE DAVIS

November 8, 1965: Bette Davis talks to Hugh Downs about acting at her home in Los Angeles.

Clockwise from Top Left: Marlon Brando, 1954, as seen in *On the Waterfront*; Warren Beatty in the 1967 film *Bonnie and Clyde*, Gregory Peck in 1962's *To Kill a Mockingbird*; and Dustin Hoffman in 1967's *The Graduate*.

In 1965, Downs interviewed another screen legend, Bette Davis, at her home in Los Angeles, and Davis turned out to have some pointed views on the relationship between acting and masculinity.

"I think as regards many men as actors," she said, "it is an odd profession for a man. It's an odd thing for a man to be made up, for instance. It's an odd thing for a man to have to sort of primp and see that his hair is right. . . . It doesn't go with being a man. And I think maybe some men have felt this way who have become actors, you know?"

Yet Davis acknowledged that Hollywood wasn't unique. "Hollywood reflects the world," she said. "I think there's a little less masculinity floating around all over the world. . . . I think it's a puzzling time for the male. Because the woman has gone so very far ahead. And he's sort of keeping his own standards. . . . I think that if the men would just sort of relax and admit that the woman is here to stay—in the world of working or whatever—then I think it would all sort of take care of itself."

Davis's perspective may have been skewed by personal experience, but she had picked up on a vibe that was, nevertheless, in the air.

In a 1986 on-air essay illustrated with movie clips, *Today* arts editor and movie critic Gene Shalit summed up decades of change in the image of men in American movies. "At midcentury," he said, "the American male can choose from disparate role models in model roles. Pretty boys proliferate. Tab Hunter and Troy Donahue seem picture-perfect. Then, with a crash, James Dean. Moody, touchy . . . a raging rebel who inflames the youth of the mid-fifties. Dean's shattering end makes him even more revered in death than he was in life. . . . The sixties arrived. The old order is replaced by disorder. *Easy Rider* carries Jack Nicholson to a dark-time meeting with Peter Fonda. . . . The ideal of tall, dark, and handsome changes to copper-faced, receding hairlines, not-so-tall, hardly handsome. Gene Hackman, with a face only a truck tire could love, becomes a hero in *The French Connection*. Young Dustin Hoffman upsets adult authority as *The Graduate* in 1967. . . . "

The year 1967 was a pivotal one for American cinema—the year of *Bonnie and Clyde*, *In Cold Blood*, *Cool Hand Luke* and *In the Heat of the Night*, as well as *The Graduate*. But as Shalit noted, the sense of uneasiness evident in these films—not to mention the unconventional attributes of its protagonists—didn't suddenly materialize in 1967. It evolved.

In 1955, *On the Waterfront*—director Elia Kazan's black-and-white film about a dock worker betrayed by his family and undermined by union corruption—earned Academy Awards for best picture, best director, best lead actor (Marlon Brando), best supporting actress (Eva Marie Saint), and best screenplay (Budd Schulberg, brother of *Today* producer-to-be Stuart Schulberg). It won additional Oscars for art direction, cinematography, and editing, and might have won another for best supporting actor if three cast members—Lee J. Cobb, Karl Malden, and Rod Steiger—hadn't been competing against each other.

Just two years earlier, the Oscar for best picture had gone to director Cecil B. DeMille's *The Greatest Show on Earth*, a frothy film about circus performers.

Waterfront's mainstream triumph by no means ended the era of the big-studio epic, but it did indicate something was afoot. Movies had been turning

inward and getting more intense in the process, examining big social and psychological themes by zeroing in on individuals in crisis. In a way she never intended, the character of Norma Desmond in Billy Wilder's 1950 classic, *Sunset Boulevard*, was right when she said, "It's the pictures that got small."

More often than not, it was the smaller-scope pictures of the fifties and sixties that proved more compelling, more provocative, and more unsettling; films like *The Apartment*, *Marty*, *Separate Tables*, *The Wild One*, *East of Eden*, *Rebel Without a Cause*, *Butterfield 8*, *To Kill a Mockingbird*, *Paths of Glory*, *Twelve Angry Men*, *Who's Afraid of Virginia Woolf?*, and *A Thousand Clowns*.

Factor in the anxiety created by the Cold War and the bomb, the sorrow and disillusionment left after the assassination of President John F. Kennedy, the distrust of authority fed by the Vietnam War, and the disaffected, rock-and-roll, electroshock of a so-called counterculture, and movies were primed for the tectonic shift of 1967.

The cult of the antihero took root and developed a unique potency. Moviegoers found themselves hurting for, if not always identifying with, a deluded male prostitute and a withered street scammer in *Midnight Cowboy*, a deeply troubled cop in *The French Connection*, a numbed female prostitute in *Klute*, a manipulative former cheerleader in *The Last Picture Show*, a ruthless mob boss and his sons in *The Godfather*, a shlub in love in *Annie Hall*, and physically and psychologically battered Vietnam vets in *The Deer Hunter* and *Coming Home*.

The next great shift in American films came in 1975 at the hands of a not-quite-rookie director named Steven Spielberg. *Jaws*, released on June 20, was a brilliantly crafted thrill ride about a giant killer shark and the clashing personalities of its pursuers. And it created not so much a genre as a phenomenon: the summer blockbuster.

Soon, industry jargon like "first-weekend grosses," "opening wide," and "worldwide box-office" became obsessions of the mainstream press and points of discussion for just about everyone.

Indeed, so ingrained had these terms and concepts become that Spielberg—having dazzled his business partners and delighted audiences with a string of blockbusters that included *Close Encounters of the Third Kind*, *Raiders of the Lost Ark*, *Indiana Jones and the Temple of Doom*, and *E.T. the Extra-Terrestrial*—was expected to explain the audacity of his wanting to try something different: *The Color Purple*, a film adaptation of Alice Walker's novel about rural black women surviving abuse and violation by men.

"I considered it a risk," Spielberg told Shalit in 1986, just before the film was released, "but I had a safety net, and the safety net was, at this point in my career, that I didn't care anymore about failing or wildly succeeding. I just didn't care about those things. I wanted to go out and make a movie that tested parts of me that I hadn't really challenged before. And that sounds real selfish and glib, but it's really true. The book knocked me out, and I really wanted to make that story on an emotional level. And my attitude was, well, why not? Why can't I?"

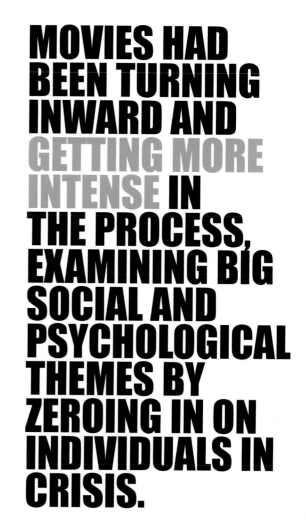

MOVIES HAD BEEN TURNING INWARD AND GETTING MORE INTENSE IN THE PROCESS, EXAMINING BIG SOCIAL AND PSYCHOLOGICAL THEMES BY ZEROING IN ON INDIVIDUALS IN CRISIS.

1956: James Dean in the movie *Giant*.

I DIDN'T CARE ANYMORE ABOUT FAILING OR WILDLY SUCCEEDING. . . . I WANTED TO GO OUT AND MAKE A MOVIE THAT TESTED PARTS OF ME THAT I HADN'T REALLY CHALLENGED BEFORE.

STEVEN SPIELBERG

January 10, 1986: Steven Spielberg is interviewed about his movie *The Color Purple* on *Today*.

BRYANT GUMBEL: Steven Spielberg's film *The Color Purple* opens this weekend in movies theaters all across the country. While I'm sure many of you know that Spielberg is undoubtedly one of Hollywood's best directors, *The Color Purple* boasts neither spaceships, Martians, nor Indiana Jones. When Gene Shalit talked with him, he talked about Spielberg's view that the movie's a personal risk.

STEVEN SPIELBERG: Yeah, I considered it a risk, but I had a safety net, and the safety net was, at this point in my career, that I didn't care anymore about failing or wildly succeeding. I just didn't care about those things, I wanted to go out and make a movie that tested parts of me that I hadn't really challenged before. And that sounds real selfish and glib, but it's—it's really true. The book knocked me out, and I really wanted to make that story on an emotional level.

And then my attitude was, well, why not? Why can't I? 'Cause often, you know, sometimes if you're told you're good at a certain thing, you don't want to stray away from that too far, and this was a—this was a departure for me.

GENE SHALIT: How do you respond to people who said, "How come a woman didn't direct that movie? How come a man did it, and a white man at that?"

STEVEN SPIELBERG: I don't know, I guess I got the book first. I got to it first, and read it and loved it, and put in my bid to direct it.

GENE SHALIT: How hard was it to persuade Alice Walker, the author of the book, to have you direct the movie?

STEVEN SPIELBERG: Well, I don't know if it was a matter of persuading Alice to let me direct it. It was a matter of my wanting to be convinced that she would accept my presence over her vision.

GENE SHALIT: She was on the set some time, wasn't she?

STEVEN SPIELBERG: Yes. Sometimes she would come down from San Francisco, and she would spend some time with us, and she would watch. She was always a spiritual presence. She'd always sort of be there in the background. And even when she wasn't in North Carolina, we would kind of feel Alice. And the question I would always ask Menno Meyjes, who wrote the screenplay when we went to find new dialogue—we would often, you know—write new lines for the characters, 'cause the movie changed every day. "Well, how would Alice say this?" And we'd often go back to the book and look through the prose. Not just the dialogue, but the prose, which she writes so wonderfully, and try to find her ideas, you know, contained therein. She was there, she was always hovering around the movie somewhere.

GENE SHALIT: Steven, tell me about Whoopi Goldberg.

STEVEN SPIELBERG: Whoopi has a gift of communication which I've never experienced before directing actors and actresses in pictures. When the pictures had special effects in them or not, I've never experienced somebody who can communicate more with an expression, more at a glance, than—through monologues, or long moments of character explanation. Whoopi Goldberg doesn't need that. She is so communicative. And when I first saw her, she performed for me. She came to my office, and she did forty-five minutes of her act that she eventually brought to New York, about nine months before she ever brought it to New York.

GENE SHALIT: You weren't alone when she did all this for you.

STEVEN SPIELBERG: Oh no, I packed the house. I mean, I would have been too embarrassed to just have her do her club act for me. So I packed the house with—

GENE SHALIT: With intimidating people.

STEVEN SPIELBERG: Yeah. Michael Jackson and Quincy Jones, and a lot of people came down to see her. And we loved her. We absolutely loved her. I mean—the first thing I did was to hug her. And that was a real key that I wanted her for Celie, 'cause some people, you know, you have to get to know before you even shake their hand. And with Whoopi, she was just so vulnerable. 'Cause in *Color Purple* she's a victim, but she's not victimized. Even when she is a mouse in a den of lions, she has a kind of wisdom and a kind of strength that says, "I will survive this. I'll just be very quiet, but someday I will survive this." And she was that way when I met her. And she was very frightened of all of us. And after her show, everybody, not just myself, but we all went over, people, complete strangers, and put our arms around Whoopi. And she felt good in my arms, so I gave her the part, what can I tell you?

GENE SHALIT: One of the great pleasures, and overwhelming effects in this movie, is the performance of a woman named Oprah Winfrey, who plays Sophia. And Oprah Winfrey is not a professional actress. How did you find her, and how did you direct her, and how was she in the movie?

STEVEN SPIELBERG: I saw a videotape of Oprah doing her Chicago confrontive talk show.

GENE SHALIT: She's a talk-show hostess on television—

STEVEN SPIELBERG: That's right.

GENE SHALIT: —in Chicago.

STEVEN SPIELBERG: That's right. And I saw this dynamic individual running around the stage with a microphone—hanging on every word of her guests. I thought, "God, this is a real risk, but here's somebody who has experience in an entirely different way. Shall I even send for her and meet her?" And I thought, "Absolutely. Why not take the chance and get her out to Los Angeles?" And she flew out to L.A., intimidated and unbelieving that this was happening to her. And there was no promise that she would get the part. She was just one of the many candidates for Sophia that came in and saw me. And I asked her to prepare a monologue from the novel, not from the screenplay, which I did not let anybody read, but just from the novel. And she prepared a monologue based on the "Why did you tell Harpo to beat me?" speech. And we started the video camera, and she was alone in the room, and she just began. And if somebody hadn't taken the camera and unplugged it out of the wall and stopped the tape, she would have gone for four days. She knew Sophia. For that moment, she was Sophia, and that part belonged to her from the moment she opened her mouth.

I'll tell you one great story about everybody, all the cast members. Most movies that I've made, when I say, "Okay, you've got four days off," people like to say, "Thank God!" and they get in a car, and they go to the big city, and they do their shopping, they live their real lives, their families come in. They enjoy themselves. On this movie, the minute somebody was released for four or five days, they wouldn't leave the set. They would stand or sit in the background, watching the performers who were working that day perform, and that's unheard of on a movie for me, in my experience. And the minute somebody did good work, it wasn't just me that would walk over and put my arms around someone. The whole cast would run onto the set, like someone had just made a touchdown, and had just finished spiking the ball. And they'd pick the person up, and they'd hug and kiss, I mean the relationship and the ambience created by this repertory ensemble cast, on the movie, making the movie, and behind the scenes kept increasing the love quotient. So I think I did a better job on the movie based on how they were responding to the experience of making the movie.

... HAVING GIVEN MY FAMILY A WONDERFUL LIFE AND PROVIDED FOR ALL THEIR NEEDS IN A VERY FINE WAY, I'VE ALSO GOTTEN TO TAKE A FLYER ON ABSOLUTELY EVERY HUNCH AND EVERY DREAM I EVER HAD.

FRANCIS FORD COPPOLA

April 7, 1989: Francis Ford Coppola discusses his career and his life on *Today*.

Besides launching the big-budget, special-effects-laden summer-spectacular wave, Spielberg also represented a new generation of filmmakers. Two years after *Jaws*, for example, Californian George Lucas exploded into space with *Star Wars*, the first installment of what became a multipart epic that's still being churned out. It became the basis for a vast advanced-technology, multimedia production empire of his own.

Arguably more intriguing was Francis Ford Coppola, a new-generation director who found both commercial and critical success with his classic three-part American-gangster saga *The Godfather*, launched in 1972. *The Godfather II* followed in 1974, and *III* in 1990.

Though his success began earlier than Spielberg's and Lucas's, Coppola never seemed to enjoy the professional stability they did—perhaps because he took enormous financial and creative risks. The 1979 release of his Vietnam War allegory, *Apocalypse Now*, was the final act of an almost impossibly difficult production that nearly broke him financially and almost killed him, period. *One From the Heart*, a clamorous, strikingly photographed 1982 musical set in Las Vegas, took him close to bankruptcy, and *The Cotton Club*, a 1984 gangster picture set in Harlem in the jazz age, left him hanging by a fiscal thread.

In a 1989 interview with *Today* contributor Nancy Collins, Coppola insisted that he never really regarded money as a problem. "I feel I'm a fabulous manipulator of money," he said. "Not only am I here at the age of fifty having given my family a wonderful life and provided for all their needs in a very fine way, I've also gotten to take a flyer on absolutely every hunch and every dream I ever had."

The most poignant moment in the interview came when Collins asked Coppola if his success had brought him honor in his own family. "You know, it's funny," he replied. "You go your whole life, they'll never say once, 'You know, I'm proud of you.' You hear it through other people. 'Oh, your dad's so proud of you.' But he always, you know, 'Oh, that film. I couldn't understand that film you made.' Or worse, my father won't even go to [my] movies that he didn't write the music for. . . . You will never get what you want from your parents," he said without bitterness. "You have to just imagine it."

Small, crystalline moments like those have become ever rarer as movie studios and the industry's giant promotional machinery increasingly regard TV appearances solely as elements of methodical marketing campaigns. Despite that, circumstances and personalities sometimes align just right, producing something special that transcends the hype and the practiced answers. *Today* co-host Matt Lauer enjoyed just such a moment in a 1997 interview with Tom Hanks, just before *Saving Private Ryan* completed production in London. One of the topics was money, and how Hanks now earns infinitely more per picture than he did for early movies like *Splash*.

"When you go to the bank with the checks for the movie, what goes through your mind?" Lauer asked.

"I—it's ridiculous," said a chagrined and slightly flustered Hanks. "I mean, I feel—I feel like Mr. Mulwray in *Chinatown*. You know, when Jack Nicholson comes and says, 'How much better can you eat, Mr. Mulwray?' It—it—it's ridiculously huge numbers. But that's what the thing is."

BRYANT GUMBEL: Director Francis Ford Coppola is celebrating a birthday today, his fiftieth. As a known figure, Mr. Coppola's life has been a matter of public record for some time now, but he remains a very private man, one who's had to deal with a lot of triumph and tragedy. He talked of both in part two of a special interview with our contributing correspondent Nancy Collins.

NANCY COLLINS: Francis Ford Coppola grew up in a large Italian family. His sister's [the] actress Talia Shire. His father, Carmine, was a solo flutist with the NBC Symphony under Toscanini. He later went on to write the music for his son's movies, picking up an Oscar for scoring *Godfather II.*

FRANCIS FORD COPPOLA: I've come from an extreme(ly) good-looking, talented family, and I always thought that I was homely and didn't have any gifts like they had, you know, in music or things or writing, and I wanted to. I wanted very much to—as I said, talent was always held up as like the big thing in our family. It was, you know, does he have talent? Does she have talent?

NANCY COLLINS: I was fascinated to read that you had—when you were a child—you had polio for a year and essentially were bedridden, I gather. Were you totally paralyzed?

FRANCIS FORD COPPOLA: Well, I found out the next morning. I woke up in this hospital and there were kids crammed everywhere, three high in the bathrooms and the hallways. It was a very big epidemic. And I looked around and I thought I'd get up, and I get up, and I ended right on the floor and I couldn't get up. After a couple of weeks in the hospital, I was just stuck in a room, you know, with a television. And I had a little toy movie projector and a tape recorder and a radio and some puppets. They just didn't want any kid to come near me. So for a year and a half, I would just like entertain myself in this bedroom.

NANCY COLLINS: In the early seventies, *Godfather I* and *II* put Coppola on the Hollywood map. But with *Apocalypse Now,* his money troubles began. By 1983, a string of failures, including *One From the Heart,* left him $40 million in debt. His studio, Zoetrope, always underfinanced, was on the verge of bankruptcy.

FRANCIS FORD COPPOLA: I knew that I didn't have the money to really carry off the dream that I had. I was just hoping that if I started it that maybe either someone would look and say, "Well, that's a good thing," and help me, or say, "Listen, I'll be a partner."

NANCY COLLINS: Money. You and money seem to have a very complicated relationship. You either have none or you have a bunch. Do you feel comfortable with money?

FRANCIS FORD COPPOLA: I feel very comfortable with money. I think that may be what separates me from other people. The main thing is that I have no value for money or I don't value money other than what you can do with it. I feel I'm a fabulous manipulator of money because not only am I here at the age of fifty having given my family a, you know, wonderful life and provided for all their needs in a very fine way, I've also gotten to take a flyer on absolutely every hunch and every dream I ever had.

NANCY COLLINS: But there are some things money can't buy. In 1986, Coppola's twenty-two-year-old son Giancarlo was killed in a boating accident. The boat was driven by Griffin O'Neal, Ryan O'Neal's son.

NANCY COLLINS: Yeah. How do you cope with that? Losing your child has got to be the hardest thing in the world.

FRANCIS FORD COPPOLA: Well, there are no words that I could really get into with you that could express—the only thing I'll say is that he died at twenty-two years old. And even though he was twenty-two years old, he had an extremely great life with parents and a brother and sister that really were crazy about him and we did great things. He got to fall in love. He got to direct. He got to do so many things that I have to say that he had a very happy, complete life. It just was shorter than other people's.

Today
April 7, 1989
Nancy Collins
and Francis Ford Coppola

—THE MAIN THING IS THAT I HAVE NO VALUE FOR MONEY OR I DON'T VALUE MONEY OTHER THAN WHAT YOU CAN DO WITH IT.

FRANCIS FORD COPPOLA

MATT LAUER: Tom Hanks is one of the most beloved actors of his generation. He won back-to-back Oscars for his roles in *Philadelphia* and *Forrest Gump*. And now with more clout than just about any actor, Tom is back in front of the cameras as another American hero in Steven Spielberg's *Saving Private Ryan*. Before filming wrapped, I visited Tom on the London set, where I asked him if it's true that he could have his pick of any role out there.

TOM HANKS: Well, I think maybe any role that's out there—okay. First of all, that's not really true.

MATT LAUER: You thought that didn't sound very modest.

TOM HANKS: That sounds really—that sounds hideous, doesn't it? I could probably generate interest in some things, but obviously the studios would like to do business with a guy like me at this point because I'm doing okay. But that's still a myth as far as honestly being able to do any damn thing you please because the studios are not totally stupid.

· ·

MATT LAUER: I looked back at the filmography and I think for *Splash*, you made $70,000.

TOM HANKS: No. I made $100,000.

MATT LAUER: Okay, $100,000. It was a lot of money.

TOM HANKS: After that, Matt, how much better can you eat? No, honestly.

MATT LAUER: When you go to the bank today with the checks for the movie, what goes through your mind?

TOM HANKS: It's ridiculous. I mean, I feel like Mr. Mulwray in *Chinatown*, you know? When Jack Nicholson comes and says, "How much better can you eat, Mr. Mulwray?" It's—it's ridiculously huge numbers, but that's what the thing is.

MATT LAUER: How ridiculously huge are we talking? There is a lot of talk about, you know, the—the Jim Carrey $20 million, the Harrison Ford—

TOM HANKS: Yes, yes. And I've been lumped into that group of people who get paid that much money and it's—it's just not true. No matter how many times I say that, it's just not true. But—there's ways in order for you to receive a big payday which I have received. There's no question about that.

MATT LAUER: Right.

TOM HANKS: But that is not predicated on huge, massive salaries up front.

MATT LAUER: The way you got here to this point where things are so good is that you had these wonderful movies, these great projects, in a row. You won two Academy Awards in a row equaled only, I think, by Spencer Tracy, who won—

TOM HANKS: Well, yeah.

MATT LAUER: —two Best Actor Oscars in a row.

TOM HANKS: Well, the back-to-back thing, yeah.

MATT LAUER: Yeah, that little back-to-back thing. Those two speeches you made.

TOM HANKS: Yes, yes.

MATT LAUER: Consecutive years.

TOM HANKS: I remember. Right. A while back now.

MATT LAUER: Yeah. You said somewhere that it was a tough time after that. Why?

TOM HANKS: Because of the attention. Only because of the white-hot attention that goes along with it. It got to be tough just because the questions were no longer about the work. It just became about the facts. "What are you going to do if you don't win? What's it like to win? What are you going to do if you win back-to-back? What are you going to say this time?"

WHEN JACK NICHOLSON COMES AND SAYS, "HOW MUCH BETTER CAN YOU EAT, MR. MULWRAY?"

TOM HANKS

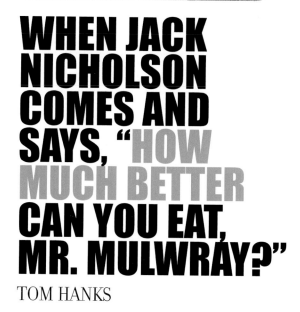

November 18, 1997: Tom Hanks is interviewed by Matt Lauer just before *Saving Private Ryan* is completed in London.

MARRIAGE IS A RETAIL STORE. SOMEBODY HAS TO WATCH THE REGISTER, AND SOMEBODY HAS TO GET THE PRETZELS DOWN FOR THE KIDS. . . .

MEL BROOKS

As delightful and even revealing as such moments can be, what seems to have become an ancient relic is the interview in which a star has nothing new to promote—an interview that occurs for no reason other than that the performer thought it might be fun to do. In that vein, it would be hard to top the December 16, 1983, interview by *Today*'s Gene Shalit with the comedy/musical writer, producer, director, and actor Mel Brooks and his wife, actress Anne Bancroft. Though the exchanges brimmed with wisecracks and Brooks's fast-talking freneticism, there was also some honest conversation about the pain and frustration of the creative process.

And when Shalit asked, simply, "Do you still love each other?" the couple felt comfortable enough with him—and themselves—to respond with something other than platitudes. "All we know," Brooks said, "is that we are a raft in the ocean, and we swim to each other, and cling, because life is . . . fraught with all kinds of disaster, uncertainty, unhappiness, and at least we have each other. . . . Look, as far as I'm concerned," he said, about to mix metaphors, "marriage is a retail store. Somebody has to watch the register, and somebody has to get the pretzels down for the kids. . . . Life is very hard. I think you need a partner that you love and who loves you to get through it successfully. And I think we were very lucky."

Shalit asked Bancroft if they were content to be with each other. "I'm more than content," she said. "I mean, when he comes home at night, when that key goes in the door, I mean, my heart's fluttering. I am so happy he's home, you know. I mean, it's like the party's going to start. . . ."

At that point, Brooks decided there had been enough poignance: "I get my party hat. I throw confetti, and I run in! And we dance all night, we eat spaghetti and dance, and it's wonderful! You come to our apartment," he yelled at Shalit. "You just wear something gay and bright and come dance with us. That's what we do. . . . Every once in a while, we run into the toilet and cry for half an hour."

August 1, 1964: Newlyweds Anne Bancroft and Mel Brooks in New York City after their wedding ceremony.

Today: It opens today. It's a drama about the congressional witch—witch hunts in Hollywood in the 1940s and fifties. Since De Niro can pick and choose his movies, Gene Shalit asked him why he chose *Guilty by Suspicion*.

ROBERT DE NIRO: When I was a kid, I had been around. I had a sense of what it was about. And as I got older, the subject always interested me because I know some people who were involved in it. And I've always felt very, very badly about the whole situation for both people who gave names and who didn't give names and whose careers were ruined. And it must have been a very, very tough situation for everybody, you know.

This phenomenon or whatever you want to call it could so easily happen again in another form. And you say, "Well, it won't happen again," but it always happens in a way that's new. So it's in another package. So it becomes very possible, probable.

And as an actor, I could see—I mean, I wouldn't know myself actually being in that situation what I would do. I don't know. You could say you'd do this, you could say you'd do that, but when it comes down to it, you really don't know.

GENE SHALIT: The climactic scene of *Guilty by Suspicion* takes place in the hearing room in Congress when you stand up for your rights. Whether or not you were a member or not a member, you say, is not the point. The point is that under the American system, you don't have to tell these Congressmen anything because you have a right not to speak up. You're very impassioned in that hearing. Would Robert De Niro be that impassioned?

ROBERT DE NIRO: Well, I'd like to think of myself being impassioned the right way, but I wouldn't be so bold as to say I would be. I don't know. You know, it's one thing to do it in a movie. It's another to do it in life.

GENE SHALIT: *Guilty by Suspicion*, just opening, has as your wife Annette Bening.

ROBERT DE NIRO: Yeah.

GENE SHALIT: Annette Bening's getting a lot of publicity. All of a sudden, she's sort of zooming—

ROBERT DE NIRO: Yeah, yeah.

GENE SHALIT: —for a number of roles, *The Grifters* and *Guilty by Suspicion*, some others that she's done. What's your assessment of her? Has she got a big future?

ROBERT DE NIRO: I think so, yeah. She's got like this fifties movie actress, star, whatever thing about her. It's interesting. She's got that real aura. She's very good, terrific.

GENE SHALIT: I hope that *Guilty by Suspicion* has a very big success because not only is it a very good movie to watch, but it tells something about our recent history that a lot of people in America either never knew in the first place or have forgotten.

ROBERT DE NIRO: Exactly. Yeah.

GENE SHALIT: So that alone makes it worthwhile.

ROBERT DE NIRO: Uh-huh.

GENE SHALIT: Of course, as a little extra, you get Robert De Niro. Looking very good in that picture, by the way. You combed your hair differently in that picture.

ROBERT DE NIRO: Only my hairdresser knows for sure *(laughter)*.

GENE SHALIT: Thank you very much for being with us. Send him over to me. I could use him, by the way.

Today
March 15, 1991
Gene Shalit
and Robert De Niro

March 15, 1991: Robert De Niro is interviewed by Gene Shalit on *Today* about his new movie, *Guilty By Suspicion*.

KATIE COURIC: Her performance in the Broadway production of *Gigi* ignited a spectacular film career now spanning over forty years. Audrey Hepburn defined a style uniquely her own, influencing women around the world. American critics described her as magical, fawnlike, not of this world. However, she has chosen to be of this world by her commitment to its children as UNICEF's goodwill ambassador. But it's her achievement in film that will be recognized tonight by the Film Society of Lincoln Center in New York. I spoke with Audrey Hepburn and asked her how it all began.

You were a dancer in England. You had some small film roles. And you were on the set of *Monte Carlo Baby* when a very, very famous writer discovered you. What happened?

AUDREY HEPBURN: Well, I was on the set of *Monte Carlo Baby*, which was being shot in France; in Monte Carlo, in fact. And the scene was being shot at the Hotel de Paris, where Colette, the great French writer, used to winter. She was very much an invalid already then and she was there with her husband. And they stood and watched a bit of shooting in the lobby and asked to meet me, and the rest is history.

KATIE COURIC: *Voilà!*

AUDREY HEPBURN: She did say to me, you know, "Would you like to do a play?" And I said, "Yes, I'd like to do a play, but I can't. I'm sorry." She said, "Why not?" "It's because I never have. I've never spoken on the stage and I wouldn't know how."

KATIE COURIC: How old were you at this point?

AUDREY HEPBURN: I was then twenty-two. Twenty-two, twenty-three. I'm not quite sure. It's so long ago. And—but she said, "But you're a dancer. So you know how to work hard. So, you know, it will be okay." And that was August of that year and in that very same month, somebody called William Wyler came to London.

KATIE COURIC: And he cast you in your first leading role.

AUDREY HEPBURN: Yes. He had five hundred girls, they said, or two hundred or three hundred, whatever, a great many.

KATIE COURIC: And what did he see in you?

AUDREY HEPBURN: There again, I don't know. But it was just my great good luck that they did pick my test and—

KATIE COURIC: I know you've been directed by many of Hollywood's finest directors, but you really still have a very special fondness for William Wyler.

AUDREY HEPBURN: Of course, you know. But he was the first and one could say certainly one of the greatest directors ever, you know. And to start right off with the very best, and that goes for Greg Peck, too. Fancy, you know, acting for the first time in your life on the screen with Greg Peck, to whom I owe so much to because he could very well have said, "I don't want an unknown in this picture. We don't know, you know, what will happen." But he approved Willie's choice, and so I did get to do the picture.

KATIE COURIC: So everyone really made you feel comfortable. But it was your first leading role.

AUDREY HEPBURN: They certainly did.

KATIE COURIC: Were you a nervous wreck?

AUDREY HEPBURN: In a way, but still a very sort of—I was so ignorant that I was nervous, perhaps, about the wrong things. Was I going to be able to know where the camera was? But it was a whole new world which I was, you know, jumping into, and I think I became much more nervous as the years went by because that's when I started to fully understand, you know, what the demands were, what was expected of me, and I had to become a professional. Then, I was just a beginner.

KATIE COURIC: You won an Oscar for best actress in *Roman Holiday*. The fame came incredibly quickly. You were once a dancer in England. Now all of a sudden, you're the toast of Hollywood. Was that hard to take?

AUDREY HEPBURN: No—it was divine.

Today
April 22, 1991
Katie Couric
and Audrey Hepburn

AMERICAN CRITICS DESCRIBED HER AS MAGICAL, FAWNLIKE, NOT OF THIS WORLD.

April 22, 1991: Audrey Hepburn is interviewed about her career by Katie Couric.

Photo Left: Audrey Hepburn as Holly Golightly in the 1961 movie *Breakfast at Tiffany's*.

February 9, 2000: Sarah Ferguson interviews Leonardo DiCaprio in Hawaii about his starring role in *The Beach*.

MATT LAUER: Our special correspondent, Sarah Ferguson, is across the Atlantic this morning at our London bureau. She recently traveled quite a way to catch up with Leonardo DiCaprio. Good morning, Sarah.

SARAH FERGUSON: Good morning, Matt. It's been two long years since the gigantic hit movie *Titanic* touched off Leomania, and many people have been anxiously awaiting the young star's follow-up movie. Well, the wait is over. I recently sat down with Leonardo in Hawaii on the island of Maui to talk about his starring role in *The Beach*.

· ·

SARAH FERGUSON: Since DiCaprio's record-setting box office success with *Titanic*, grossing over $1.8 billion worldwide, he's tried to maintain a relatively low profile. But despite his efforts, he can't seem to avoid the media, which hasn't always been kind to the twenty-five-year-old superstar. You deal with the press negativity quite well. I mean, it must be very difficult for you.

LEONARDO DiCAPRIO: I don't do anything is how I deal with it.

SARAH FERGUSON: But I mean, I walk out and I teach my girls, Beatrice and Eugenie, eleven and nine, they're going to have it the rest of their lives. And so when we get out of car, I always say, "Smile. Just keep smiling and you'll just go through it." I mean, how do you deal with it?

LEONARDO DiCAPRIO: Negative press is what sells about a person. And the truth is always so much more boring than the juicier bits of what could be wrong with somebody's tortured supposed life. And I'm of the school of thinking that, number one, I'm going to let my work speak for who I am. That's how I choose to do it. But on the other side, as far as every little rumor that comes up, it's a monster that you cannot control and it's completely out of your hands. And I think most of the time by commenting on it or trying to fight it is like a forest fire, you know what I mean? It's—it only feeds the problem. And just let it be. Then the truth will inevitably come out in the end about what kind of a human being you are.

SARAH FERGUSON: You've got a very intense side to you, haven't you, Leonardo? Because, I mean, you're very young and yet you're still very spiritual. It certainly shows through the movie.

LEONARDO DiCAPRIO: An intense side. I suppose that there's an intense side to me. I don't show it very often, but I get to do that in the characters that I play, certainly. I mean, being able to, you know, really get into the psyche of different characters is like a journey for me. It's like a vacation, you know what I mean?

SARAH FERGUSON: Yeah, because then you can lose yourself in the part.

LEONARDO DiCAPRIO: I can lose myself in the character and lose myself in the part and it's like the best job I could ever imagine. It's the only thing professionally that I could ever do, be an actor.

· ·

SARAH FERGUSON: Actually, I'm really pleased to have met you because you're completely different from the person that is being portrayed in the press. And likewise, you'd probably say the same about me. I don't know. But it's really good to meet you because you have sort of—you are just yourself, which is really nice. Diana told me just before she died, she said, "It's okay for you folks because you're at the bottom and you can only go up. I'm on the top of the pedestal and I can only fall off." I'll never forget it, and I guess you're really at the top of your career at this moment.

LEONARDO DiCAPRIO: I suppose I have nowhere to go but down from here. . . . This is all perception and how you look at it. I don't think any-thing could ever compare to the success of a film like *Titanic*, and I don't think anyone expects that and nor would I ever put that upon myself. The main thing for me is to grow as an actor and, you know, be the best that I can with the opportunity that I've been given.

DEBORAH NORVILLE: After a stint doing stand-up and the years on *SNL*, Martin aimed for the big screen and scored a huge success with his first major film, *The Jerk*. *The Jerk* was a megahit. It grossed over $100 million. But Martin's next five films were less successful. It wasn't until *Roxanne*, a labor of love he wrote, produced, and starred in that Martin felt a sense of achievement. You told some interviewer that you were afraid if this movie failed, it would be the end of your career. Do you go through that kind of angst?

STEVE MARTIN: Well, if I said end of my career, I didn't really mean it. I meant because I wrote *Roxanne*, it could represent a failure of enormous proportion. You know, you failed as a writer. You failed as an actor. You failed as a producer, too, really, because it was your idea to start with.

But what has emerged for me from that film was respect, and you can't put your finger on what it is. But you can fail now and you can succeed, but this respect constant is always there, and it feels good.

DEBORAH NORVILLE: But Martin has had a string of hits, which means he's not only in demand by producers, but reporters as well. On this day, he gave five dozen interviews.

STEVE MARTIN: The only thing bad about it is the length of the day. You know, when you suddenly go, "I'm going to do fifty-five interviews" and eventually what happens is you start to—you know, by the twentieth interview, you've crystallized your own thoughts a little bit and it's almost easier to talk about it.

DEBORAH NORVILLE: Playing happy and jovial characters has made Steve Martin a wealthy man, but it hasn't won him a shelf of acting honors.

STEVE MARTIN: When you go to awards, you'll always—even though you have this like really well-made comedy, it might deal with something very frivolous. And maybe the performances are fabulous, but over here you have something that people are throwing things and crying and talking about life and death. And so that naturally when you come to vote, you go, "What kind of person am I? I'm really a highfalutin person."

DEBORAH NORVILLE: When Steve Martin appeared on *Saturday Night Live*, ratings went up by over a million homes, ensuring his stardom and an identity that's been a little tough to shake. Do you ever think people will ever stop putting "wild and crazy" in front of your name?

STEVE MARTIN: I don't know. It's been ten years since I've even uttered it.

DEBORAH NORVILLE: Right.

STEVE MARTIN: It doesn't seem to go away.

DEBORAH NORVILLE: What also hasn't seemed to go away is the stereotype of Martin as the class clown who hit the big time of making people laugh.

STEVE MARTIN: Comedy is learned. I mean, you have a certain inspiration in your youth. And acting is also learned. I mean, it's taken me five or six films to really start to understand it. And I just want to be able to act well enough to get through the dramatic parts so I can be funny, you know.

Today
August 11, 1989
Deborah Norville
and Steve Martin

COMEDY IS LEARNED. I MEAN, YOU HAVE A CERTAIN INSPIRATION IN YOUR YOUTH. AND ACTING IS ALSO LEARNED. I MEAN, IT'S TAKEN ME FIVE OR SIX FILMS TO REALLY START TO UNDERSTAND IT.

STEVE MARTIN

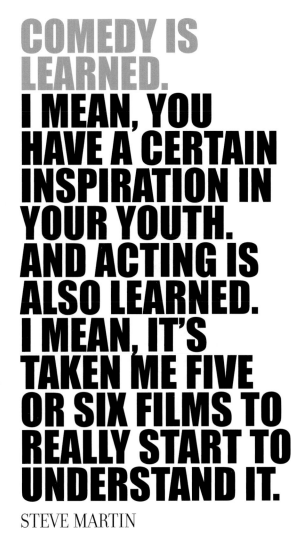

Steve Martin is interviewed on *Today*.

TODAY DREW HEAVILY ON THE RESOURCES OF NEW YORK CITY ... THE HOME TO TIN PAN ALLEY AND MORE JAZZ CLUBS THAN ANY OTHER CITY ON EARTH.

Duke Ellington laughs with Hugh Downs, during one of his many *Today* appearances.

Duke Ellington accompanies Ella Fitzgerald on *Today*.

The rundown for the January 14, 1952, debut of *Today* listed ten prerecorded songs used as transitions between segments during the two-hour show, including tunes by Artie Shaw, the Modernaires, Hugo Winterhalter, and the husband-and-wife duo of Les Paul and Mary Ford.

Half a century later, the lineup of musicians who've performed live in Rockefeller Plaza as part of *Today*'s Summer Concert series includes David Bowie, the Dixie Chicks, James Taylor, Shakira, Santana, Sheryl Crow, and on and on.

One way or another, music has always played a part in *Today* broadcasts, whether through live performances (indoors and out), interviews and profiles, tributes to extraordinary artists, feature pieces or segments spun off music-related stories in the news.

In its early years, *Today* drew heavily on the resources of New York City, the capital of musical theater and classical music, the home to Tin Pan Alley and more jazz clubs than any other city on earth. So, naturally, Duke Ellington dropped by in 1956 and played a few of his dazzling compositions. And, naturally, shows in 1963 saluted composers Jerome Kern and Arthur Schwartz, with live performances by guest singers, including former *Today* Girl Florence Henderson, backed by Skitch Henderson and the NBC Concert Orchestra.

For its eighteenth birthday in 1970, *Today* put together a special tribute to jazz. Saxophonist Budd Freeman and his band and Doc Severinsen, then the leader of the NBC Concert Orchestra, demonstrated different styles of jazz, and Willie "the Lion" Smith played ragtime and stride piano.

Today closed the year by devoting an entire two-hour broadcast to Beethoven's two-hundredth birthday. Interviews with musicians and authors alternated with live performances of Beethoven compositions by the Guarneri String Quartet and pianist Lorin Hollander.

For a three-part ninetieth-birthday salute to Irving Berlin in 1978, Shalit invited composers Alan Jay Lerner, Sammy Cahn, and Arthur Schwartz in to talk about Berlin's incomparable legacy and play some of his songs.

All this time, of course, pop music was undergoing radical transformation. Black performers in the fifties—including Louis Jordan, Little Richard, Ike Turner, Chuck Berry, and Fats Domino—had created a new sound, and radio deejays like Alan Freed spread it across the country. Singers like Elvis Presley, Carl Perkins, and Bill Haley took the rock and roll sound and drove into the consciousness of white teenagers and up the pop charts.

The music influenced a young generation of British musicians, who returned the favor via the so-called British invasion of the mid-sixties. The Beatles became international superstars and pulled the rougher-edged Rolling Stones and a host of other British rockers along with them.

By the summer of 1969, the multidimensional energies of American youth—rock music, anti-Vietnam War fervor, and a fashion rebellion—reached critical mass. The peaceful, passionate Woodstock music festival drew roughly a quarter of a million kids to pastureland in upstate New York, and observant American corporations took note of the youth market's massive economic potential. The counterculture was about to become the mainstream.

In the seventies and eighties, rock, bluegrass, and folk music started showing up on *Today* with increasing frequency, and it wasn't always easy. In a 1978 *Today* report from Atlanta, NBC's Jack Perkins could barely contain his disgust at what he'd seen covering a concert by Johnny Rotten and the Sex Pistols: the group's anarchic lyrics and music, its gross onstage behavior, the safety pins through fans' cheeks, the demand by a couple of band members for ten dollars before they'd do an interview.

Other segments went more smoothly. Tom Brokaw interviewed folk legends Pete Seeger and the Weavers prior to a Carnegie Hall appearance, and Shalit sat down for a chat with Jerry Garcia of the Grateful Dead. *Today* contributor Rona Elliot profiled, among many others, former Beatles Paul McCartney and George Harrison in separate multipart features in 1986 and 1987, and later introduced viewers to a little-known smoldering rockabilly singer named Chris Isaak.

And for any *Today* viewers unfamiliar with the musical genius of Ray Charles, Elliot's multipart interview, aired in the summer of 1986, was a revelation.

February 9, 1964: The Beatles perform on *The Ed Sullivan Show* in New York. From left are Paul McCartney, George Harrison, and John Lennon. Ringo Starr plays drums.

"I think the key word is *singer*," Charles told Elliot. "I'm a singer. I mean, I'm not a jazz singer or I am not a blues singer. I am not a country-and-western singer. I am a singer that sings the blues. I'm a singer that sings love songs. In other words, I think of myself as a real good utility man, you know, who can play first, second, and shortstop, and catch and pitch a little bit every now and then. . . ."

A more apt comparison, given Charles's talent in so many different musical genres, might have been to an athlete who plays all-star-caliber ball at all positions.

Not that *Today*'s attention to rock and pop displaced the show's musical traditions. In 1984, for example, Bryant Gumbel interviewed the profoundly influential jazz trumpeter Miles Davis.

"Miles has had his problems," Gumbel said in his introduction. "He's been through drug addiction, at least four broken marriages, numerous illnesses, and repeated operations for a hip injury sustained in a car accident. . . . Reviewers have sometimes criticized his ever-changing style, so much so that in the mid-seventies, he withdrew."

"There's two ways you can listen to music," Davis told Gumbel. "You can listen to it and copy it, or you can listen to it and feel it. So I felt it. And I didn't play. I didn't try. . . . When I stopped, I stopped because the business part of it made me sick."

As the nineties began, changes in the way the industry tracked record sales produced some startling results. Although country music had always been popular, results from Nielsen's new SoundScan system indicated that country records were actually outselling every other genre, including rock. One of the early beneficiaries of the shift was a transplanted Oklahoman named Garth Brooks, who appeared on *Today* in 1990 to promote his just-released second album, *No Fences*.

"You just picked up a couple of country music awards," Gumbel said. "You had four number-one hits off the first album. Are you real conscious of being hot?" he asked Brooks.

"Sure," Brooks replied. "I mean, there's good and bad to everything. And the bad side of being hot is, you've got to try and stay hot now, or you burn out and you're gone. So I'd like to do this the rest of my life."

The 1990s also saw the public's obsession with celebrity expand exponentially, and no show-business figure more completely embodied this than Madonna. Although primarily a pop singer who rocketed to prominence through music-video exposure on MTV, she soon became a multimedia phenomenon, starring in movies and publishing books. In 1993, shortly after the release of her pricey *Sex* book of provocative photographs, Madonna was feisty in a *Today* interview with Gumbel.

"What is it about you [that] people find so fascinating?" he asked.

"I don't know. I think you should ask them," she said.

"I also heard that you recently went home for the holidays," he said. "First time in a long time? How was it?"

"It was weird," she said. "I had to sleep on the floor in a sleeping bag."

Gumbel was incredulous. "You had to sleep on the floor in a sleeping bag?"

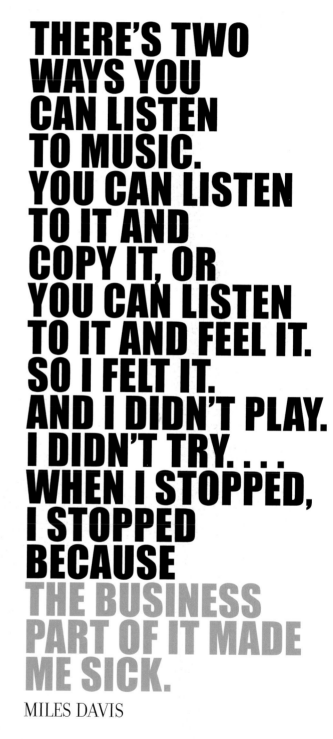

THERE'S TWO WAYS YOU CAN LISTEN TO MUSIC. YOU CAN LISTEN TO IT AND COPY IT, OR YOU CAN LISTEN TO IT AND FEEL IT. SO I FELT IT. AND I DIDN'T PLAY. I DIDN'T TRY. . . . WHEN I STOPPED, I STOPPED BECAUSE THE BUSINESS PART OF IT MADE ME SICK.

MILES DAVIS

Photo Left, October 1, 1970: Miles Davis escorts a friend to funeral of rock-guitarist Jimi Hendrix in Seattle, Washington.

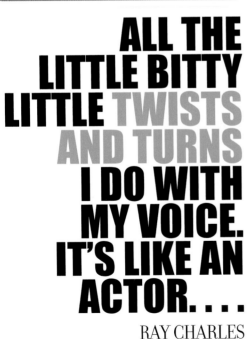

ALL THE LITTLE BITTY LITTLE TWISTS AND TURNS I DO WITH MY VOICE. IT'S LIKE AN ACTOR. . . .

RAY CHARLES

July 28, 1986: Ray Charles discusses his music on *Today*.

RONA ELLIOT: Ray Charles is recognized in all quarters of music, and his latest album, *From the Pages of My Mind*, makes over a hundred albums in his career. In part one of our interview, he provides the definitive explanation of his art.

RAY CHARLES: I think the key word is *singer*. I'm a singer. I mean—I—I am not a jazz singer or—I am not a blues singer; I am not a country-western singer, or—I am a singer that sings the blues. I am a singer that sings love songs. In other words, I—I figure myself as a—a real good utility man (*laughter*). You know, when you play first, second, and shortstop, you catch, you pitch a little bit every now and—you know, one of those kind of people, you know.

RONA ELLIOT: Earlier in your career, you said when you were young, music was the only thing that could stop you in your tracks as a kid. What was that experience like for you, when you heard music?

RAY CHARLES: It had drawing powers. In other words—it—when—when I would hear the—music, I don't know what it was about it—because I was—I guess I was too young to know what it was. But whatever it was, I couldn't stay away from it. I was raised in a Baptist church, you know, we went to all the revival meetings—during the week when they had them, and—and every Sunday, you went—you went and you stayed all day and—so a lot of training and—listening to gospel music. So if some of that comes out in me, so—so be it, you know, what can I do.

RONA ELLIOT: You took church music and then un-sanctified it.

RAY CHARLES: I sing the way I sing. Now, if some people think that that—that sounds religious, well, maybe I'm close to God or something, I don't know.

RONA ELLIOT: Even your grunts and groans are completely expressive.

RAY CHARLES: Obviously, that means something. All the little bitty little twists and turns I do with my voice. It's like—an actor or an actress playing a part so well that you become—so involved that—you know, tears can come from you.

RAY CHARLES: Soul is, to me, is music that you can feel. "Girl, you oughta come on home." You can—you put your heart in it. It's like—a uniquely—really relieves—that really must have happened, 'cause there's no way you could sing that song that way unless—"I believe—I believe." It becomes so real to you. It brings your emotions alive.

RONA ELLIOT: What's that feeling that you look for, when that goes—"Mmm, hits the spot—" when you interpret somebody else's work?

RAY CHARLES: Well, I always like to be able to do something that I feel makes me feel good when I sing a song. And, although I may like a lot of songs, but that don't mean that I can sing them. Myself, for me, you see. You know—like I—I love Nat Cole's—"Nature Boy." But I figure, after he sung it, that was the end of it (*laughter*). You understand, you—you see what I mean? So it's that kind of a thing— "The corn is as high as an elephant's eye—" I took a song called "Oh, What a Beautiful Mornin'" and I wanted to do it my way, because I could hear something that made my insides feel good. See, it's hard to explain that to anybody.

RONA ELLIOT: What are the things you're still going after? The what—what do—what do you need to satisfy you?

RAY CHARLES: I don't need anything to satisfy me except good health. I don't have any mountains to—to climb, or—any rivers to—to cross to satisfy me. "America, America—" I've had some wonderful things happen to me. I've talked to three presidents of the most powerful country in the world. Gee whiz, I play my music, you know, and the people, they seem to be so happy, and I—I've been around for just about forty years, doing exactly what I love doing. "From sea to shining sea."

"Okay. I didn't sleep on the floor. . . . I had to sleep on the floor on an air mattress, okay? That's just as bad."

Madonna loosened up a bit when Gumbel noted that she had become a lightning rod for criticism. "Everybody tries to brush it off," he said. "How much of it sticks?"

"Depends on what kind of mood I'm in," she said. "Some days . . . some weeks, months go by, and things that people say about me don't affect me at all. And then, I could be in a really sensitive mood and read something and feel wounded about it. But life goes on and I get past it."

Today's fascination with Madonna continued. Matt Lauer interviewed her early in 1997, when she was promoting the movie *Evita*, and at one point the subject turned to television. "I just wanted to kill my father when I was growing up, because he never let us watch TV," she said. "And it was the greatest thing that he could have done for me, because I love to read, and I know how to entertain myself. Whereas I think children that grow up watching television all the time are, like, used to . . . being taken care of all the time. . . ."

Lauer said it seemed peculiar to hear her, of all people, complain about the effects of television. "Is there no irony," he asked, "in the fact that so much of your career—that has created this enormous popularity for you—has been almost a constant presence on television, on MTV?"

It wasn't ironic to her. "Yeah, well, that's not because of me. I mean, I started out as a singer and a songwriter and performing live onstage, you know. . . . The media, you know, has brought what I do to the masses through television. But I could still do what I do without television."

She came back to television, *Today*, and Matt Lauer, however, to promote her next movie, *The Next Best Thing*. Lauer's questions included one about a rumor that she was pregnant again. She said she wasn't. Her pregnancy was announced about two weeks later.

Not all *Today* encounters with music superstars are so maddening, though. In the spring of 2002, Katie Couric spoke live via satellite with Paul McCartney, who was in London and about to set off on a new concert tour. McCartney told her that he had decided to tour after helping to organize and performing at the Madison Square Garden benefit after the September 11 terrorist attacks the year before.

"I just like to do it, you know," he said of performing. "It's one of those things. Every so often I come out of hibernation and get on the road. After I did the Madison Square Garden concert, I just thought, 'You know what? I like this. This is what I do. Let's do a bit more of it.'"

McCartney also shared some thoughts about George Harrison, his boyhood friend and fellow former Beatle, who had died three months earlier.

"You know, I'd known George forever," McCartney told Couric. "He was my little mate who used to get on the bus, and we used to ride into school together for about half an hour, talking about guitars, and rock 'n' roll and stuff. So, you know, I'd known George longer than anyone in the group, actually. So it was very sad, you know. It's always sad to see a dear friend go, someone like George, who's younger than me. It was very sad. For him, obviously, for his wife and son. It was a very sad time for all of us, and he'll be sorely missed by everyone, you know. So many people loved that man."

January 15, 1993: Madonna is interviewed by Bryant Gumbel about her music.

January 10, 1997: Madonna talks with Matt Lauer.

January 15, 1993: Madonna discusses her career with Bryant Gumbel on *Today.*

BRYANT GUMBEL: Of all the things that can be said to or about Madonna, what supposedly irks her most are statements that center on the way she's marketed herself. She feels it minimizes her talent. Whatever the merits of her complaint, there's no minimizing her success. At thirty-four, she is the most famous woman in the entertainment business. She sells albums by the millions (and) has a reported $60 million deal with Time Warner that includes specials and her own record label. And her recently released book, called *Sex,* supposedly sold a million copies at fifty bucks a pop.

There's even a collection of scholarly studies on her entitled *The Madonna Connection: Representational Politics, Subcultural Identities, and Cultural Theory.* It's a book that tries to understand why so many are so fascinated by her, a fact that seems to even puzzle her.

In all the years I've been doing this—

MADONNA: Yes?

BRYANT GUMBEL: I have had the pleasure of doing a zillion and one different people from all walks of life. And my friends who know me have never asked to come on to any other interview. And yet for this one, doctors, lawyers, designers, friends, family, everybody wanted to come along. What is it about you people find so fascinating?

MADONNA: I don't know. I think you should ask them.

BRYANT GUMBEL: They just wanted to meet you.

MADONNA: Uh-huh.

BRYANT GUMBEL: Does that happen all the time?

MADONNA: Yeah, I guess. I mean, I'm sure there's plenty of people who don't want to meet me. I don't know.

BRYANT GUMBEL: It doesn't strike you as bizarre, unusual?

MADONNA: Well, I'm a celebrity, and I think a lot of people want to meet celebrities. Isn't that how it works?

BRYANT GUMBEL: It has become fashionable in a lot of circles to dis Madonna, to criticize her, to put her down.

MADONNA: To throw a shade on me.

BRYANT GUMBEL: Yeah. Everybody wants to be loved. Everybody tries to brush it off. How much of it sticks?

MADONNA: It depends on how kind of a mood I'm in. Some days, you know, some weeks, months go by and things that people say about me don't affect me at all. And then I could be in a really sensitive mood and read something and feel wounded about it. But life goes on and I get past it.

BRYANT GUMBEL: Are there any mechanisms you use to get past it? I mean, some people binge themselves on eating. Others go out and grab a bottle. Some people run it off. Some people write letters. Some people cry.

MADONNA: I don't know if a bad review ever made me cry. I get a lot of aggression out when I work out. I also have a lot of good friends who are very supportive of me. And if I say like, "Oh, God. I can't believe somebody said that about me," I have people going, "What are you complaining about? There's so many people that love you. You have a great life," whatever. I mean, you know what I mean? It's—

BRYANT GUMBEL: Yeah.

MADONNA: So that—that helps.

BRYANT GUMBEL: You never had the urge—I mean, like, for example, Roseanne Barr. We were talking earlier about Roseanne. She likes to pick up a pen and a pencil and—

MADONNA: Write notes?

BRYANT GUMBEL: Yeah. Scribble nasty things off to people. Never?

MADONNA: It's not worth it. No.

BRYANT GUMBEL: A couple of wrap-up questions. You're a very young lady. What do you see yourself doing, let's say, fifteen years from now?

MADONNA: I have no idea.

BRYANT GUMBEL: Oh, come on. Everybody has some idea.

MADONNA: I'm not a fortune teller.

BRYANT GUMBEL: Maybe being—maybe being retired. Being a—

MADONNA: Retired?

BRYANT GUMBEL: Yeah.

MADONNA: No way.

BRYANT GUMBEL: No way?

MADONNA: Retired? Doing what? Like gardening or something?

BRYANT GUMBEL: What do you feel like doing?

MADONNA: I have—I have no idea.

BRYANT GUMBEL: *Sex II*? I don't know.

MADONNA: No. I—I don't know what I'll be doing in fifteen years. I just don't.

BRYANT GUMBEL: If you could write the script, okay, for the next ten, twenty years, what's it include if you had your druthers?

MADONNA: What does it include? More free time.

BRYANT GUMBEL: Everything I read about you says that if you had a spare moment, you would try to read something, to look for a script, that you would try to listen to a new group, that you would try to write something, that you would try to work on something, that you are a compulsive worker and compulsively ambitious.

MADONNA: I am. I am. I am. But on the other hand, I still want more free time.

BRYANT GUMBEL: To do what?

MADONNA: To have fun. To hang out. To do nothing. To read. To play Pictionary with my friends. To, I don't know, be silly.

BRYANT GUMBEL: Do you think that your fans will allow you to age with their blessing?

MADONNA: It's not my concern whether—what my fans think of my aging. That's not important.

BRYANT GUMBEL: What is?

MADONNA: Being true to myself as an artist and being happy in life. That's important.

BRYANT GUMBEL: Are you happy now?

MADONNA: Yeah.

....

MATT LAUER: Her name is Lourdes Maria Ciccone Leon. And although she's only three months old, she's already received more media attention than most people get in a lifetime. It's because she's the daughter of Madonna, who earlier this week explained to me how motherhood has changed her life . . .

MATT LAUER: I read somewhere you won't let her watch TV.

MADONNA: Nope.

MATT LAUER: Not at all.

MADONNA: She's only allowed to watch the *Today* show and that's it.

BEING TRUE TO MYSELF AS AN ARTIST AND BEING HAPPY IN LIFE. THAT'S IMPORTANT.

MADONNA

Today
January 10, 1997
Matt Lauer
and Madonna

January 10, 1997: Madonna
is interviewed by Matt Lauer.

September 8, 1988: Former Beatle Paul McCartney discusses the life of John Lennon on *Today*.

DAVID FROST (GUEST HOST): Earlier this week, Jane spoke with author Albert Goldman about his controversial new biography of John Lennon. In an exclusive interview at a luncheon in London yesterday, Paul McCartney exclusively told music correspondent Rona Elliott that even though Goldman claims that his book is based on published reports, the author doesn't have his facts quite right.

PAUL McCARTNEY: I think that—all I really think about that book is that—there are probably a lot of things, as you say, that are from other books, that are on the record, and that John did say, and John did do. He certainly has some wild theories that he admitted to. But [a] lot of people have that. I think where he starts to exaggerate and says that John was possibly homosexual—I think he throws that in with some of the truth, and it starts to have the same credence as the real truth. I think that's the problem with the book. There certainly are things—I've only dipped into it, actually. But—revelations. Well, you know. But—there's a bit about me, where John's supposed to come around to my house and put his foot through a picture of somebody. I mean, it never happened, you know. So if one of them never happened, it's quite possible that a lot of the stuff in the book never happened. And I say, if he's homosexual, I woulda thought he'd make a pass at me in twenty years, darling.

RONA ELLIOT: Do you think more people are likely to believe this book because John Lennon isn't here to defend himself?

PAUL McCARTNEY: Well, that's the other thing about it, obviously, is that—you know, he's not here to defend himself, and—I think that's a big problem with a book like that. It's too cheap a shot, I think. It's only my opinion.

RONA ELLIOT: As a friend of his, do you feel a need to go public to refute these accusations?

PAUL McCARTNEY: Yeah—I mean the truth is, John was really a great guy, and really a nice fellow. But fame is a crazy thing. When you get the kind of fame that the Beatles got, if you're not that stable, it's tough. Now if you look at John for his stability, you've got to look at a guy whose mother left him, his father left home when he was three. He was brought up by his auntie and his uncle. His auntie was lovely but the uncle died. Then his mother, who used to live nearby, was visiting one night. She left, she got run over by a drunken policeman, and got killed stone dead when he was sixteen. His first marriage failed. So you know—and on top of all of that, it's remarkable that he was as straight as he was, really.

RONA ELLIOT: Does a book like this make you think there's too high a price for being a celebrity?

PAUL McCARTNEY: Who cares, you know? Who listens? I mean, I don't read that stuff. Like I say, it's the kind of stuff you just dabble. The first time I ever came to America I saw the *National Enquirer*, that mighty organ, and in its center pages, you know, we—we were just British kids, and looking at this, we'd never seen this. Now we do it better than you. But you know. But I looked in the center pages, and there's a horse in quarters. A horse, just had been cut in four. And this was a picture from the newspapers. You know? And for me, I just think it's trash, you know. What are you going to do about it? I'm not gonna—I can't fix it.

RONA ELLIOT: If a book like this were about to come out on you, what would you do?

PAUL McCARTNEY: About me? I don't know, I'd probably read that one.

MATT LAUER: . . . Let's talk a little bit about what's happening to you two. It's been a wild couple of months. How are you handling all the attention, Ben, that's come, with not only you personally, but this—but this relationship?

BEN AFFLECK: Well. It's a little crazy. And it's a little bit more, I think, than I—either of us anticipated. But it's all, you know, basically good. And most of it seems pretty nice, and we're very happy. And she's doing great. And the album's great and the movie's great, and she's happy, and so I'm happy, and I'm just having a good time.

MATT LAUER: I want to talk to you about some of the things she wrote about you in this album. She dedicated it to you, saying that basically it came about because of your support. She wrote lyrics in a song about you. So now it's your turn. And you've got some—a tough act to follow. So what has this relationship meant to you?

BEN AFFLECK: Well, if I were half as talented at songwriting as she is, then I would attempt to. But obviously she means a great deal to me. I was enormously flattered. And . . .

JENNIFER LOPEZ: I'm waiting for my movie. He's going to write me a movie and win another Oscar for it.

BEN AFFLECK: That's right. I'll write her a screenplay. No, obviously, I'm very happy and she's great. And as all of you can see, what an incredible wonderful talent and what a wonderful woman and person. So I was just here as a fan, and very excited and had a wonderful time.

MATT LAUER: So what are the future plans? When are you two getting hitched?

JENNIFER LOPEZ: We don't know yet.

BEN AFFLECK: I'm sure we'll do it on the *Today* show, however.

MATT LAUER: Promise? I'm going to hold you to that.

BEN AFFLECK: What's the point of getting married, if you don't do it on the *Today* show?

Today
December 6, 2002
Matt Lauer and
Ben Affleck and Jennifer Lopez

WHAT'S THE POINT OF GETTING MARRIED, IF YOU DON'T DO IT ON THE TODAY SHOW?

BEN AFFLECK

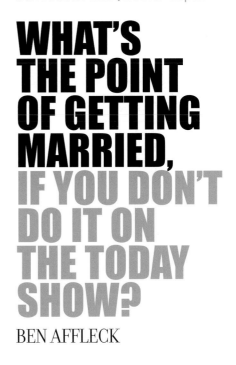

December 6, 2002: Jennifer Lopez and Ben Affleck talk with Matt Lauer about their relationship.

HARPO THOUGHT FOR A SECOND, THEN FLIPPED THROUGH THE BOOK, RIPPED OUT A BUNCH OF PAGES, AND SCATTERED THEM ACROSS THE FLOOR.

When Dave Garroway said on the 1952 premiere of *Today* that the show would be substantive and enlightening but would "not get stuffy about it," he wasn't kidding.

On one show a few years later, by way of example, Garroway did a segment about the value of paintings by *Today*'s resident chimpanzee, Kokomo. After only a brief break for a weather update, he then plunged into an interview with George Kennan, a former U.S. ambassador to the Soviet Union and author of *Russia Leaves the War: Soviet-American Relations, 1917–1920*.

A year later, Kennan's book won the Pulitzer Prize for history, and Kokomo, who had succeeded J. Fred Muggs, was told his services were no longer needed—including the artwork. With high culture and low sitting side by side, stuffiness is an impossibility.

Today started talking to authors about books on the day it was born, and it has never stopped. In 2002, it launched the Today Book Club, which invites established authors to designate books by lesser-known writers as the club's monthly selections.

Since its premiere, *Today* has broadcast thousands of segments on writers and their works of fiction and nonfiction in a dizzying array of fields—with an arguable tilt toward current events and show business. That's not exactly startling, given the show's basic news-and-features identity.

Entertainers who've become authors, though—and even authors who have become celebrities in their own right—can be unpredictable. Among the wildest of *Today* book segments was a 1961 encounter between substitute host John Daly and Harpo Marx of the Marx Brothers. Harpo had written a memoir, *Harpo Speaks*, a title that played off the madcap pantomimist persona he had assumed for his entire career.

It was that persona—mute, excessively expressive and comically literal in interpreting questions—who showed up for the interview. One exchange conveys the essence of the segment. Daly asked Harpo what his favorite story in the book was. Harpo thought for a second, then flipped through the book, ripped out a bunch of pages and scattered them across the floor.

March 13, 1957: George Kennan is interviewed by Dave Garroway about his book on the Soviet Union.

Photos Right 1961: Harpo Marx expresses his feeling about his book *Harpo Speaks* with John Daly and Jack Lescoulie on *Today*.

I MEAN, WITH THE BOOZE AND THE PILLS AND THE FOOD, IT WAS ALL CROSS-ADDICTIVE. AND I WAS SLOWLY SORT OF LETTING MYSELF DIE.

ELIZABETH TAYLOR

By the time über-celebrity Elizabeth Taylor appeared on *Today* in 1988 to promote her diet book, her wondrous acting performances had been all but replaced in the public's collective memory by trivia about her not-very-private private life and personal attributes. Yet in an engaging interview with *Today*'s Jane Pauley, Taylor seemed completely conscious of her fame's mutated state and used it to her advantage.

"I stopped weighing [myself] after about 175," she told Pauley. "I assumed I was in the [one]-eighties. I stopped looking at myself in the mirror. You can tell that by the way I didn't do my hair and the way I dressed. I just didn't care what I looked like. It's like I wanted to kind of disappear."

Taylor attributed her excessive weight gain to profound unhappiness in her marriage to Virginia Senator John Warner, but Taylor insisted that only she was responsible for her self-destructive behavior.

"I'm not blaming Washington or John or anyone," she said. "I could have, I'm sure, made more of an effort and gotten out and done more to regain my sense of identity. But instead, I just allowed myself to submerge, and I wallowed in it toward the end. I mean, with the booze and the pills and the food, it was all cross-addictive. And I was slowly sort of letting myself die."

Books dealing more directly with politics, both foreign and domestic, have provided fodder for countless *Today* segments. But for startling political effect, a pair of *Today* interviews with writer David Brock, separated by nine years, stand out from the others.

JANE PAULEY: *Elizabeth Takes Off* is Elizabeth Taylor's new diet book. But as you would expect, she tells us more than how she lost sixty pounds. I spoke with her in Los Angeles, and she explained why she decided to write the book, and how she put on the weight in the first place.

ELIZABETH TAYLOR: I had to fight to have [certain photographs] put in. And I said, "Well, that really is the point of the book. To show exactly how obese I was, and that I managed to lose it." I mean, if I don't have the courage to show that, why am I writing the book? It's to try and help other people, and show that it actually can be done. I mean, in those photographs, I'm obscene.

JANE PAULEY: You published the facts and figures. Your high point in weight was 180-something. How do you know? Did you ever get on a—

ELIZABETH TAYLOR: I—I st—I stopped—

JANE PAULEY: —scale in those days?

ELIZABETH TAYLOR: —I stopped weighing after about 175. I assumed I was in the [one] eighties. I stopped looking at myself in the mirror. You can tell that by the way I didn't do my hair, and the way I dressed. I just didn't care what I looked like. It's like I wanted to—kind of disappear.

JANE PAULEY: You write about the Washington days. When Washington comes up, it's with words like where—"I derailed in Washington." Do you associate Washington with a bad time in your life?

ELIZABETH TAYLOR: Well, a very lonely time, because—I'd always been acting—well, since I was nine years old. And I was very active in the campaigning. When I really started eating, because of the odd hours, and you really sort of eat on the run, and you eat standing up, or in a car, and you eat Colonel Sanders, and all those—you know, all the junk food in the world. And you don't have time to think about correct eating, or proper food or—there is no such thing as dinnertime. Breakfast time could be six thirty in the morning, or four thirty, or eight o'clock. It was an unbelievable schedule. And from that kind of activity, and feeling that I was doing something to help my husband, to becoming totally redundant, and not knowing anyone in Washington, I went through a kind of phase where I really didn't know who I was, what purpose I was serving as a human being.

JANE PAULEY: You write about how after John Warner was elected to the U.S. Senate, he would say, "Well, I've got quite a lot of work here to do. Why don't you go upstairs and watch a little TV, Pooters?" Pooters?

ELIZABETH TAYLOR: Pooters.

JANE PAULEY: Pooters. I cannot imagine Elizabeth Taylor being told by a man that, "I've got some work to do, honey, go upstairs and watch TV."

ELIZABETH TAYLOR: Yes, oh, I did. I'm a very committed wife. I should be committed, too, for being married so many times. But I keep trying. Or kept trying. I may have given up now. But I always gave a hundred percent. And I realized that he was giving a hundred percent of himself to the Senate. He married the Senate. I was married to him.

JANE PAULEY: You said that you would find no reason to get up in the morning. You have so much in your life. What was it about Washington that your particular gifts or skills or whatever were not used?

ELIZABETH TAYLOR: I think they were suspicious of me. I think they thought—sort of the—the Washington crowd thought that I would—I had in mind someplace that I would come in and be the Pearl Mesta of Washington. That I had some kind of social ambitions or something. Which was totally untrue, so I became so laid-back to prove them wrong, that I went inside out, and I had no friends. I was treated a bit like a freak. I was Elizabeth Taylor, the celebrity who was a politician's wife, and they—it was like they were afraid to ask me to do senatorial wife's duties . . .

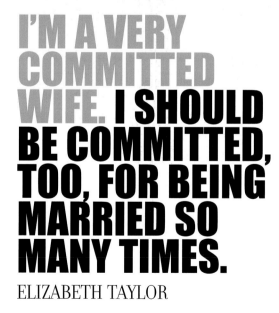

I'M A VERY COMMITTED WIFE. I SHOULD BE COMMITTED, TOO, FOR BEING MARRIED SO MANY TIMES.

ELIZABETH TAYLOR

123

In 1993, Katie Couric interviewed Brock about his book *The Real Anita Hill: The Untold Story*. Brock's book savaged the credibility of law professor Hill, who two years earlier had accused Clarence Thomas of sexual harassment after Thomas had been nominated to the U.S. Supreme Court. Thomas got the position, but only after televised Senate committee hearings on Hill's charges had provoked a national discussion about sexual harassment.

Brock, whose book grew out of articles he wrote for the conservative magazine the *American Spectator*, told Couric that he nevertheless had approached his subject without bias.

"I'm just a journalist here," he said. "I'm not representing one party or another. I'm not representing Professor Hill; I'm not representing Clarence Thomas. I was perfectly willing to write this book the other way if the facts and the evidence turned out that way. Unfortunately, it didn't."

Brock insisted his book was fair. "If an open-minded reader sifts through the evidence with me in this book," Brock insisted, "they're going to see that there was nothing more to Professor Hill's charges than character assassination. Clarence Thomas committed not the crime of sexual harassment, but the thought crime of being a black conservative, and that's what this is all about."

As it turned out, that is not what it was all about at all, as Brock admitted when he returned to *Today* in 2002 with a new book, *Blinded by the Right*.

Co-anchor Matt Lauer lost no time getting to the point. "You're someone who admits he lied," Lauer said to Brock. "You wrote things that weren't true. You were posing as a journalist when you were really a political operative. And now you come and sit with me and look at our viewers and say, 'Here's the truth.' And the question is, why should they believe this version of the truth?"

Brock said that when he was reporting for the conservative magazine, "I had a mission. There was a check written to that magazine to go after Anita Hill. It was checkbook journalism. And I was doing that kind of job."

Lauer then asked Brock about a newsmaking *Today* interview Lauer had done in January 1998. "After the Monica Lewinsky story broke," he said, "and Mrs. Clinton was on this program and she talked about the now-famous 'vast right-wing conspiracy,' you were watching that day. Were you a part of that right-wing conspiracy?"

Brock replied instantly: "I was. And I was stunned when she said it because I said, 'Finally, someone gets it.' And I think maybe she and I were the only ones who got it that day because a lot of people laughed off what she said."

I'M JUST A JOURNALIST HERE. I'M NOT REPRESENTING ONE PARTY OR ANOTHER.

DAVID BROCK

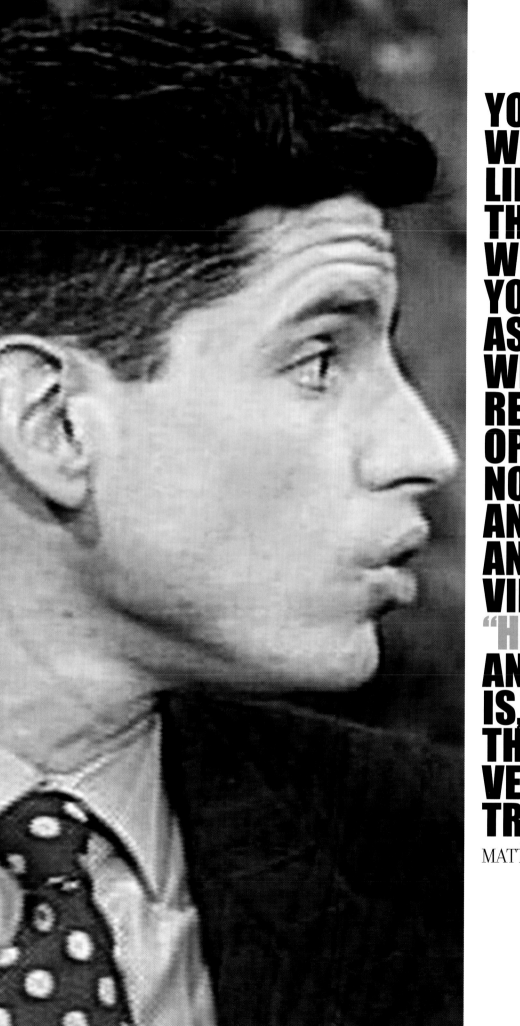

YOU'RE SOMEONE WHO ADMITS HE LIED. YOU WROTE THINGS THAT WEREN'T TRUE. YOU WERE POSING AS A JOURNALIST WHEN YOU WERE REALLY A POLITICAL OPERATIVE. AND NOW YOU COME AND SIT WITH ME AND LOOK AT OUR VIEWERS AND SAY "HERE'S THE TRUTH." AND THE QUESTION IS, WHY SHOULD THEY BELIEVE THIS VERSION OF THE TRUTH?

MATT LAUER

125

KATIE COURIC: Anita Hill's testimony that Clarence Thomas sexually harassed her shocked the entire nation. Of course, Thomas was eventually confirmed as an associate justice of the United States Supreme Court. But when the hearings were over two years ago, left unanswered was the crucial question of who was telling the truth? Author David Brock believes he has found the answer. . . .

DAVID BROCK: Well, you know, at the time of the hearings, I believed Anita Hill. I watched Clarence Thomas. I believed Clarence Thomas. And I accepted the media image that these were two people of equal credibility. And as I got into reporting a story for the *American Spectator* on the subject, I found a number of discrepancies in Professor Hill's testimony, problems with her corroborating witnesses, things that questioned her credibility as a witness. So what I did for the book was to compare the sworn testimony of Clarence Thomas with third-party testimony, with documents, with records. When I did that, I found no problems. When I did that with Professor Hill's testimony, I found problems. I found false statements, incorrect statements, and I think the accumulation of all of that settles the question of credibility hands down in favor of Clarence Thomas.

KATIE COURIC: We're going to get to all those points or at least some of them that you raise in the book in just a moment. But I just want to ask Professor Ogletree: You've read the book. What are your impressions of it?

CHARLES OGLETREE: Well, the problem is that it's a great investigative effort, but he's careless with the truth. It's a great piece of fiction, but he doesn't deal with fact. He makes countless errors of fact. He tells outright lies. He refers to statements that have been proven false and it's a dupe. I think that the most important thing is that journalists should take a look at David Brock's book and find out about the real David Brock, not the real Anita Hill. The untold story is that he's relied on lies, on distortion, on misrepresentations, on inaccuracies, and has put them in a book. Many of those were pointed out in an article he wrote last year in the *American Spectator*. He was aware of that. He retracted many of those lies. He's done it again in the book in even larger form. And if people look at this book objectively, they'll say here he goes again. It's not surprising from David Brock. It's not surprising from the *American Spectator*. It's not surprising that someone would try to retaliate against Professor Hill. She was a victim of sexual harassment. There's never been any question about that. She's never changed what happened to her. It was confirmed by the polygraph test. And David Brock's book is a crock.

KATIE COURIC: I've got to give you a chance to respond, of course.

DAVID BROCK: Okay. Well, first of all, I never retracted anything from my *American Spectator* piece. But more importantly, as I told Professor Ogletree when we met in his office a year ago, I'm just a journalist here. I'm not representing one party or another. I'm not representing Professor Hill. I'm not representing Clarence Thomas. I was perfectly willing to write this book the other way if the facts and the evidence turned out that way. Unfortunately, it didn't. I'm sorry. This has not been easy for me. I'm sure it's not easy for you. But there is not one fact and not one shred of evidence to support Anita Hill's case. The case is a house of cards.

KATIE COURIC: You do, though, Mr. Brock, have some innate biases, don't you? I mean, the *American Spectator* is an ultraconservative magazine and it seems as if you are an advocate for Justice Thomas in the book. Is it really fair to call yourself an objective journalist when it comes to this book?

DAVID BROCK: Yeah, I think it is. My politics, first of all, are not in this book. As I say at the beginning, you know, I probably agree with Professor Hill more than Clarence Thomas on a number of social policy questions. For example, I'm pro-choice. That's not the issue. The issue really isn't my politics. The issue is character assassination. Character assassination, Katie, is wrong, whether it's done against a conservative, a liberal, a white person, or a black person. . . .

May 3, 1993: Katie Couric interviews David Brock about his book *The Real Anita Hill: The Untold Story*. Charles Ogletree challenges Brock's views.

MATT LAUER: His specialty was character assassination, and throughout the 1990s he made a living as a right-wing hatchet man. But after years of lies and some would say malicious journalism, this Washington insider wants to clear his conscience. In his new book *Blinded by the Right*, best-selling author and ex-conservative David Brock exposes how he says the GOP tried to destroy the Clinton presidency through a series of well-plotted smear campaigns. David Brock, good morning.

MATT LAUER: Are you a journalist now?

DAVID BROCK: No. This book is a memoir. This is not a journalistic exercise. This is what I did and what I saw conservatives say and do during this entire decade of really—inside story of a dirty tricks operation that the Republicans ran. So, it's really a firsthand account.

MATT LAUER: So you're not gonna be back sitting in front of me in four years with another book that says, "Okay, that was not true. Now here's the real truth"?

DAVID BROCK: No, this is it, Matt.

MATT LAUER: What was the straw that broke the camel's back for you?

DAVID BROCK: Well, I think it was partly—my own conscience when I went that far to defend Clarence Thomas on something that I knew wasn't true. And then I had—the next project, which was my book on Hillary Clinton.

MATT LAUER: Right.

DAVID BROCK: And that's when I really started to have both a change of heart and mind and that was real tough, because I was under enormous pressure to trash Hillary Clinton as I had trashed Anita Hill. And I didn't do it. And I think I did the right thing there, and I think that says something for my credibility.

MATT LAUER: You infuriated conservatives when you did not trash her.

DAVID BROCK: Right.

MATT LAUER: And you wrote that line that—that stuck with you for a long time and stuck with her. You called her "a little bit nutty and a little bit slutty." Coming from someone who's posing as a journalist, that can be incredibly damning to someone's character.

DAVID BROCK: Sure. I mean, in some ways, it was, and that line has stuck with me. But if you look at the other side of it, Rush Limbaugh read that article on the air, and that really made my name on the right, which tells you something about what they value.

MATT LAUER: After the Monica Lewinsky story broke and Mrs. Clinton was on this program and she talked about the now-famous vast right-wing conspiracy, you were watching that day. Were you a part of that right-wing conspiracy?

DAVID BROCK: I was, and I—I was stunned when she said it because I said, "Finally somebody gets it," and I think maybe she and I were the only ones who got it that day, because a lot of people laughed off what she said. But this book really documents, Matt, and I think that's the historical value of it, that you can't really judge the Clinton presidency without a documentation of the implacable opposition he faced. There were millions of dollars spent, and I name names, and I show you how all that worked.

MATT LAUER: Who drove that conspiracy?

DAVID BROCK: Well, mainly someone named Richard Mellon Scaife put more than $2 million into a dirt-digging operation on the Clintons. And then the conspiracy came to center on the Paula Jones case and the secret conservative advisors around that case. So—I mean, it really is clearly documented that there was a conspiracy. The only thing I quibble with is the word *vast*. It—there weren't that many people involved, and it's kind of scary that so few people with a lot of money could abuse our political process the way they did, and try to disable and destroy our system.

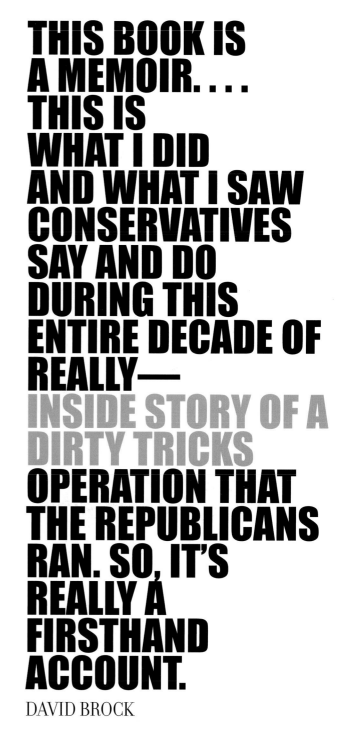

THIS BOOK IS A MEMOIR. . . . THIS IS WHAT I DID AND WHAT I SAW CONSERVATIVES SAY AND DO DURING THIS ENTIRE DECADE OF REALLY— INSIDE STORY OF A DIRTY TRICKS OPERATION THAT THE REPUBLICANS RAN. SO, IT'S REALLY A FIRSTHAND ACCOUNT.

DAVID BROCK

KATIE COURIC: His critics call him a belligerent racist who demeans women and minorities. But Howard Stern, the self-proclaimed king of all media, is still expanding his empire. His radio show is now heard in twenty-three cities. His radio antics can be seen on E! Entertainment Television. . . . When he penned his first book two years ago, it was an instant best-seller. And when his second book, *Miss America*, went on sale last week, Stern's fans were lined up outside bookstores waiting for the doors to open.

CROWD: Eight, seven, six, five, four, three, two, one. *(Cheering)*

KATIE COURIC: And selling books was the reason why he wanted to do this interview.

HOWARD STERN: And if I was single and you were single and we hooked up as a couple, can you imagine what that—would you imagine the headlines? "Howard Stern Fouls Katie Couric, Ruins Her."

KATIE COURIC: That's right.

HOWARD STERN: The demon has, you know—oh!

KATIE COURIC: But it wasn't easy getting his mind back to the book.

KATIE COURIC: Okay. Let's talk about—

HOWARD STERN: Go ahead.

KATIE COURIC: —*Miss America*.

HOWARD STERN: Yeah.

KATIE COURIC: Why the title and how long have you been into cross-dressing, Howard?

HOWARD STERN: Why *Miss America*? When I was a kid growing up in high school, I would come down the steps. My parents were disgusted by me. I had started this growth spurt. I looked like a big, hairy pencil. I'm walking down the steps and my father would look at me and I'd be in my underpants. And he looked at his son who was sprouting facial hair and he'd go, 'Oh, look. There's Miss America."

KATIE COURIC: How long did your parents try desperately to work on you, Howard, and when did they just throw their hands up and say, "This is not exactly a boy who's going to grow up and be a doctor?'

HOWARD STERN: Well, my father was always very disappointed in me. My father was the type of guy who wanted me to be a lawyer. He wanted me to go into politics. He felt that I would be a great politician. And I was always a disappointment to him because all I ever wanted to be since the age of five was a disk jockey. And I had this grand plan to go on radio and change the face of radio, to make it completely different. I had the idea for this show when I was five years old.

KATIE COURIC: Come on.

HOWARD STERN: I swear to you. And my father would say to me, "You are horrible. You have—you don't have a voice. You do not have a delivery. You don't read the newspaper. You don't study any books. You have to be well-versed to be in radio. You have nothing going for you. This is a ridiculous career choice." And yet I defied him and I went into radio and I proved that he was wrong. And that has been the whole basis of my life.

KATIE COURIC: Do you worry, though, Howard, about being hurtful or demeaning?

HOWARD STERN: No. I think the majority of people know it's a joke.

KATIE COURIC: But the Federal Communications Commission doesn't see the humor. The FCC has found Stern's show indecent on several occasions. And just last week, the company that employs Howard paid the first installment of a whopping $1.7 million fine. Stern calls it extortion.

Infinity pays FCC

Infinity Broadcasting has sent the Federal Communications Commission more than half of the $1.7 million it is paying to settle indecency charges against **Howard Stern**.

Infinity made a $1 million payment Monday, with an additional $715,000 promised by March 31.

January 14, 1995: Katie Couric
is subjected to Howard Stern's antics when she
interviews him in his studio for *Today*.

HOWARD STERN: . . . indecent or obscene, nor do I think any court would have. And the United States government extorted $1.7 [million] to save face.

KATIE COURIC: Is anything at all off limits to you?

HOWARD STERN: Absolutely not. I would talk about anything.

KATIE COURIC: Nothing.

HOWARD STERN: As—as witnessed by talking about how attractive I think you are. By the way, the whole interview, I'm looking at your legs. Fabulous.

KATIE COURIC: Let's talk about what you're going to do next. Are you going to be doing this show on radio for—for as long as you can or do—I know that you talked about doing a movie and there is a movie of *Private Parts* in the works?

HOWARD STERN: There's a movie of *Private Parts*. The script is completed.

KATIE COURIC: So are you going to stop doing the radio gig and become a full-time actor?

HOWARD STERN: No. I—I still have a lot to accomplish in radio because there's a lot of people who very never heard a guy pass wind into a microphone yet and they need to hear that.

KATIE COURIC: Oh, God. Can you imagine?

HOWARD STERN: Do you realize there's somebody in Minnesota right now who has never heard a guy pass wind into a microphone?

KATIE COURIC: Gosh.

HOWARD STERN: To actually take his buttocks and put it up to the microphone and pass wind?

KATIE COURIC: They're deprived.

HOWARD STERN: I feel—I feel that that's something I have to do, you know. I have still that—that desire to make sure they hear it.

BY THE WAY, THE WHOLE INTERVIEW I'M LOOKING AT YOUR LEGS. FABULOUS.

HOWARD STERN

One summer morning in 1953, *Today* host Dave Garroway got a pointed lesson in how ticklish the business of television could be. He was on 49th Street in midtown Manhattan, chatting live on the air with some of the folks who gathered every morning to look through *Today*'s glass windows and maybe get on TV, much as people do today.

Garroway moved easily among the crowd, asking innocuous questions about the specific location of TV sets at home, morning viewing routines, and what people liked about the show. One youngster piped up that he liked watching J. Fred Muggs, the show's resident chimpanzee. Then he added, "If someone wants to watch the thing all the way through, it gets boring the second hour because you repeat everything."

Everybody's a critic.

The moment underscored what would be a continuing dilemma for *Today*: Its coverage of television, which eventually became the predominant force in American popular culture, would sometimes be constricted by self-interest.

Although there were only two prosperous networks when *Today* premiered in 1952 (NBC and CBS) and two others battling for the advertising scraps left over (ABC and Dumont), there was no escaping that television was a competitive business, and one network would hardly be expected to promote another's products. So when movie superstar James Cagney showed up on *Today* a few years later to promote his first performance in a live TV drama, it came as no surprise that the show in question was NBC's own *Robert Montgomery Presents*. And there doubtless were some raised eyebrows in the *Today* control room when Cagney—ever the straight shooter—mentioned that it would not exactly be his first live TV appearance. "I did a bit with Dave—Ed Sullivan, rather, on his show about two years ago to publicize *Mr. Roberts*," Cagney pointed out. Ed Sullivan's show aired on CBS.

But there were other, much stickier, complications ahead. In 1959, *Today* found itself not at the center but certainly on the uncomfortably close periphery of the quiz show scandal that shook television to its foundations.

Charles Van Doren, a brainy and boyish academic who had won big on NBC's *Twenty-One*, had subsequently become a regular *Today* contributor covering culture, traveling with the show overseas, and sometimes even filling in for Garroway as host.

When his name first came up in connection with game-rigging, Van Doren denied any chicanery. But he later admitted his complicity, and NBC first suspended him from his *Today* duties, then fired him. In an extraordinarily personal moment, Garroway spoke directly to *Today*'s viewers about it.

"I want to talk a few minutes about Charlie Van Doren, my friend," Garroway said. "Up until now, I've said nothing, not presuming to judge my fellow man until he was judged by my betters—including Charles Van Doren, who has judged himself now. As you know, Charles Van Doren's contract has been terminated by NBC. . . . And I wonder what you want me to say?

"What I want to say is, I knew Charles. Quite well, I think. You get to know a person when you're with him at five o'clock in the morning, five days a week. There's a certain openness about five o'clock in the morning. You get to

Today fans watch through the studio windows.
James Cagney is interviewed by Dave Garroway on *Today*.

DAVE GARROWAY: Let me state the facts simply and directly. On Monday evening on NBC, *Robert Montgomery Presents* offers a drama entitled *A Soldier From the War is Returning*. And the star of that drama is one of America's great actors, James Cagney. Jimmy, Monday will be the first time you're performing in a live television show at all, isn't it? What made you take the step?

JAMES CAGNEY: Well, it's not exactly the first time. We—I did a bit with Dave—Ed Sullivan, rather, on his show about two years ago to publicize *Mr. Roberts*.

DAVE GARROWAY: I remember that—

JAMES CAGNEY: It was about a two-minute piece or something like that.

DAVE GARROWAY: —now that you speak of it, yeah. You've been rehearsing for several days now. How would you compare TV rehearsals with movie rehearsals?

JAMES CAGNEY: Oh, they're essentially the same. We've got a script. The only difference is that there is a constant flow of movement and the cameras, of course. You operate with three or four. We operate with only one. And the only thing that's the difference essentially is that there is a strict continuity in this, whereas we do a straight hour. We will shoot the script in five or six weeks and there's nothing that holds us to it.

DAVE GARROWAY: Well, let me check some statistics here now. *Who* says—the *Who's Who* says you were fifty-two on your last birthday. You're five foot nine. You weight about 160, I would guess.

JAMES CAGNEY: Yes.

DAVE GARROWAY: You have two children, a sixteen-year-old son named Jim and a fifteen-year-old daughter named Cathy.

JAMES CAGNEY: That's about right.

DAVE GARROWAY: Is that correct?

JAMES CAGNEY: That's about right.

DAVE GARROWAY: So *Who's Who* is still in business then.

JAMES CAGNEY: Yeah.

DAVE GARROWAY: People, you know, who have never seen your work, young kids just growing up, still know you by the imitations that are done of you everyplace. Could you imitate an imitator imitating you?

JAMES CAGNEY: Well, I'll tell you, to me it's a very—imitation has been a part of show business ever since the start of it, of course. And I do remember when I was a kid, I used to go to the theater and see imitators do—impersonate the people of show business, and it's still a part. Somebody's making a living from it. What's better than that?

DAVE GARROWAY: Nothing that I know of.

JAMES CAGNEY: Yeah.

DAVE GARROWAY: Of all the movie roles that you have played, which one gave you the most satisfaction?

JAMES CAGNEY: I think *Yankee Doodle Dandy*. That was a very satisfactory—because I had everything to work with, you know. It was all phases and show business and they did it interestingly, I thought. It was a good job.

Today
Dave Garroway
and James Cagney

AND THERE DOUBTLESS WERE SOME RAISED EYEBROWS IN THE TODAY CONTROL ROOM WHEN CAGNEY— EVER THE STRAIGHT SHOOTER— MENTIONED THAT IT WOULD NOT EXACTLY BE HIS FIRST LIVE TV APPEARANCE.

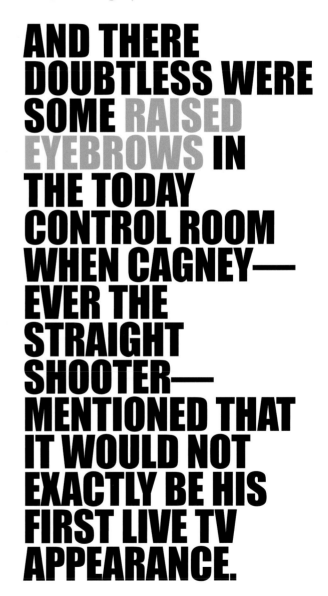

James Cagney talks about his guest role on *Robert Montgomery Presents* on *Today*.

WHAT DO YOU WANT ME TO SAY? HE WAS ONE OF OUR FAMILY; WE ARE A LITTLE FAMILY ON THIS SHOW. . . .

DAVE GARROWAY

Dave Garroway makes a very personal speech about his friend Charles Van Doren.

December 1978: John Houseman is interviewed by Gene Shalit.

know each other on plane flights ten, fifteen hours at a time sometimes. You get to know each other when you're fellow Americans abroad, as we were in Paris. . . . I came to love Charles, to love his inquiring mind, his enthusiasm, his rifeness—and I wonder what you want me to say. He wronged himself, of course. He erred. I think you agree on that. Here on the *Today* show, Charles said, and I quote him now, 'I believe in the honesty of the contestants on that program, *Twenty-One*, whom I know. . . . I also believe in the honesty of the questions used on that program. I myself was never given any answers or told any questions beforehand. And as far as I know, none of the contestants received any coaching of this sort.'

"What do you want me to say? He was one of our family; we are a little family on this show, strange as it may seem. Whatever Charles did wrong was, of course, wrong. I cannot condone it or defend it, and I have no intention of doing so. . . . I'm sorry to break up this way. . . . I know his family. I know his charming wife. I've watched his little girl grow up at his home. . . . What do you want me to say? I can only say, I'm heartsick."

As television became even more intensely competitive in the sixties, seventies, and eighties, patterns began to emerge on all the network morning shows, *Today* included. (ABC's *Good Morning America* premiered in 1975.)

When there was genuine news to report about the medium—studies on the supposed effects of televised violence or the relationship between TV programming and social attitudes and mores—*Today* reported it straight. Significant milestones were not ignored: On April 28, 1989, *Today* devoted the entire show to a substantive look at the state of the medium on its fiftieth anniversary.

But when coverage is optional—say, talking to stars of new entertainment shows—the parent network gets priority, although there have always been exceptions for shows and personalities that become so widely popular and talked about that to ignore them would be foolish.

In the early years of *Today*, for example, the universally renowned Jackie Gleason and the aforementioned Ed Sullivan, both CBS stars at the time, came around to chat with Dave Garroway. And in December 1978, *Today* took advantage of a juicy opportunity to promote the competition and zing it at the same time. "This segment may very well wind up in the Guinness Book of World Records," arts editor Gene Shalit told viewers. "We are about to talk to John Houseman, who is a producer, director, the university professor who a few years back won an Academy Award for his first major role in a movie. It was called *The Paper Chase,* and he played a law professor. Now CBS—yes, I said CBS—hired Mr. Houseman to play that same role, that of a law professor, in a television series which is also called *The Paper Chase.* Well, the quality of the program was so high that the ratings were low and it seemed the show would be canceled. Then something happened; it was decided not to cancel *The Paper Chase* for the seemingly incredible reason that the show is very good. Now who would believe that could happen in television? And who would believe that Mr. Houseman would wind up talking about his CBS program on the *Today* program?"

In another notable exception, Katie Couric interviewed Roseanne in 1994, even though *Roseanne* was a hit for ABC at the time. But it also was the most popular and most talked-about entertainment show on any network at the time, and it had been breaking ground with its sharp comedic treatment of the real problems of working-class families. On top of that, the ups and downs of Roseanne's private life had become something of a national fixation.

More recently, early in 2001, Matt Lauer sat down with actress Sarah Jessica Parker for an interview about a new movie she was in, and ended up also discussing *Sex and the City*, her award-winning and often bawdy HBO comedy about single professional women in New York.

And early in 2003, *Today* paid close attention—in several segments aired over a period of weeks—to the amateur performers and celebrity judges on Fox's smash reality-show hit, *American Idol*.

But if any non-NBC show ever earned the right to a segment on *Today*, it was the one featured on October 17, 1980.

"Who did shoot J. R.?" asked anchor Tom Brokaw. "We may never get the answer to that question. I mean, the people who produce that program [*Dallas*] are going to keep us in suspense for as long as they possibly can. J. R. himself is here—doesn't look bloody or wounded or anything. Right out of the hospital, here's Larry Hagman. And I can't think of anybody having a better time in that whole role than you are."

Hagman was, indeed, having the time of his life. As the character J. R. Ewing on the CBS nighttime soap *Dallas*, he was the lead performer on the most-watched show on television, and he had become the focus of a worldwide frenzy over who had shot J. R. in the final episode of the previous season.

Hagman, in fact, did not know at that point which *Dallas* character had shot J. R. or how the writers had resolved the mystery. Scripts he had received for the key episodes, he said, were missing the revelatory pages.

Given the *Dallas* hysteria that gripped the land, Brokaw wondered, could Hagman venture out in public anymore?

"No," he admitted. "It's real hard. It really is, because [everyone] says J. R, you know, J. R. this and J. R. that." Even so, Hagman said he was enjoying the ride. "I know it'll only last another thirty or forty seconds, so I'm living with it, you know?"

As the segment ended, Brokaw thanked his guest. "Real glad to have you here, even though you're on another network," he said.

"Are we?" Hagman kidded him. "What network is it?"

"That one with the bloodshot eye," Brokaw shot back.

The "Who Shot J. R.?" episode of *Dallas* aired November 21, 1980, on CBS. Of the homes in which TV sets were on at the time, 76 percent were tuned to *Dallas*. In the modern era of television, only the final episode of *M*A*S*H* has attracted a higher percentage of TV homes. And, by the way, Kristen shot J. R.

September 8, 1994: Roseanne discusses her personal life with Katie Couric.

October 17, 1980: Tom Brokaw interviews Larry Hagman about the much-anticipated outcome of the "Who Shot J. R.?" episode of *Dallas*.

MATT LAUER: You may remember yesterday that Sarah Jessica Parker was here to talk about her new movie *State and Main*. Well, when we broke away to go to your local news, she stayed with us to talk about her very popular TV show *Sex and the City*. And I asked her if she enjoyed working on the HBO series now as much as when it first began.

SARAH JESSICA PARKER: It's just been one of the great jobs of a lifetime. It's hard to explain because I've never worked harder. I don't work harder. And it's just a thrilling job to have. I shoot on the streets of New York, a city I love and care deeply about, and I feel like I have this responsibility to represent it well.

MATT LAUER: Are women still coming up to you on the streets and at airports and kind of sharing their sexual secrets and fantasies with you?

SARAH JESSICA PARKER: Yeah.

MATT LAUER: What a great job.

SARAH JESSICA PARKER: It's bizarre. I think—also, and I feel very touched that they feel comfortable enough to share intimate details. But you know, a lot of times, and I don't want to discourage anybody from coming and sharing things with me, but it does make me feel uncomfortable to know and visualize because immediately when people tell you things, you start—you know, that's how the mind works.

MATT LAUER: You picture them naked, basically?

SARAH JESSICA PARKER: Well, any number of things. I mean, some of it has nothing to do with not being clothed. You can't imagine the things people show me and tell me and share with me.

MATT LAUER: Don't you think they're trying to get this stuff on the show? I think people come up to you because they think maybe this is a good storyline for *Sex and the City*.

SARAH JESSICA PARKER: You know, I still am such an innocent, I don't believe that everybody wants to be in show business. But I suppose that there is some degree of, like, perhaps this will make it onto the show. But I also think people just feel that television, as you know probably better than anybody, there is a muddied line between the person—

MATT LAUER: Yeah.

SARAH JESSICA PARKER: —that visits their home for free except actually in my case, where they actually pay for it—

MATT LAUER: Exactly.

SARAH JESSICA PARKER: —but you know, it's so often in their home, I think there is accessibility and they feel comfortable. And for that, we're delighted.

MATT LAUER: Theater. Still like to do theater. You said this back in 1996. "A woman's movie career is much shorter than a man's and it's awfully nice to have a career in theater, where a woman can work longer. So I do this out of love, but not without a certain degree of calculation. I want a career in theater because in a couple of years, my opportunities will change drastically." Do you see a time in the near future in thirty seconds, deep answer, where your choices in television and movies will—

SARAH JESSICA PARKER: Absolutely.

MATT LAUER: Really?

SARAH JESSICA PARKER: It's the inevitable. The best actresses that you can see sort of struggle. I'm not equating myself with the best actresses, but even they have to make peace with the type of roles that are offered. I think the theater has always been open to actresses of an older age group and they always will be. And there's great parts.

MATT LAUER: Hopefully, there'll be great parts for you in movies and television, too.

January 9, 2001: Sarah Jessica Parker talks with Matt Lauer.

The *Today* fashion segment that aired July 15, 1953, wasn't just low-tech; it was below-tech. Arrayed in the studio was nothing more than a batch of oversized photographs, which *Today*'s Dave Garroway strolled past with Eugenia Sheppard, fashion editor of the *New York Herald Tribune*.

"I'll explain to you very simply," Sheppard said, "that the new fall fashions are going to be both natural and elegant. And by natural, I mean that they're going to follow the contours of a woman's figure. And by elegant, I mean that the fabrics are going to be especially elegant. . . . This dress follows the body line through here and down here," she said, pointing to one of the photos. "Nothing sticks out too much here. That's what I mean by the natural look. Do you like it?"

Garroway wasn't sure. "Is that the same as kind of simple?" he asked warily.

"Simple, natural," Sheppard affirmed. "But natural following the lines."

A moment later, Sheppard offered similar praise for another dress. "Now we have another simple dress, but showing the very trick seaming that the designers like for fall. You notice here how they accent all the body lines of the dress? I think that's most attractive."

Garroway disagreed. "It looks very ugly to me," he said.

"I think you'll like it when you see a beautiful girl wearing it," Sheppard said knowingly.

The cocktail dresses came next. "And necklines are pretty exciting," she said. "They're never square necklines this fall. They're all cut across this way, scooped out like a boat or a plunging neckline, which you're going to see in a minute."

But Garroway stopped her. "I can just barely stand to say this, Eugenia, but we're not going to have time for the plunging necklines," he said. "Next fall, perhaps."

It wasn't long before *Today* replaced photos with living models wearing real clothes and shifted responsibility for the segments to the show's *Today* Girl.

Fashion, a vast and varied topic appealing particularly to *Today*'s principally

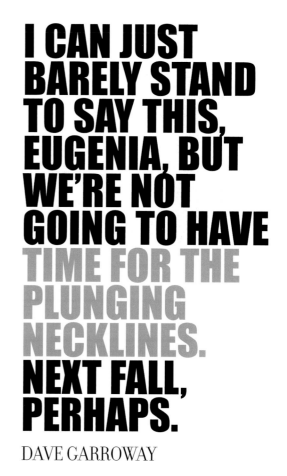

I CAN JUST BARELY STAND TO SAY THIS, EUGENIA, BUT WE'RE NOT GOING TO HAVE TIME FOR THE PLUNGING NECKLINES. NEXT FALL, PERHAPS.

DAVE GARROWAY

July 15, 1953: Eugenia Sheppard, fashion editor of the *New York Herald Tribune*, discusses trends in fashion with Dave Garroway.

HEMLINES ROSE, FELL, ROSE, FELL, AND ROSE MORE TIMES THAN ANYONE NOW BOTHERS TO COUNT AS THE FASHION INDUSTRY TRIED TO EXPLOIT EXISTING TRENDS WITH ONE HAND WHILE CREATING THEM WITH THE OTHER.

female audience, has been integral to the show ever since. And its perpetually spinning cycles—that which is in will be out; that which is out will be in again someday, then out again—has assured the show of a limitless supply of raw material. Consider the changes—some fundamental, some fleeting—of the last fifty-plus years:

High-maintenance natural fabrics, which predominated at the middle of the twentieth century, gave way to supposed "miracle" synthetics promising convenience for ever-busier homemakers. These were later displaced by easier-care natural materials that offered greater comfort, and those eventually slid over to peacefully co-exist with successive generations of improved synthetics. Blue jeans and T-shirts, once the almost exclusive province of schoolchildren and farm workers, spread to American cities and suburbs and then conquered the world, redefining the concept of casual. Skirts made room for pants in women's closets. Cuffs flared into sloshy bell-bottoms, then tapered to pencil width, then spread again. Shoulders got padded and sharpened, then softened and sloped. Hemlines rose, fell, rose, fell, and rose more times than anyone now bothers to count as the fashion industry tried to exploit existing trends with one hand while creating them with the other. And once-rigid, instantly recognized generational boundaries melted away, as *Today* contributor Christy Ferer noted in a fashion segment from the summer of 1985. "There's no more generation gap in women's wardrobes," Ferer declared. "As long as the size is right, three generations can really dress out of the same closet." A salesman in Bergdorf Goodman's ball gown department emphasized the point. "I guess if you want to categorize them," he said, "they're somewhere between [age] fifteen and death, my customers."

Today's archives catalog endless variations on the fashion theme: simple Swiss cottons for the fifties housewife, the earthy simplicity of the flower-child/peasant look, playful metallics and vinyls for nighttime clubbing, outlandish hats, conservative hats, affordable style via home-sewing patterns, the Carnaby Street craze, incredibly shrinking swimwear, women's business suits, illegal knockoffs of designer brands, the explosion of vintage-clothing shops, the return of the sixties look, the return of the seventies look, the erratic business fortunes of couture houses, spring fashions, fall fashions, thongs, and shoes, shoes, shoes.

A fairly recent addition to the mix descends from the decades-old fashion tradition of best-dressed lists, but stirs in the contemporary obsession with celebrity and adds a robust dash of biting, anything-is-fair-game commentary. On *Today*, the result has been frequent, free-wheeling contributions by Steven Cojocaru, west coast style editor for *People* magazine.

In a segment aired just before the Grammy Awards in 2001, for example, Cojocaru showed viewers the kinds of free party favors the academy gives to its celebrity presenters, specifically, Madonna.

"This is a $20,000 goody bag that she's getting," he said. "It's a haul, absolutely. . . . This is a seven-strand chakra necklace. It's supposed to open up your chakra, your energy. Enlighten you. I wore it yesterday; it didn't even open up my clogged nose." Other free booty: "Oh, this is really cool," Cojocaru said slyly. "This is a bejeweled earpiece for your cell phone. Very Madonna. So L.A. Very Zsa-Zsa Gabor."

Photo Right; an early *Today* fashion segment.

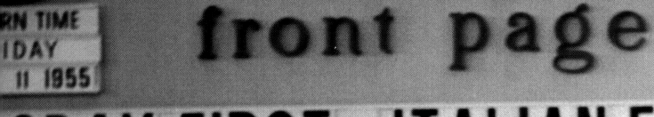
front page

ODAY FIRST – ITALIAN FASHIO

CAN I JUST ANSWER BLAH BLAH BLAH, OR WHATEVER—

ANDY WARHOL

ALINE SAARINEN: I've just said a lot of very pompous things about your work and what it means and the twentieth century and everything. Do you agree with any of it?

ANDY WARHOL: Can I just answer blah blah blah, or whatever—

ALINE SAARINEN: Yes, you can.

ANDY WARHOL: Blah blah blah blah blah.

ALINE SAARINEN: Back in 1962—or '61 or '62, around in then—when you and Rosenquist and Lichtenstein all were working very independently of each other but evolving a same kind of attitude, does that seem odd to you that—you all began to look at the world in the same way?

ANDY WARHOL: I think we just read a lot of—comic books and it just happened to come out then.

ALINE SAARINEN: Well, I'm—

ANDY WARHOL: 'Cause comic books make things—the way they are really today. I mean the way things happen in New York now it's like being in a Western movie. I mean it's just so scary. Now the newspapers are more like the comic books then. I mean you pick up a newspaper now. It's just like a comic book of, you know, eight years ago. It's—really strange.

ALINE SAARINEN: With all the—the horror?

ANDY WARHOL: There's so much action. Yeah. All this action I guess that's happening.

ALINE SAARINEN: Why are you going to change your name to John Doe?

ANDY WARHOL: Well—well I—after I thought about it now is—if I told everybody what my name was then that's sort of silly. So I—I think I'm going to take another name.

ALINE SAARINEN: I mean you're not gonna take John Doe.

ANDY WARHOL: Well, I'm not sure. I was working on it and stuff but then—I thought it would be easier to just take some other name and—and just work under that.

ALINE SAARINEN: Why?

ANDY WARHOL: Because if they—well if they knew it was John. Well, John Doe was my favorite name and—if they know what it is then they know that it's really me. But—but I think it's better to actually take a whole new name—name that somebody doesn't know. And actually, the name is spelt wrong. It's D-o-u-g-h.

ALINE SAARINEN: Why do you wanna be anonymous?

ANDY WARHOL: Well, I think you can just—do more.

ALINE SAARINEN: You don't think people will recognize what you do even if it's under another name?

ANDY WARHOL: No, I don't think so.

ALINE SAARINEN: You don't think your style is like a signature?

ANDY WARHOL: No, because there's so many different things and new things to know about.

ALINE SAARINEN: When you first started painting, people said this was so very American. But it—but there's—you've—there's sort of universal now, isn't it?

ANDY WARHOL: Well I think everything is coming sort of—English or American or somethin' like that all over the world.

ALINE SAARINEN: England and America set—

ANDY WARHOL: Yeah.

ALINE SAARINEN: Setting the tone.

ANDY WARHOL: Yeah.

ALINE SAARINEN: If I—if you were I and—and were interviewing yourself, what (would) you ask?

ANDY WARHOL: That the lights go out.

May 4, 1971: Andy Warhol is interviewed by *Today* art critic Aline Saarinen on *Today*.

NOW THE NEWSPAPERS ARE MORE LIKE THE COMIC BOOKS THEN. I MEAN YOU PICK UP A NEWSPAPER NOW. IT'S JUST LIKE A COMIC BOOK OF, YOU KNOW, EIGHT YEARS AGO.

ANDY WARHOL

CAST

DAVE GARROWAY
JACK LESCOULIE
FRANK BLAIR
JOHN CHANCELLOR
HUGH DOWNS
JOE GARAGIOLA
FRANK McGEE
BARBARA WALTERS
GENE SHALIT
TOM BROKAW
JANE PAULEY
WILLARD SCOTT
BRYANT GUMBEL
KATIE COURIC
MATT LAUER
AL ROKER
ANN CURRY

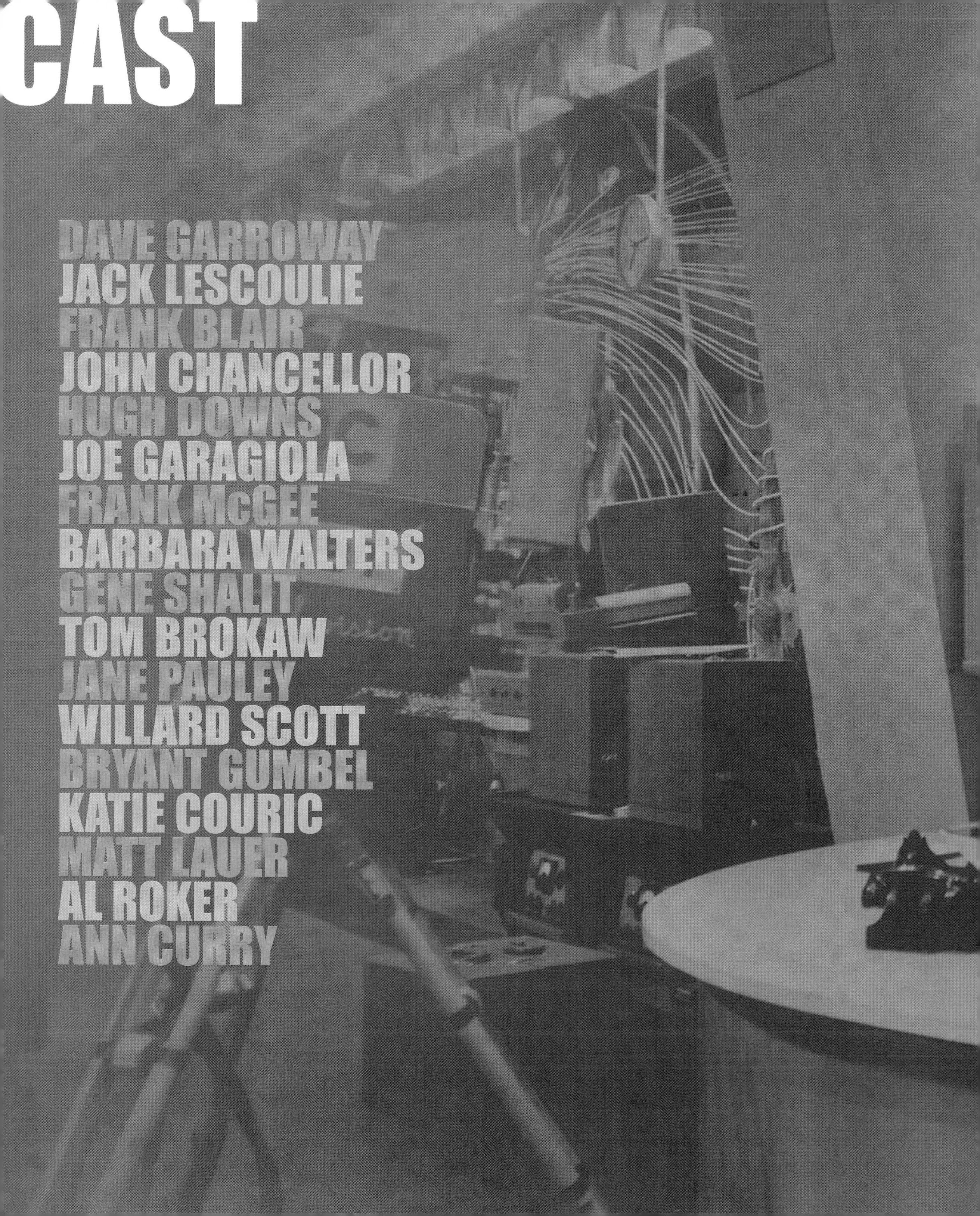

CAST

Today's on-air patriarch, Dave Garroway, was born in Schenectady, New York, and spent his formative teenage years in University City, Missouri, a suburb of St. Louis. He became a radio newsman and disk jockey, then a pioneering TV star in Chicago. His principal Today sidekick, Jack Lescoulie, was a California-born actor and broadcast announcer with a knack for mimicking the voice of Jack Benny.

Katie Couric started in entry-level jobs at network news bureaus in her native Washington, D.C., then worked her way into local-TV producing, political reporting, and, eventually, an NBC spot covering the Pentagon. Bryant Gumbel, a Chicagoan, first hit his professional stride as a TV sportscaster. Barbara Walters grew up in Boston, New York, and Miami Beach in homes often teeming with celebrities, all of them friends or associates of her father—a sometimes flush, sometimes broke nightclub owner.

Frank McGee was a born-and-bred southerner who cut his teeth covering the hard news of the early civil rights era. St. Louisan Joe Garagiola played major-league baseball before sliding into broadcasting at the major-league level. Tom Brokaw, born near tiny Bristol, South Dakota, was a young radio deejay in Yankton before taking a job in TV news in Omaha and later landing an NBC correspondent's spot in Los Angeles. Hugh Downs, an Akron native, was an announcer and comic foil on NBC late-night shows starring Steve Allen and Jack Paar. Matt Lauer, born and reared in New York City, worked through several reporting, producing, and hosting jobs in local and cable TV before settling at WNBC-TV back in his hometown.

This hodgepodge of people—and just a very few others—constitute the Today cast of the past fifty years, a tight circle indeed. Their geographic origins stretch from coast to coast. Their economic and social backgrounds are far from uniform. And they clearly did not follow the same career path to Today.

But whatever their differences, success on Today required of them a distinctive combination of character traits and professional skills that they either possessed or managed to develop as they went along.

"I think you have to be accessible," says Couric, "meaning, I think people need to feel like they'd be comfortable having a cup of coffee with you. I think people need to trust you and feel that you're honest. I think they want to believe that you're fair. And I also think you have to have a lot of self-confidence, the self-confidence that makes you feel comfortable being spontaneous. And I also think you have to have very good split-second judgment, because there's a fine line between being spontaneous and being a train wreck. You have to know when you can have fun with things, when you can't, how much is enough, how much is too much."

And in dealing with arcane subjects that turn up in the news, Couric says, "You have to be able to distill complicated material fairly easily. And you have to find the right level of respecting an audience's intelligence and yet not making it so complex and inside-baseball that only experts in a particular area would understand. So I think that that's a sort of delicate balance, too."

For Brokaw, success in morning television requires an even harder-to-define quality. "I think you have to be user-friendly," he says. "That's the first criterion. And, it's a tricky piece. You have to be at once user-friendly but

This Page and Opposite, Today cast members through the years.

Photo Above, Dave Garroway.

Charles Van Doren, Lee Meriwether, Jack Lescoulie, Dave Garroway, and Frank Blair.

Photo Below, Joe Garagiola and Frank McGee.

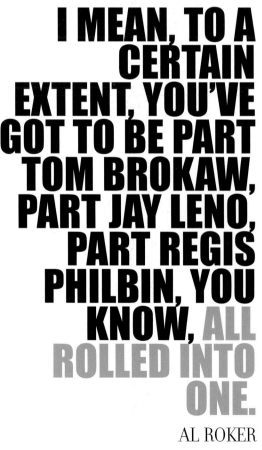

I MEAN, TO A CERTAIN EXTENT, YOU'VE GOT TO BE PART TOM BROKAW, PART JAY LENO, PART REGIS PHILBIN, YOU KNOW, ALL ROLLED INTO ONE.

AL ROKER

Al Roker out in Rockefeller Plaza.

informed and kind of businesslike, because you're getting [the viewers'] day started for them. And you try to do that in an engaging way—with what's happened overnight, what's likely to happen that day—that doesn't curdle the milk in their coffee."

Today's current weathercaster and feature reporter, Al Roker, thinks viewers don't understand how demanding the host's job is. "I mean, to a certain extent, you've got to be part Tom Brokaw, part Jay Leno, part Regis Philbin, you know, all rolled into one," he says. "And not everybody can do that."

Those who can, says Gumbel, tend to share not only broadcasting skills but a certain kind of disposition.

"You have to be able to stay calm. You have to be able to streamline your thoughts. And you have to have, oddly enough, a sense of endurance in front of the camera," he says. "It's two hours a day. It's a grind. There are a lot of people who jump in front of the camera and do something for a half hour. You know, you maintain your focus for a half hour, then you get out of there. But two hours is a lot of television, and it beats a lot of people down. You have to be able to pretty much keep on an even keel, because if you get too sky-high, you're not going to make it through two hours. You're really not."

What complicates the task is the need to routinely deal with a wide range of material, both in subject matter and tone. To do that well, Gumbel says, the ability to focus is key. "I think that you have a lot of things that you have to do. I mean, on any given morning, you may have to debrief somebody from the State Department on a crisis overseas. You may then have to turn tables and talk economics. You may then deal with the latest ingenue from Hollywood. You then may have a best-selling author, and then you wind up cooking with someone. And I think if you go into the morning going, 'Oh my God, how am I going to do all of these things?' and if you're talking to the economist and thinking about the ingenue, or you're talking with the ingenue and thinking about the author, it tends to blur what you're trying to do. I think you have to be able to compartmentalize and stay focused, so that you're very much in the moment. You make sure you do what's in front of you as well as you can do it, and then move on."

Much of a person's ability to thrive in this environment, says Matt Lauer, depends on his or her connection to the world. "The first thing you need is what you need not only on this show but to do news in any form, and that's curiosity. You've got to be a curious person. You've got to be someone who doesn't hear a story and take it at face value and say, 'That's enough information.' You always have to be the person who wants to know more. That's the first thing."

At the same time, Lauer acknowledges, the very nature of a morning show all but precludes specialization. "You have to be what I sometimes call 'cocktail-party smart.' You have to have that level of and foundation of knowledge in a hundred subjects that's a quarter of an inch deep," he says, "as opposed to a level of and foundation of knowledge in one subject that's forty miles deep. You know, we have to be comfortable in a lot of different areas. The people who've been successful at this show have been very well rounded. Probably the best word is *versatile*. You've got to be versatile on this show. You've got to be willing and ready to cover hard news, breaking news, at a moment's

notice. And then at some point, you have to be able to take a breath, take a beat, and cover something very different. As different as a cooking segment, as a celebrity. As travel. As pop culture, music, movies, you name it."

Willard Scott, the veteran *Today* weathercaster and contributor, offers a bigger-picture perspective. "It was true in radio for a hundred years, and it's true in television," he says. "Morning shows are different animals. They trade on warmth and personality. Jane [Pauley] was America's sweetheart. Katie is America's sweetheart. I mean, if Katie Couric—and she's a very smart woman, we know that; she's a great interviewer—but if she had spinach in her teeth, and was sitting there just saying, 'Isn't that lovely?' people would like her, because she's so warm, and they love her for her personality and warmth and charm. The same thing with Jane. The same thing, really, with Tom [Brokaw]. If I've heard it from one [local station] affiliate, I've heard it from a thousand: 'He's a really nice man. He's a good guy,' they say. I think that's what it takes. Al is a good guy. Matt is one of the most sensitive, warm, loving human beings I've ever known in my entire life."

Scott rejects, in fact, the stereotype of on-air talent being ruthless, career-minded sharks. "I think probably some of the most warm and wonderful people I've known come from TV and radio," he says. "Because they're childlike in many ways. That's part of their charm. They want to be loved. They want to please. It's not just the fame and fortune. When you're a kid and starting out in radio, you want to please people. You want to be accepted. I think that's more important than anything else in this business and especially in a morning show."

Being on the air at that hour of the day creates a unique kind of connection, past and present *Today* cast members agree, between the people who appear on the show and the people who watch the show.

"Morning is simply different," says Jane Pauley. "It's new. It's fresh. You're vulnerable. You're waking up. You're not dressed yet. You're not shaved yet.

MORNING SHOWS ARE DIFFERENT ANIMALS. THEY TRADE ON WARMTH AND PERSONALITY. JANE [PAULEY] WAS AMERICA'S SWEETHEART. KATIE IS AMERICA'S SWEETHEART.

WILLARD SCOTT

July 1981: Jane Pauley and Willard Scott at the Royal Wedding in London.

145

You haven't gotten down that first cup of coffee. You know, in saying that, I feel a little ridiculous because I always used to kind of smirk at people who defined morning television as special in that way. But I think it's true."

The very act of watching television at that time of day, argues Gene Shalit, gives people a sense that they're sharing their prepublic selves with the people they're watching on the screen. "If you succeed in the show, you are a member of ten million families or whatever the number is," Shalit says. "When [viewers] see any of these people in person on the street, or in restaurants or something, they think they know them. They approach a person like me as if we've known each other for years because they see me in the morning. You know, they're brushing their teeth, they go into the bathroom, they're having breakfast, they're sending their kids to school. I mean, we're in their household in the morning."

To illustrate how strong the morning connection can become, Shalit tells the story of a peculiar request that came in from a viewer some years ago. "There is a famous letter that I saw once," Shalit recalls, "that said, 'Could you write a letter to my mother and tell her that you cannot see her? Because when she gets up in the morning, she won't sit in front of the set until she takes the curlers out of her hair and puts on a good dress, because she's convinced that you can see her like she can see you.'"

That may be extreme, but Lauer points out that just being present in someone's home in the morning, even electronically, lends substance to the oft-promoted cliché of the cast being like a family. "As you're waking up with your family, it's like you're joining our family as well. It's the meeting of the families for the morning," he says. "The fact that we say we're like a family doesn't necessarily mean we go out and spend Thanksgiving together. But while we're on the air for the three hours a day, we treat it very much like a family. Because you come to expect certain things within your own family, and we want you to be able to expect those things from us as well. We want you to know that there's going to be a certain banter between us, that there's a comfort and an ease between us, that there's a familiarity among the group, that we know each other's likes and dislikes. And, as a result, we can carry on conversations and produce segments that play to our strengths and sometimes poke fun at our weaknesses. And I think that's what people find in their own families. You know, we all know the dynamics of our own family. And it is nice to start to get to know the dynamics of someone else's family, too. It makes you comfortable. It makes you feel like an insider. It draws people in and says, 'Come witness our family a little bit.'"

Today cast members also agree that these elements—the cast-as-family comparison, the early-morning hour, the three-hour daily broadcast schedule—make it not just impossible but undesirable to stick to hard news for a whole show, except at times of major breaking news. In order to survive, much less prosper, in the morning, they say, the show must contain some moments of lightness, some softer stories and segments, a bit of bantering among the cast, sometimes even some frivolity. Indeed, these have been part of *Today*'s identity since the day it premiered in 1952.

"*Today* show hosts don't only report the news," says Jane Pauley. "They have fun. They get silly. You know, every now and then, we forget to put our microphones on, and we look foolish. And if we're charming about looking

AS YOU'RE WAKING UP WITH YOUR FAMILY, IT'S LIKE YOU'RE JOINING OUR FAMILY AS WELL. IT'S THE MEETING OF THE FAMILIES FOR THE MORNING.
MATT LAUER

Photo Left, Gene Shalit and Jane Pauley.
Katie Couric, Matt Lauer, and Al Roker enjoing the morning.

147

foolish, well, that's endearing. And just the fact that the *Today* show can do the variety of topics it does is part of the reason the people on the *Today* show are more approachable and familiar than someone like Uncle Walter [Cronkite]."

Not that all cast members have been comfortable with the show's mix of hard and soft, heavy and light. The late John Chancellor was famously and all too obviously ill at ease during his fourteen-month tour of duty as *Today* host in 1961 and 1962—even though the seasoned journalist was highly regarded for the quick wit and sometimes stinging sense of humor he displayed off the air.

For others, the adjustment took a little time. Tom Brokaw, who became the show's anchor in 1976, admits he was uneasy at first. "I went into it worried that it was going to somehow diminish my hard-news credentials," he says. "And that was always a rear-guard fight for me, because some people had said, 'Oh, he's just another pretty face,' or 'He's a guy who did local news and he doesn't know what he's doing.' And the fact is, my entire career had been contrary to that, and I didn't want to give those people an excuse to define me in ways they were already inclined to."

Eventually, though, that concern faded. "I just got to a point where I thought that my traditional journalistic credentials were pretty well established by now, and if I could show another side, it would serve me well. And, I mean, I still have people talking today about some moment on the *Today* show where something funny happened, and they'll say, 'God, you had a great sense of humor that you don't show on *Nightly News*.'"

Having to deliver the news every thirty minutes, says *Today* news anchor Ann Curry, often limits how much she can participate in the easy bantering of the cast. But she recognizes its value. "I think that it gives people a chance to feel connected," she says. "I think that people watching can connect to the host and laugh about something amusing."

Beyond that, Curry says, sometimes even silly moments can have unexpected effects on viewers. She cites an appearance by *Today* contributor Steven Cojocaru, the west coast style editor for *People* magazine, whose segments often involve him dishing about celebrities' fashions with the cast. "I heard from a woman whose father had recently died. Her mother was in agony; they had been married for many, many years. And this woman called me up and said that watching the bantering during one of those segments, her mother laughed for the first time. Now, there is a value to that. There is a great value to allowing people to stop whatever problem, worry, or issue is distressing them, and enjoy a moment."

Lauer rejects any suggestion that these sorts of moments detract from the show's more serious mission of reporting the news. "I disagree completely," he says. "But we're also human beings. We also know that there has to be some respite, that there has to be a break, a change of pace. And I think that's as valuable as sitting there and beating people over the head with the same delivery of hard news over and over again."

Still, interaction among cast members has to arise from a natural dynamic, not an artificial one, especially on a morning show, which tests the consistency of its personalities over long periods of time. "The viewers are so sophisticated

I WENT INTO IT WORRIED THAT IT WAS GOING TO SOMEHOW DIMINISH MY HARD-NEWS CREDENTIALS.

TOM BROKAW

John Chancellor as *Today* anchor.
Tom Brokaw as *Today* anchor.

TOM BROKAW: . . . I, during a trying time in my life, I dropped out of college—because I was uncertain about what I wanted to do. And certainly, I was uncertain about how I was gonna get it done apart from drinking beer and chasing girls. I—that part, I had down to the gold. In fact, it was cum laude, but—

WILLARD SCOTT: Hopefully the beer was cold.

TOM BROKAW: So, I dropped out of school and—because I thought I could get a job—and I couldn't right away, which meant that I had nowhere to go. I had no money. And I had to go home. And—my parents really knew how to handle that. My dad got the worst jobs you have ever seen, menial jobs around town. He went—the word went out. Red's kid needs work. And Dad would say, "You need—post holes dug for your new fence? I—Tom'll do it, buck and a quarter," or whatever it was an hour. And he'd make the deal for me and it—and that night, he—he'd say to me, "Seven o'clock tomorrow morning, you're gonna be down at Bob Roper's. You're putting a new fence in." Well, you—digging post holes is real hard, isn't it?

WILLARD SCOTT: Awful. Awful.

TOM BROKAW: It's just a really bad job.

WILLARD SCOTT: Yeah.

TOM BROKAW: I did get a letter from the guy the other day who said that corner of the house is still standing, so he figures I must have done a good job. That was a long time ago. Then you go out at night, and you don't have any money, and you know, you kind of go to your mother for a quarter, and you're twenty years old. And you feel awful about it. Well, I—the pressure grew enormously, and finally, one of my brothers always had a little loose change around. I borrowed twenty bucks from him, and I got out on the street, and there was a fair standoff about this as I recall. I was hitchhiking over to Minnesota where I heard there was a radio job, and I thought if I could just get over there, I could have a crack at that job. But living under those circumstances is tough. I mean, we live in a variety of ways, but if you're an out-of-sorts son, or daughter for that matter, that's far more difficult than what we're talking about here.

JANE PAULEY: I was so anxious to get, to get out from—

TOM BROKAW: Under.

JANE PAULEY: —under my parents' roof that—I got a job, which paid—not a lot of money. It was in politics where you were supposed to be there for the love, you know.

TOM BROKAW: Yeah.

JANE PAULEY: So that it wasn't a lot of money. But I immediately, immediately signed a lease for an apartment, small studio, and—c—bought a car.

TOM BROKAW: Sticker price.

JANE PAULEY: Well, my dad was so upset. This is a guy who prided himself—

TOM BROKAW: Paying cash.

JANE PAULEY: —on paying cash for everything. Everything. And—he had to sign a paper to cash in an insurance policy they'd had on me that had, I think, like $300 th—coming to me that I could put a down payment on this car. I didn't have a dime. But I bought a car. He was physically ill over it 'cause I was getting myself into this obligation but—but as far as I was concerned, you know, money's coming in now. Money's going out. Life is b—

TOM BROKAW: So different because your parents grew up—during the Depression—

JANE PAULEY: Yes.

TOM BROKAW: —right?

JANE PAULEY: Yeah.

AND MY MOST PROFOUND HOPE IS IT GIVES THEM SOME CONTEXT, A BETTER UNDERSTANDING OF COMPLICATED EVENTS THAT HAPPEN EVERY DAY. . . .

KATIE COURIC

Matt Lauer and Katie Couric anchor the current *Today* family.

today," says Lauer, "they spot a phony a mile away. The best compliment anyone can pay me or Katie, and I'm sure Al and Ann too, is when they meet you in public or whatever and at the end of that encounter they say, 'You know what? You are just like you are on TV.' That's a compliment. Because we are not acting. I am not playing Matt Lauer; I am Matt Lauer."

All of which is secondary, nevertheless, to *Today*'s primary mission. "I think it's the show of record and it has been for fifty-plus years at this point," says Couric. "I think it gives people a sense of what's happened overnight and what's going to happen that day. And my most profound hope is it gives them some context, a better understanding of complicated events that happen every day. . . . I just think it helps people make better sense of the world."

Its presence each morning also serves as a sign to viewers that the world order did not completely disintegrate overnight. "Sometimes, just that familiarity breeds reassurance," says Lauer. "It's not about me. It's not about Katie. It's about, you turn on the set, you see two people that you hopefully see every day and you say, 'You know what, at least I know the world is somewhat as I left it. I know that my routine goes on.' Now, you may, in the first few seconds of the show, find out that's not necessarily true, that perhaps the world isn't the same as when you went to sleep. But in just being able to see two people come up and hear the words, 'Good morning'—which we say, by the way, even on a morning that's not good—how reassuring is that? Just, you know what, that there's electricity, that there are two people who were able to get to work that day, that nothing prevented that, that the lights have gone on. Nobody's firing at them. They're not ducking under the desk, and in some places, that does happen. But these two people are sitting there, and they seem to have their composure about them. Everything can't be so bad. Even when things get so bad, and they happen live on the air, our job is to somehow say, 'You're going to make it through this.'"

It was not easy to communicate that message on September 11, 2001. Couric and Lauer agree that reporting the events of that day was by far the most challenging assignment of their careers. "It was so difficult on every level," Couric recalls. "It was so hard to believe it was happening, and then to basically talk about it as it was happening in a calm way. And it was just extraordinarily frightening because there was so much uncertainty, and as events unfolded, it was just one tragedy after another. I mean, I had covered a lot of individual tragedies before that. . . . But the magnitude of the heartbreak was so extraordinary that day. . . . I knew a lot of people who were just so shocked watching this unfold—as shocked as we were—were depending on us to help them through this and give them the information they needed. So that was one instance where just I had no choice but to put my own emotional response completely aside so that I could do what I do every day, and that is, impart information to people. It was hard."

The TV images that morning—images of real-life horror unfolding in real time—were as difficult for professional broadcasters to describe as they were to watch at home. Lauer ticks off things he was trying to deal with. "The gravity of the situation. The almost unbelievable surreal quality of what was happening live on our air. The fact that I'm a born and raised New Yorker. The fact that my family lives here. The fact that we were all concerned for our safety, that we felt as if at any moment we could be a target. The fact that we strive so often to reassure people that things will be all right, and on that particular day, I wasn't sure. It was very hard to look into the camera with any kind of assurance that this wasn't going to absolutely change the way we live," he says. "And it did."

Such days—and such events—are rare, however. And *Today* cast members past and present recall other assignments, including sad or poignant or momentous ones, not with anguish but with warmth or amusement or satisfaction or even a measure of pride.

Gumbel, for example, credits his 1984 *Today* broadcasts from Moscow with advancing his stature as a news anchor. "In September of '84," he recalls, "there were still a number of people who were saying, 'Geez, you know, this guy can't interview anybody more than a linebacker,' that he was still this sports guy who was out of his element. Suddenly we were behind the Iron Curtain, and this was at a time when the Cold War was very much an issue, and when all kinds of arms talks had broken off. It was a difficult diplomatic dance, between being viewed as the puppet of the Soviets and being an inhospitable guest. And it worked. It helped the program, and it helped me personally. To go on over there, and to come out not getting savaged, I think was a big step."

IT WAS VERY HARD TO LOOK INTO THE CAMERA WITH ANY KIND OF ASSURANCE THAT THIS WASN'T GOING TO ABSOLUTELY CHANGE THE WAY WE LIVE. AND IT DID.

MATT LAUER

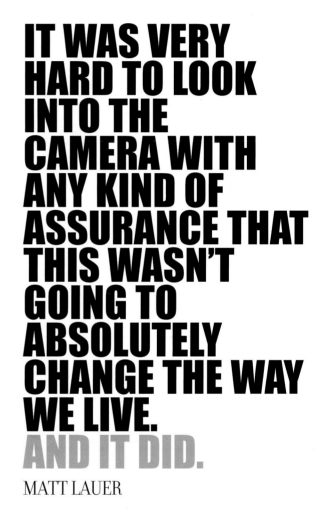

September 11, 2001: *Today* covers the World Trade Center attack.

September 10, 1984: Bryant Gumbel reports live from Moscow.

Jane Pauley fondly remembers broadcasting live in 1987 from a U.S. Navy ship. "We did the aircraft carrier, the *Coral Sea*, during Thanksgiving one year," she says. "Now, you know, a ship—it pitches, you know, and it bobs, and the tides turn it. Well, how do you keep the signal straight? It just was a miracle of television."

At one point, Pauley was on the flight deck delivering care packages from home to a few sailors. "We were going to surprise these guys," Pauley told viewers, "but we asked the Navy to, and I quote, 'make discreet inquiries' as to whether they would be here or not. I'd like you to meet Master Chief Al Murray. You're from Charlotte, Florida?"

"My mother lives in Port Charlotte, Florida," Murray corrected her.

"Well," Pauley asked, "would you describe how it was you were advised that maybe you should be here?"

"Well, yesterday morning about six thirty, they came down to my bunk and woke me up and said that Jane Pauley wanted to meet me and had something to give to me," he said.

"Yeah, that was a discreet inquiry," Pauley said wryly.

"That was a discreet—nothing, nothing is a secret on a ship," Murray pointed out.

Some sixteen years later, Pauley recalls, "It rained there too. . . . There was a saying [among producers], 'It never rains in the truck.' They'd say, 'Sorry, Bryant. Sorry, Jane. You know, it's cold, it's wet. But we're fine in here.' So we are on the deck with a couple thousand men half my age. They didn't care. And it starts to rain. And it's really raining pretty heavily. And now they want us to come in because it is raining. And Bryant and I refuse. 'If these guys are out here in the rain,' we said, 'we're out here in the rain.' It was so great."

Jane Pauley delivering care packages from home to a few sailors.

Not so great are Pauley's memories of December 9, 1980, the day after former Beatle John Lennon was shot and killed outside his New York apartment building. Almost the entire show that morning, anchored by Pauley and Tom Brokaw, was devoted to the Lennon story. As the program drew to a close, Pauley recalls, "They played a documentary that Yoko had done, I guess, with Lennon to [the song] 'Imagine.' So we finished our show and just let that tape play us out. So I'm done, they play that tape—and I just dissolved. And I think that the Associated Press must have been there that day in the studio covering us or something, and they took a picture of me with my head on the desk, sobbing, and Brokaw sitting next to me, just kind of looking stricken. . . . It was the end of my youth. It really felt like, you know, somebody had killed it. Somebody had killed him, and they killed our youth in the process. And you know, we were crying for a whole lot of reasons, but I guess just for generational reasons, that felt like my story."

Setting aside monumental stories like the terrorist attacks of September 11, Matt Lauer cites his "Where in the World Is Matt Lauer?" odysseys as "the most personally gratifying, for the strangest of reasons," he says. "The reason being that it created an enormous bond between me and the technical people who work at NBC. I've developed more great friendships and working

December 9, 1980: Jane Pauley sobbing, shortly after reporting on the assassination of John Lennon.

AND KEEP IN MIND THAT EVEREST, THE SUMMIT, IS THREE MILES HIGHER, SO IT WOULD TAKE, LIKE, 29 EMPIRE STATE BUILDINGS TO REACH THE SUMMIT OR MATCH [THE] SUMMIT OF MOUNT EVEREST. THAT'S JUST HOW HIGH WE ARE.

MATT LAUER

May 10, 1999: Matt Lauer reports from the foothills of Mount Everest on the "Where In the World is Matt Lauer?" segment of *Today*.

relationships based on those five years and twenty-seven locations around the world, because every year I would go and meet the technicians and the camera people and the grips from all our bureaus—people from London and Paris and people who would meet me in Asia. And we created this kind of fraternity, this group. We have war stories together. It is our war without covering a war. And that's been wonderful for me. Whether it's the hardest-hitting series in the world—certainly not. But it's been, kind of, my thing. It's let me see the world. It's taken me to places I never would have gone had it not been for that particular series. And I think it's also created a nice bond between me and the viewers."

On May 10, 1999, Lauer made his first "Where in the World" appearance of the year from the foothills of Mount Everest. "Just to give you an idea how we get this done," he explained to viewers, "we are so far away from New York City, that we have this incredible satellite system worked up. We're taking the live signal from Tengboche in Nepal, we're sending it up to a satellite, then we're bringing it down in Jerusalem in Israel. Then we're sending it back up to another satellite, and then it comes down in Secaucus, New Jersey, and comes by land line, I guess, to Studio 1A in Rockefeller Center. I mean, this is—as I said before, the crew has done a masterful job in pulling off this live location, Katie. . . . And let me give you an idea of just how high we are. We're at 12,700 feet. Now, everybody knows the Empire State Building is about 1,200 feet. So we estimate that it would take about ten Empire State Buildings to reach where I am right now. And keep in mind that Everest, the summit, is three miles higher, so it would take, like, twenty-nine Empire State Buildings to reach the summit or match [the] summit of Mount Everest. That's just how high we are."

Lauer admits that the rigors of the annual feature wear him down. "It's the most fun and hardest thing I ever do every year," he says. "It takes weeks to recover from. It's mentally taxing. It's physically exhausting. . . . I hate the trip from the middle of May until somewhere in the middle of summer. And then, invariably, someone walks by me in the hall, pulls me aside and whispers in my ear, like, 'Mount Everest,' as an idea of where I should go. And I go, 'That's interesting.' And all of a sudden the juices start to flow again."

Tom Brokaw looks back on his years at *Today* and lists some of the major breaking news stories for which he sat at the show's helm: the assassination of Anwar Sadat, the attempted assassination of Ronald Reagan, the death of China's Mao Zedong, presidential inaugurations and campaigns and political conventions. But he also acknowledges the sheer fun of having traveled with the show to England to cover the wedding of Prince Charles and Lady Diana Spencer.

"I had a wonderful time that whole week long," Brokaw says. "And [former NBC News executive] Gordon Manning had discovered the little-known editor of *Tatler* magazine and put her at my side, Tina Brown. And we had Robert Lacey, who'd written a lot of books about the royals and was much more conventional and mainstream, on the other side of Jane [Pauley]. And the four of us were on for two, three hours at a time with extraordinary ratings. And we just had the time of our lives."

Brokaw recalls that Brown was extremely nervous about being on television. "I'd said to her before we went on, 'Don't worry about it. It's just going to get the largest television audience in the history of morning television.'" But as the broadcast got underway the morning of July 29, 1981, Brokaw instigated a funny discussion that quickly dissipated any nervousness. "May I say something about her shoes?" Brokaw asked on the air. "Because we are covering all the minutiae of this wedding and anything that has to do with any of the principals. It's not the type of area that I'm terribly familiar with, but I saw a picture of Lady Diana the other day standing beside Prince Charles, and she's quite tall. And most people don't realize that she is, at least, almost as tall as he is because all of the photographs are staggered. He's two steps up."

Tina Brown jumped in with some background information. "That's right," Brown said. "She's a very tall girl. In fact, 'Hey, big Spencer!' is something that has been one of the little tags that has been put on her. Because she is very tall . . . and she always wears very, very flat loafers, otherwise she'd tower over him."

"Would it be impertinent of me," Brokaw added with a twinkle, "to say that she also appears to have very large feet?"

Afterward, Brokaw recalls, Brown said to him, "I knew then that I had permission to be me."

Clearly, *Today*'s various cast members focus on different segments for different reasons. Al Roker becomes emotional talking about two stories he and producer Jackie Olensky did with one of Roker's lifelong heroes, the late Charles Schulz, creator of the comic strip *Peanuts*. The first aired in conjunction with the strip's fiftieth anniversary; the second aired just six weeks later, after Schulz had been diagnosed with advanced colon cancer.

"In the month since I had seen him," Roker recalls, "he had lost a lot of weight. He was wearing a chemo pack. And it was just . . . heartbreaking. It was a very difficult interview to do, to be talking to, you know, a man . . . an idol. And somebody who meant so much to so many people. And watching him, and talking to him. And it was hard, but it meant a lot."

Gene Shalit says he's gratified by "all the wonderful people I had a chance to meet and the wonderful interviews that I was able to do with some very extraordinary people. I mean, you know, I've done everybody from Pavarotti to Isaac Stern to the Grateful Dead. . . . Mel Brooks once stopped an interview in the middle, and said, 'I can't work with this guy. He doesn't stop laughing.'"

Shalit recalls taping a wildly funny 1993 sequence outdoors in Lincoln Center with the Italian comic actor Roberto Begnini, long before his award-winning film *Life Is Beautiful* was even conceived. They ran into some tourists visiting from Italy, and Shalit asked them to applaud first for the Pope and then for Begnini to see who was more popular with the group. "I think it's a tie," Shalit wisely declared.

July 29, 1981: Tom Brokaw and Tina Brown ponder the size of Princess Diana's feet during *Today* coverage of the Royal Wedding. Also reporting at the event are Jane Pauley and Robert Lacey.

GENE SHALIT: Roberto Benigni, star of Blake Edward's new comedy *Son of the Pink Panther* is Italy's most popular comic actor. I think he's one of the best comedians in the world. Now, we had never met. We had never even seen each other when we got together in New York for a walk and talk. It was completely spontaneous, and it was filled with surprises, as are these little glimpses of his movies. Benigni directed and starred in *Johnny Stecchino,* the biggest box-office hit in Italian movie history. Benigni was cast also as a talkative taxi driver in Rome in *Night on Earth,* It was his first movie for the American director Jim Jarmusch. And now in *Son of the Pink Panther,* he demonstrates his remarkable physical comicality.

GENE SHALIT: So, Roberto Benigni, do you know where you are? Where are you now?

ROBERTO BENIGNI: Now—now we are at—at the Lincoln Center.

GENE SHALIT: Stand up here. Stand up on this chair. *(Cheers)* What is this group? Are they all friends? Or—a church, what is this? These people all came to see the Pope in Colorado. So you—you live in Italy, where the Pope lives, and you come 6,000 miles—

ROBERTO BENIGNI: They meant, the Pope and Benigni.

GENE SHALIT: I'm gonna ask them, "Pope or Benigni?" and whoever gets the loudest cheer wins.

ROBERTO BENIGNI: *(Foreign language not transcribed.)*

GENE SHALIT: First, the Pope. *(Cheering)* Okay, now, Roberto Benigni. *(Cheering)* I think it's a tie.

ROBERTO BENIGNI: *(Foreign language not transcribed.)*

GENE SHALIT: Does this happen to you when you walk in Rome?

ROBERTO BENIGNI: Yes. Yes. When I walk with the Pope, it's terrible . . . sometimes. Yeah, to have a coffee, me and the Pope together, we try it. But now we can't. Some years ago, yes. Now is difficult.

GENE SHALIT: *Ciao. Arrivederci.*

ROBERTO BENIGNI: *Ciao. Arrivederci.*

GENE SHALIT: Well, that was a very thrilling moment for me.

ROBERTO BENIGNI: Oh, yeah.

GENE SHALIT: The fact that your countrymen should come across a star that they obviously admire so much, that's wonderful.

ROBERTO BENIGNI: NBC, the best. Thank you.

GENE SHALIT: Well, that's about all I know to tell you. You look very good in my hat.

ROBERTO BENIGNI: Thank you very much. You look very good in my hair.

GENE SHALIT: I have your hair, you have my hat. *Son of the Pink Panther,* open now?

ROBERTO BENIGNI: But is—I give you if—because—this is really a—a movie—how do you say beautiful in—in Italian?

GENE SHALIT: *Bella.*

ROBERTO BENIGNI: *Bella. Bella. Ma—ma bello.*

GENE SHALIT: Thank you, Roberto.

GENE SHALIT: Thank you, indeed. Roberto Benigni returned my money, you should know that. And most important, he gave me back my hat. And we'll be back in a moment with more on *Today* after this.

September 3, 1993: Gene Shalit interviews Italian comic actor Roberto Benigni at Lincoln Center.

THIS PROGRAM IS INCREDIBLY POWERFUL IN SHAPING AND INFLUENCING WHAT AMERICANS FEEL ABOUT PUBLIC POLICY, ABOUT THE ISSUES OF THE DAY.

ANN CURRY

Ann Curry's daily duties ordinarily keep her in the studio, but a trip to Kosovo in April 1999 was one of the memorable exceptions. At the time, Curry says, "the networks were not doing these kinds of stories. Well, for a week, we went live in circumstances that were very touch-and-go—uncertain live shots, uncertain satellite hookups, at one point getting to a camp full of refugees where police officers were pointing guns at us and not letting us in. . . . And I know that the awareness in America of a great humanitarian disaster grew. And I know that subsequently the government, the federal government, sent more aid. . . . What small part we played, one cannot quantify. But it reminded me of the power of this program. This program is incredibly powerful in shaping and influencing what Americans feel about public policy, about the issues of the day. And I think we take that responsibility very seriously."

Katie Couric doesn't hesitate when asked about her most important *Today* stories. "My colon cancer work," she says, "because I think very few news stories and very few segments on the show, although there are others, actually have the power to save lives. And I think that, you know, through a combination of my personal experience [the death of her husband, Jay Monahan, from colon cancer in 1998] and our relentless efforts to educate the public about this, I was really able to save more than a handful of lives. So that's certainly the most personally fulfilling work I've done, and certainly important to the families of those people who are still around. I also hope that it was an important lesson and message for people who maybe haven't been affected by the disease in that, as hackneyed as it sounds, you can turn a tragedy into something positive. So I hope that I was a good example of that for some people."

MATT LAUER: Katie, thanks, now back to the fate of those refugees. Ann Curry has been on the scene all week. She joins us again now from the border of Macedonia and Kosovo. Ann, good morning to you.

ANN CURRY: Good morning, Matt. You know, when we first arrived here late yesterday, Macedonian police and soldiers wielding rifles [were] refusing to allow journalists inside this camp. But we managed to sneak in. Our cameramen hid here on this hillside, and NBC's Amy Roth Churnley went inside with me carrying a home video camera. And here is what we saw in the last hours of this camp. We got in just as hundreds of refugees, some who have been here as long as a week, were lining up with all their belongings waiting to be bussed out. They're carrying food with them, blankets. There are babies. We know that there were babies born here. We don't know how many there were, babies born in this no man's land. We know that people have died here. We don't know how many.

There are many, many children. We're now deep inside the camp. In this tent, there are two families and five children. . . . [One] is just seven months old. These women don't know where their husbands are. The last time they saw them was in Kosovo. You can see the anguish. You can see the conditions that they're living in.

They live in a tent where it's cold at night. They're all crammed in here. They do have mattresses and blankets, but it's very difficult. This woman has just now told us that her twenty-three-year-old son is missing in Kosovo, and she doesn't know where he is. And she's frightened for him. This is one of many stories here in this camp. You don't have to walk very far to see people suffering, not only because of the conditions here, the poor sanitary conditions, the cold at night, because of the trauma that they have felt, the trauma that they endure not knowing where all their loved ones are.

Wherever I looked in the two hours I spent in the camp, I saw faces of all ages filled with fear. I've seen a number of children who are clearly ill with runny noses. One woman told me here that she had—ex—she had—a skin condition from the exposure from being in the cold at—every night.

As a mother of two children, seeing these children herded this way, not knowing where they're going, the fear in their faces, it's overwhelming. It would be difficult for anyone who had seen what was going on in Blace not to be affected. Well, this morning all the refugees are gone. We don't know where they have gone, and this morning, not even the UN Commission on Refugees can tell us where they have been taken. The commission in fact is appalled, and we have just learned that the UN High Commission on Refugees has asked for all relocation to stop until they can figure out how to make this thing run more smoothly, Matt.

MATT LAUER: Ann, while—while that camp has now been emptied there are reports, there are thousands of Kosovar Albanians waiting on the border of Macedonia to get in, and they're not allowed in. What can you tell me about that?

ANN CURRY: Well, it's a very good question, Matt, and in fact, we can—we—we have heard, but we have not confirmed that the Serbs are now sending those refugees back into Kosovo.

Today
April 7, 1999
Ann Curry and Matt Lauer

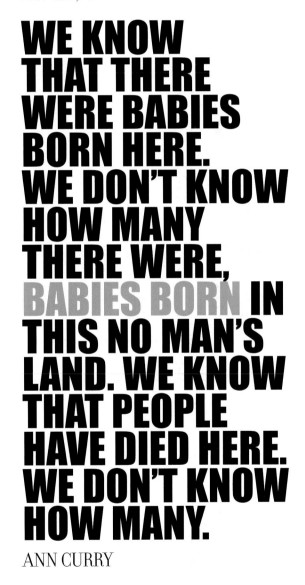

WE KNOW THAT THERE WERE BABIES BORN HERE. WE DON'T KNOW HOW MANY THERE WERE, BABIES BORN IN THIS NO MAN'S LAND. WE KNOW THAT PEOPLE HAVE DIED HERE. WE DON'T KNOW HOW MANY.

ANN CURRY

April 7, 1999: Ann Curry reports live from Kosovo–Macedonia border.

159

THAT'S NOT LIKE, OH, WE'RE THE BIG BAD, MEAN TODAY SHOW. BUT OBVIOUSLY WE DON'T SHY AWAY FROM CONTROVERSY OR FROM HARD QUESTIONS.

KATIE COURIC

October 13, 1992: Barbara Bush checks her watch while Katie Couric continues to interview her husband.

One of the most important functions of *Today*, Couric says, is to "shine a light under the various rocks that are covering the less attractive aspects of our society. The Rodney King beating . . . I think that that opened up a lot of discussions about police brutality and profiling and racism."

Sexual harassment is another of those issues, says Couric, who on August 8, 1991, conducted a key interview for *Today* with Anita Hill, the law professor who had accused then–Supreme Court nominee Clarence Thomas of having harassed her.

"You know, even though the country is still very divided on this," Couric says now, "I think however you feel about Anita Hill, she certainly brought the issue of sexual harassment to the forefront. And I felt that was an extremely important thing to do. You know, I had experienced harassment even in the twenty-two years I've been in the business. I think there's a huge change in attitude about women in broadcasting. And I think that probably is true in a lot of other fields as well. I think the discussion of harassment sort of led to an understanding that women were going to be in the workplace, and that certain attitudes were just unacceptable."

This weightier dimension of *Today*, Couric says, is sometimes misunderstood. "Sometimes I think because [the show] is such a mix, that people have underestimated the show. 'I pity the poor foo,'" she says, paraphrasing the fictional television tough guy Mister T, "who thinks that they're going to get on the show and not be asked tough questions."

George H. W. Bush, then president of the United States, found that to be the case on October 13, 1992, when he casually "dropped by" at the end of a live White House segment between Couric and the first lady, Barbara Bush.

"I was interviewing Barbara Bush about the White House," Couric recalls. "I think it was an anniversary of the White House and so she was giving me a tour. And I was so focused on the—what's it called?—the ball-and-claw legs and Dolly Madison's tea set, and remembering all these little factoids about various aspects of the décor, that I really kind of blanked out the possibility that the president would even stop by. And then I heard [one of the Bushes' dogs] Ranger's little paws scurrying across the floor. And sure enough, there was President Bush. And I think he was just going to say hi, but I went for it. And I think most good reporters would have done that."

"I came over to congratulate Barbara Bush. I thought it was a fabulous interview," the president said. "Got the facts out there. And also, to get equal time for me and Ranger. Because I didn't—I'm not saying this was a sexist tinge," he joked, "but the female dog and my wife—and Ranger and I were excluded."

Couric joshed amiably with the president a bit, but with an election less than a month away, she quickly got down to business, even as Mrs. Bush kept trying to pull her husband away. "One of the points you brought out, Mr. President, was that you were going to have James Baker as an economic domestic czar," she said. "Do you think that that's an admission that your economic policy needs work?"

Then another: "How about the upcoming debates? How crucial do you think they are to the campaign?"

Couric, picking up on an oblique reference by Bush, joked about candidate Ross Perot's comment that she asked tough questions because she was trying to prove her manhood. But then she went right back to questions. "A lot of people said that Ross Perot stole the show [at the debate in St. Louis] the other night. What did you think of his performance?" she asked.

And then this one: "[then-Arkansas] Governor Clinton had a fairly strong rebuttal to your charges of questioning his judgment and character about demonstrating overseas. He said your father, Prescott Bush, during the McCarthy days, stood up to McCarthy. And he said you really shouldn't question his patriotism. Will you continue to raise questions about his character?"

When Bush repeated that Clinton needed to "level" with the American people about his activities as a student in England during the Vietnam War, Couric said, "But in your inaugural address four years ago, you said the American people can no longer be—to paraphrase—torn apart by Vietnam. This seems to contradict that vow." And after giving the president time to reply, she then added, "On the flipside, some observers, some Democrats, say that you have not leveled about your knowledge of Iran-contra."

The lengthy exchange—the president said he enjoyed it and complimented Couric on her fairness—underscored the show's foundation in news. "Yeah," Couric says now. "We may, you know—what does my mom say? paw 'n' scratch?—whatever, act silly and have fun and clown around. But we really do deal with a lot of very serious things, and I think people are well served if they remember that before they on the program. That's not like, oh, we're the big bad, mean *Today* show. But obviously we don't shy away from controversy or from hard questions. And that makes me very proud of the product."

October 13, 1992: Katie Couric and the Bushes.

DAVE GARROWAY: I read a letter of a guy who watches the show by watching around the corner in two different mirrors. So to find out—what the people are doing when they're watching our program, we brought our friendly mike out here. Let's see what a couple of 'em are doing. And this lady's trying to get down on the floor there.

MRS. LAVENSTEIN: No, I got pushed from the back.

DAVE GARROWAY: Oh, no, did you? Tell me your name, would you?

MRS. LAVENSTEIN: Mrs. Lavenstein from Chicago.

DAVE GARROWAY: Where—where do you see our program? What are you doing—

MRS. LAVENSTEIN: I see it—

DAVE GARROWAY: —in the morning?

MRS. LAVENSTEIN: —in my—when I'm getting dressed. I watch it in my dresser mirror through the—the bedroom—mirror in the closet door.

DAVE GARROWAY: Another mirror watcher?

MRS. LAVENSTEIN: Yeah, one reflection to the other, you see.

DAVE GARROWAY: Wonderful. Sounds—

MRS. LAVENSTEIN: I wouldn't miss it for anything.

DAVE GARROWAY: We ought to put the program on in reverse for you someday so you can read all the printing, eh?

MRS. LAVENSTEIN: Well, I can do it that way 'cause I'm looking at it in two mirrors, you see?

DAVE GARROWAY: You're another double mirror watcher?

MRS. LAVENSTEIN: Yeah, one's a closet door and then the one on the dresser reflects that.

DAVE GARROWAY: I'm glad we come out all right in the end.

Spectators look through
the windows of the *Today* studio.

August 18, 1953: Dave Garroway interviews
Mrs. Lavenstein during a segment he did out
on the street about viewers' opinions of *Today*.

DAVE GARROWAY: . . . Who's this lady over here? Do you watch our show?

CAROLINE ALANGE: Yes, I do.

DAVE GARROWAY: Tell me your name.

CAROLINE ALANGE: Caroline Alange.

DAVE GARROWAY: Caroline, where are you from?

CAROLINE ALANGE: Northeast Pennsylvania.

DAVE GARROWAY Where—where are you when you watch us in the morning, then?

CAROLINE ALANGE: Well, I get up—as soon as my mother turns it on, I jump in bed with my sister and watch it from the bedroom door.

DAVE GARROWAY: Outside the bedroom—

CAROLINE ALANGE: In the parlor.

DAVE GARROWAY: Who—who watches it longest in your house? You, your mother, or your sister?

CAROLINE ALANGE: My sister and I both watch. But she gets up at nine o'clock.

DAVE GARROWAY: Do you eat breakfast while you look?

CAROLINE ALANGE: No, I wait and eat breakfast later.

DAVE GARROWAY: You're ahead.

DAVE GARROWAY: Let's find a fella here who watches. Do you watch our program there—Mr. Stackpole Motor Transport?

DAVE GREGORY: I sure do. My name's Dave Gregory and I work for—Stackpole.

DAVE GARROWAY: Where—where are you from, Dave?

DAVE GREGORY: Manchester, New Hampshire.

DAVE GARROWAY: What are your circumstances at home when you see our show?

DAVE GREGORY: Well, I just keep movin' the TV around—to the most— advantageous points. And as a matter of fact, I don't eat breakfast until you're finished [with] the show. Your show is so good.

DAVE GARROWAY: You got it on wheels or something?

DAVE GREGORY: Oh, I've got casters on my TV.

DAVE GARROWAY: You looked as though you could almost pick it up and take it around yourself.

DAVE GREGORY: Well, no. Not quite that bad.

DAVE GARROWAY: That a moving outfit? That—

DAVE GREGORY: No, it's—transport. Motor transport. Freight. And—all.

DAVE GARROWAY: Who turns it on in your house?

DAVE GREGORY: I do.

DAVE GARROWAY: Oh, you're a brave man there. Here's a young man here. Do you watch our show too?

BOY: Yes, I watch it every—well, every time I get a chance to from seven till nine.

DAVE GARROWAY: Uh-huh. That's a reasonable attitude there. What do you like best about it?

BOY: Well—the best thing I like is when—the—when J. Fred Muggs is on.

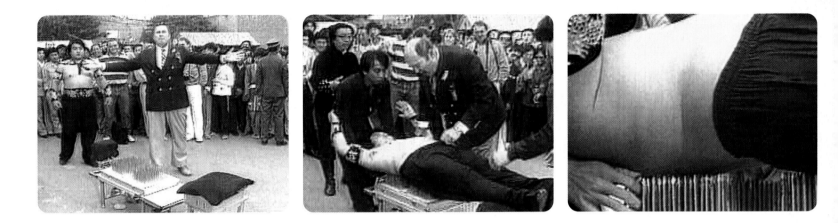

WILLARD SCOTT: It's something I couldn't resist doing. I promised my friends at home, little Willy Scott from Alexandria, Virginia, has finally hit the big time. Sitting on the Great Wall with Bryant Gumbel. I have an RC Cola and a Moon Pie. That's America. Now back to Jane Pauley. She's in Indiana.

JANE PAULEY: Thank you, Willard.

. . . .

BRYANT GUMBEL: Willard Scott has drawn a crowd. Willard?

WILLARD SCOTT: Hey, good morning to you again, Bryant. We are here at the Great Wall. I had a ball at the mall at the Great Wall. We are surrounded by beautiful people. And we're gonna show you one of the great acts of all times. Ladies and gentlemen, so many great things of antiquity started right here in China. Six thousand years ago, the first emperor, Conrad Hilton, invented the bed. And we have it right here.

Look at this bed, my friends. I guarantee you each one is a pearl and each one is going to present to you a challenge for my friends, the Yuan family, who for the last two generations have done this trick. Are you ready? Very good. Okay, here we go. Here.

Okay, this man is going to show you something you may have never seen before. These are the Yuan family again. Again, the Chi Gong art has been practiced for six thousand years. First, you lay your head back very gently and quietly. And this man's 210 pounds will be placed on this bed of nails. And he will sit there, he will lie there with absolutely no pain whatsoever. Well, maybe a little needle here or there. But after he finishes this act, you will see him stand up. Lady, how about this? Look at this. Let's go. *(Applause.)*

How about this? Ladies and gentlemen, isn't that fantastic? Take a look. Absolutely one of the great acts of all time. There you—incredible. There you go. Services will be held in one hour right beneath the Great Wall, as we wish this man good-bye. Thank you. Here, is everything okay?

Now, watch this. You've only seen part of the act. We have taken a stone out of the Great Wall and we're going to attempt to place this stone on this man's stomach as he lies there, proving to you once and for all, this is no trick, this is no sham, this is no flim flam. This has been done, and watch that two hundred–pound boulder. Good morning, folks. How about it? Let's hear it. *(Applause.)*

Is that not an act? Look at that. Now, watch this. He will now attempt— this is known as Excedrin headache number seven. Watch this. Hey. That's one. That's two. On the third one, you will see three. And now, as the fourth stroke comes, there you go. Watch his navel pulsate. You have— there's five. It is going to be one of the true acts of—it does not hurt. Hey, there you go. Hey, bravo. Bravo. *(Applause.)*

Incredible. Truly the best. There you go. Let me take a look here and see, just to prove. Oh, my God. Oh, I have never seen anything—don't let the kids watch this. He's all right. Send him back to the Hilton. Okay, let's check the weather this morning and see what we have. What an act that is. Thank you.

Today
September 28, 1987
Willard Scott

September 28, 1987: Willard Scott and Bryant Gumbel report from the Great Wall of China, as a nearby man practices the challenging art of Chi Gong.

January 14, 1952
Today is the first two-hour morning news program on television.

February 6, 1952
For the first time, *Today* devotes an entire program to one subject: the death of King George VI.

July 18, 1952
First use of television on wheels. NBC uses its new "Disaster" Mobile Unit, which has its own generator and power and microwave transmitter. Landmarks of Chicago were described.

June 2, 1953
Coronation of Queen Elizabeth II is covered on *Today*. First use of Mufax, a trans-Atlantic radio-photo machine that sends pictures taken from a television screen in England across the Atlantic so they appear on our screen in nine minutes. First picture of the coronation seen by this method at 5:35 A.M.

June 9, 1954–July 28, 1954
First series of Color Mobile Unit pickups ever presented. NBC's Mobile Unit travels through the Midwest and Eastern states making pickups in color from ten different cities. All color pickup segments are seen on the *Home* program; some are also seen on *Today*. This is the first live television network colorcast from the Midwest.

July 30, 1954
First public presentation of films of the Polish uprising against German oppressors in 1944.

December 29, 1954
For the first time, live television cameras are allowed on the floor of the New York Stock Exchange.

January 30, 1956
Today televises the first news conference aboard a ship, with Prime Minister Sir Anthony Eden of Great Britain. The *Queen Elizabeth* was docked at West 50th Street pier in New York City.

March 2, 1956
Today airs the first complete papal audience filmed for television, with Pope Pius XII.

March 21, 1956
For the first time, a TV crew, with *Today* reporter Paul Cunningham, goes on a simulated "bombing" mission carried out by the Strategic Air Command. The films aired on *Today* the following day, showing highlights of the mission, which covered 5,000 miles across the United States, and lasted for twenty-nine hours nonstop.

April 30, 1956
Today becomes the first daily television news show to be transmitted directly from New York to Los Angeles.

September 4–6, 1957
Today originates from Toronto, Ontario, Canada, marking the first time any single American network program has telecast so many hours from a point outside the United States (nine hours).

October 8, 1958
Today presents the first live two-hour origination entirely from a mental hospital, Central Islip New York State Hospital, Long Island.

April 28–May 1, 1959
Today originates via videotape from Paris, France, marking the first time a regular U.S. network television program televises from Europe in entirety on videotape.

March 27, 1964
First live television broadcast from Japan to the United States, transmitted by the Relay II satellite, lasts for one minute and ten seconds between 8:30 and 9:00 A.M. on March 27. It was the first television exchange in history between the United States and Japan.

May 3, 1965
Today becomes the first regularly scheduled program to originate live from Europe via Earlybird Satellite. Hugh Downs was based in London, Frank Blair was at the BBC Studios, and Peter O'Toole was a guest. Barbara Walters was at the Paris location with Yves Montand; Jack Lescoulie was in Amsterdam, art critic Aline Saarinen was in Rome, and Pope Paul VI made a brief address in English from the Apostolic Palace, beginning, "Dear people of the United States, we are very happy to be with you today by means of this new communications satellite. . . . Who would have dreamed . . ."

September 13, 1965
Today is broadcast in color this day and hereafter. Aline Saarinen discusses how to

enjoy paintings with an example of a print of Gainsborough's *Blue Boy;* George Ball, Undersecretary of State, discusses the India–Pakistan conflict and his meeting with French President Charles de Gaulle. Pretaped in Hollywood was a Barbara Walters interview with Richard Chamberlain and Raymond Massey regarding *Dr. Kildare* series, and Fred Freed and Len Giovannitti, NBC News producers, are interviewed about their book, *The Decision to Drop the Bomb* (the title of their NBC News special, which aired in January).

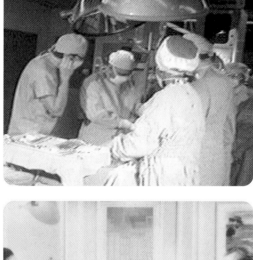

June 17, 1971
Today airs the first live color coverage via satellite (8:07–8:30) of treaty-signing ceremonies in Tokyo and Washington, D.C. It is simultaneously telecast in both countries. The treaty provided for the return of Okinawa to Japan, and was signed by Secretary William P. Rogers in Washington and Japan's Foreign Minister Kiichi Aicki in Tokyo.

October 15, 1971
Today airs the first live broadcast from Persepolis, Iran, covering the festivities celebrating the 2500th anniversary of the founding of the Persian Empire.

July 15, 1975
A special three-hour edition of *Today* presents live color coverage of the Soviet *Soyuz* launch. This was the first live television coverage of the launch of a manned Soviet spacecraft.

January 1, 1976
The NBC logo is introduced on *Today*. The logo replaces the peacock, which was phased out during the last half of 1975.

February 26, 1976
The first nationwide coverage of a kidney transplant operation is broadcast on *Today* live from the Downstate Medical Center in Brooklyn, New York.

January 26, 1978
The first live television broadcast from the underground command post at SAC Headquarters in Omaha, Nebraska. Tom Brokaw reports on the current status of our strategic forces.

November 4, 1982
Bryant Gumbel interviews former President Richard M. Nixon, his first live network television interviews since leaving office. In his conversations with Gumbel, Nixon discussed the current elections, offered one-line descriptions of political leaders, and spoke about foreign policy.

May 6, 1983
Dr. Mark Gold appears for the first time live on network television announcing the 800-COCAINE hotline that had been set up to help users. In a follow-up appearance later that month, Gold notes that the hotline had been receiving about 100 calls a day before *Today*'s segment; thereafter, it receives about 1,500 calls a day.

September 10, 1984
Bryant Gumbel conducts an unprecedented interview with both Soviet Deputy Foreign Minister Georgi F. Kornienko and newly appointed Soviet Military Chief of Staff Marshall Sergei F. Akhromeyev. This is the first time such highly placed Soviet officials have been interviewed together.

January 28, 1985
Today becomes the only American television news program to be broadcast daily via satellite to Australia.

April 1, 1985
Today airs the first live telecast from the Colosseum in Rome, and the first time American TV cameras have been inside the Pauline Chapel, the Pope's private chapel. Pope John Paul II celebrates mass for the *Today* staff and greets them afterward (on tape).

April 26, 1985
During the week-long NBC News project, "Vietnam—Ten Years Later," the first live TV pictures in international communications history were beamed from Ho Chi Minh City to the United States via an NBC-installed and -operated portable ground station. *Today* was a part of this effort, with Bryant Gumbel anchoring from Ho Chi Minh City from April 25 to May 1, and Jane Pauley co-anchoring from Washington, D.C.'s Vietnam War Memorial on April 29.

May 20, 1985
Anchors Bryant Gumbel and Jane Pauley took the *Today* Express, an Amtrak train specially converted to accommodate the program, to Houston, New Orleans (Gumbel's birthplace), Memphis, Indianapolis (Pauley's hometown), and Cincinnati; this "first" marked five consecutive days of live programming from a train.

HE HAS TO OVERSEE AND MOTIVATE AN ON-AIR CAST OF NEWS SUPERSTARS WITH NECESSARILY POTENT EGOS WHILE CONTINUALLY EARNING THEIR RESPECT AND TRUST.

Imagine the conductor of an acclaimed metropolitan opera company standing at his podium before an immense orchestra and sprawling chorus of high-strung professional musicians and singers. Consider his potentially explosive relationship with his company's primo dons and prima donnas— officially their supervisor yet, in the public's eye, subordinate to them.

Think of the maestro's obligations to that finicky public, which hungers for newness but invariably protests change. And picture him entangled in the separate and often conflicting agendas of his organization's internal bureaucracy and an outside clique of demanding financial backers.

Such is the life of the executive producer of *Today*.

He (and so far, all have been men) must tap into the talents, experience, and expertise of segment producers, field producers, bookers, the staffs of NBC News bureaus at home and abroad, and a host of correspondents and outside contributors, all of whom know that every editorial decision and production choice is subject to obsessive second-guessing.

He must manage a technical staff expected to deliver three hours daily of essentially flawless video, sound, lighting, editing, switching, and multiple simultaneous live satellite connections, often patched together on short notice.

He has to oversee and motivate an on-air cast of news superstars with necessarily potent egos, while continually earning their respect and trust.

And he has to make dozens of snap decisions while stitching the show's disparate elements together into a compelling network-quality television program, with none of the seams showing.

On top of all this, *Today*'s executive producer has to deal with two fascinating and frustrating realities that even opera conductors generally do not: First, on a moment's notice, he must be willing and able to get his team to throw out their meticulously made plans and respond to major breaking news stories. Second, he must accept as a virtual certainty that nothing said or done within the confines of the show's offices and studio will remain secret for long. Indeed, the likelihood is that every internal discussion, dispute, and decision, every conflict with corporate management and every confrontation with talent will eventually splash across the feature pages, gossip columns, and critics' reviews of the nation's newspapers, hum through the wire services at the speed of light, and morph into melodrama on TV's entertainment-news shows.

Of course, over a span of fifty-plus years, circumstances change. When *Today* premiered in 1952, it was an odd-duck TV entertainment show trafficking in news and information, and it was disdained by many of NBC's hard-news veterans. (*Today* didn't officially become a news program until 1961.) Corporate jealousies and resentments, an uncertain future, and the emergence of a fresh crop of idiosyncratic stars created unique challenges for the show's early producers.

Fifty years later, NBC's news professionals now covet exposure on *Today*, and the network's parent company, General Electric, cherishes the show's ability to generate hundreds of millions of dollars in annual profits. But *Today* also deals daily with fierce competition that was all but nonexistent a half century ago, with an increasingly fragmented and distracted audience and with a daunting degree of pressure to perform and deliver.

Photo Above, Tom Touchet.

Here, then, are the names and tenures of the men who have dealt with these forces as executive producer of *Today*:

1951–52: Abe Schechter

1952–August 1954: Richard Pinkham

August 1954–September 1955: Mort Werner

September 1955–September 1956: Gerald Green

September 1956–October 1958: Jac Heinz

October 1958–August 1960: Robert Bendick

August 1960–January 1961: Robert "Shad" Northshield

January 1961–March 1961: Norman Kahn

March 1961–July 1961: Fred Freed

July 1961–June 1962: Robert "Shad" Northshield

June 1962–November 1968: Al Morgan

November 1968–June 1976: Stuart Schulberg

June 1976–April 1979: Paul Friedman

April 1979–May 1980: Joseph Bartelme

May 1980–July 1987: Steve Friedman

August 1987–January 1990: Marty Ryan

January 1990–January 1992: Tom Capra

January 1992–May 1993: Jeff Zucker

May 1993–September 1994: Steve Friedman

September 1994–December 2000: Jeff Zucker

May 2001–October 2002: Jonathan Wald

November 2002–present: Tom Touchet

THINK OF THE MAESTRO'S OBLIGATIONS TO THAT FINICKY PUBLIC, WHICH HUNGERS FOR NEWNESS BUT INVARIABLY PROTESTS CHANGE. . . . SUCH IS THE LIFE OF THE EXECUTIVE PRODUCER OF TODAY.

Photo Above, Jeff Zucker.

PHOTO CREDITS

ERIC MINK has been writing about television for more than twenty-four years, first at the *St. Louis Post-Dispatch* and then at the *New York Daily News*. His freelance work has appeared in such national publications as *TV Guide*, the *New York Times*, *Time* magazine, the *Atlantic Monthly*, and the *Washington Journalism Review* (now the *American Journalism Review*).

He has been a featured guest on a wide variety of programs including *Nightline*, *The News with Brian Williams*, *Good Morning America*, *CBS This Morning*, CNN's *Reliable Sources* and *Moneyline with Lou Dobbs*, PBS's *MacNeil/Lehrer NewsHour* (now *The NewsHour with Jim Lehrer*), *Entertainment Tonight*, *Access Hollywood*, and, of course, *Today*.

Since 1989, Mink has served on the jury of the duPont-Columbia Awards for Television and Radio Journalism, widely regarded as the most prestigious honors bestowed exclusively upon electronic news.

Born in St. Louis and reared in the suburb of University City, Mink is a proud inductee of the University City High School Hall of Fame. In April 2003, he moved from New York back to his hometown to become the commentary page editor and op-ed columnist at the *St. Louis Post-Dispatch*.

LAURIE DOLPHIN is the award-winning designer, producer, and editor of *This Is Today*. Recently she edited and produced *Flash Frames* (Watson-Guptill, 2002), a book and DVD on the popular form of Web animation with her husband, Stuart S. Shapiro. Her other publishing credits include *Neve Shalom/Wahat Al-Salam* (Scholastic, 1993), which received a 1994 National Jewish Book Award Honor, *Om Yoga: A Guide to Daily Practice* (Chronicle, 2002), *Om at Home: A Yoga Journal* (Chronicle, 2003), and *Evidence: The Art of Candy Jernigan* (Chronicle, 1999), which received a certificate of excellence. She is also the author of several critically acclaimed children's books. Currently she is working on several new books: *Om Yoga Today*, *Tao of Wellness*, and *Chuck D's Hip-Hop Hall of Fame*. Laurie Dolphin lives in New York City and Los Angeles.

CHRISTIAN BROWN was a reporter for the *New York Times* and then a writer and field producer for *Today* for more than three decades.

STUART S. SHAPIRO produced the DVD accompanying *This Is Today*. A pioneering producer for film, television, DVD, and the Internet, his production credits include USA Network's award-winning series *Night Flight*, the live Internet Webcast of Woodstock 99, the feature films *Mondo New York*, *Comedy's Dirtiest Dozen*, featuring the career launching performances of Tim Allen and Chris Rock, and the motion picture *Only the Strong*, in which he introduced the now-famous Mazda theme song, "Zoom Zoom Zoom." He is the co-editor and producer with Laurie Dolphin of the *Flash Frames* book and DVD (Watson-Guptill, 2002). He is now at work on his next book, a career path handbook for young adults and a book/DVD, *Chuck D's Hip-Hop Hall of Fame*. He is currently president of Constituents Direct and Democratic Network, an e-mail political and legislative network. Stuart S. Shapiro lives in Los Angeles and New York and is married to Ms. Dolphin.

Photos from top to bottom: Eric Mink, Laurie Dolphin and Stuart S. Shapiro.